— a selection of magazine artic[les] occasion of the 100th anniversary of the conversion of JHN

— a bibliography of books, pamphlets & articles issued on that occasion

— Biographical sketches of the authors represented in this book, 2 laymen + all the other clergymen.

— Good index, but French names incorrectly handled.

AMERICAN ESSAYS

FOR THE

NEWMAN CENTENNIAL

AMERICAN ESSAYS

FOR THE

NEWMAN CENTENNIAL

EDITED BY

JOHN K. RYAN

AND

EDMOND DARVIL BENARD

WASHINGTON, D. C.

THE CATHOLIC UNIVERSITY OF AMERICA PRESS

1947

NIHIL OBSTAT:

Edward A. Cerny, S.S., S.T.D.,

Censor Librorum

IMPRIMATUR:

✠ *Michael J. Curley, D.D.,*

Archbishop of Baltimore and Washington

February 27, 1947

The Chandler Printing Company, Baltimore, Md.

iv

PIAE MEMORIAE

JOANNIS HENRICI CARDINALIS NEWMAN

1801 - 1845 - 1890

CUJUS ANIMA IN PARADISO

Contents

ACKNOWLEDGMENTS

"Cardinal Newman and America," "The Tone of the Centre," and "University—Actuality or Idea?" first appeared in *America* for October 13, 1945. "Most Consoling Intelligence from England . . .", "Newman and Modern Educational Thought," "Newman and Papal Infallibility" (under the title of "John Henry Newman and the Vatican Definition of Papal Infallibility"), and "The Salvation of the Hearer" were first published in *The American Ecclesiastical Review* for October, 1945. "For the Modern Reader" was published under the title of "Cardinal Newman Is Easy Reading" in the same review for December, 1945, and "The Beauty Ever Ancient, Ever New" in its October, 1946, issue, where it was called "The Ancient Newness of Dogma." "The Psychology of a Conversion" was published in *Theological Studies* for December, 1945, under the title "Psychological Reactions before Newman's Conversion." "Newman Letters in the Baltimore Cathedral Archives" appeared in *The Catholic Historical Review* for January, 1946. "Newman and the Liberal Arts" was first published in *Thought* for June, 1945, and "Maker and Thinker" under the title of "Newman as Poet" in *Thought* for December, 1945. New material has been added to some of these articles and minor changes have been made in others.

The editors of *American Essays for the Newman Centennial* wish to acknowledge with thanks the kind permission to republish these articles granted by the editors and publishers of the above-named reviews.

INTRODUCTION

From his years at Oxford Newman was a man to whom other men were attracted. During his own lifetime he was a center of interest and influence. Friends came to him, "unasked, unhoped," but he aroused opposition and enmity as well. The fierceness of these last died down even within his own life, although it is understandable that hostility to Newman has never completely disappeared. It is more important that in the six decades since his death Newman's greatness as a thinker and writer has become established as something beyond dispute or cavil.

In witness to this fact may be adduced the books and articles that have been brought forth during the centennial of Newman's conversion to the Catholic Church. If these latter years had been a time of peace and order, they would have produced much more in commemoration of that event. Students of Newman's life and thought upon the continent, in France, Germany, Italy, and elsewhere, would have paid tribute in larger measure. That so much was done in the course of the most destructive years in history—the bibliographical article in this volume gives some of the record—is proof both of Newman's historical stature and of the living character of his appeal. The twentieth century remains the unhappy offspring of the nineteenth. It is no slight thing that at least a part of our generation finds guidance, not in nineteenth-century prophets of communism and fascism and state absolutism, but rather in one who expresses best that Christian humanism which a lost world needs. It is the Oxford Plato whose voice still is heard more clearly over the strident calls of the materialist, the skeptic, and the atheist.

In America a regard for Newman has been traditional. It is a regard that is stronger and deeper than that found in any country except his own. The movement that he led at Oxford had its effect upon the Protestant Episcopal church in America. Here, as in England, the accession of no small number of con-

verts to the Church was among its results. Newman's own conversion and his subsequent career were matters of interest to
American Catholics. Their generosity during the trying period
of the Achilli trial was great and may still be recalled with pride.
It is significant too that more than fifty years ago, when the first
societies for Catholic students at secular unversities were formed,
they were called Newman Clubs. Still more important and
characteristic is the long series of Newman studies produced by
American writers, both Catholic and non-Catholic. From the
days of Brownson to our own, Newman has been read by Americans and has been written upon by them.

Out of the large number of articles published in Catholic
magazines in America upon the occasion of the Newman centennial, the present selection has been made. It is thought that
the volume is representative in more than one sense. Not only
does it again reveal how widespread is contemporary interest in
Newman's thought, but it again reveals how varied were his
powers and interests. It indicates as well how his modes of
thought have stimulated other thinkers and writers, including the
authors of the several chapters of the book itself.

Of these essays some are historical in character: "Most Consoling Intelligence from England. . ." gives for the first time the
story of how the news of Newman's conversion was received in
the United States; in Dr. Ellis's article some interesting correspondence is made public; Monsignor Hawks, with the advantage and authority of personal experience, tells of Newman's
impact upon the religious thought of America. Historical, too,
as well as being a genuine contribution to the literature of religious experience, is the thorough and penetrating study of the
long process of growth found in "The Psychology of a Con
version."

In the America of today, with its unceasing debate about the
nature and function of the university, it is natural that Newman's educational doctrines should be a source of light. The
articles by Father Donovan, Prof. Leddy, and Father Wise are
interpretations of Newman and are also original contributions
to educational theory. Dogmatic problems are discussed in the
article upon Newman's attitude towards papal infallibility and

in "The Beauty Ever Ancient, Ever New." It is not too much to say that Dr. Fenton's "Newman and Papal Infallibility" is the most thorough and authoritative treatment of this important subject and that it will remain as a permanent corrective of much that was previously written upon it.

No book on Newman would be complete without consideration of his character and achievement as a writer. In "For the Modern Reader" Father O'Connell unites the teacher and the missionary to show some of the many aspects and attractions of Newman's writing. In "Maker and Thinker" Newman's poetry, perhaps the least known and least appreciated part of his literary production, is evaluated. In "The Salvation of the Hearer" the technique of one of the greatest and most original of all speakers is displayed and is shown to have its present-day meaning and use. Finally, Dr. Reilly's "The Tone of the Centre" is an appraisal of Newman as thinker and artist so succinct and yet so complete and incisive as to deserve to become a *locus classicus* of what criticism in general as well as criticism of Newman in particular should be.

Of making books upon any great figure there is no end. On the great artist, as on the great man, the last word can never be said. It is part of their greatness that they arouse other to imitate them in some measure. It is of their gift that they stimulate lesser minds to think, and that they silently encourage poorer men to speak and act.

> Hither, as to their fountain, other stars
> Repairing in their golden urns draw light.

So it is with Newman. For over a century he has been the most truly vital force in modern English thought. Who is there of his own great era to compare with him in his possession of all the talents, in his supremacy in his chosen fields, in his continued vigor and originality, and in his unfailing ability to evoke a response to his program and appeal? Victorian divines, once men of renown and power, are now but forgotten names, or perhaps are names remembered only in connection with his. Victorian thinkers—Spencer, Mill, Ruskin, Carlyle, and the lesser lights—are now passed by or perhaps are even discredited and contemned. Victorian painters and sculptors are today of little more than historical or academic interest. Beyond Newman, only the names of the great Victorian storytellers and poets remain bright and cherished. Yet even they do not grow as does Newman. Little that is new can be said of Thackeray, Dickens, and Trollope, or of Tennyson and Browning, and little more can be learned from them. Voices of adulation and of depreciation tend to die away, and the poets and novelists are seen in their true condition and standing in their final place.

Newman's greatness lies in the complexity of his character and in the variety of his deeds as well as in their magnitude. As a non-Catholic he played a leading role in the Oxford movement. As a Catholic he equalled and surpassed his previous successes, both as a religious leader and as a preacher of the Word. He extended his mastery over the English language and put English prose to new and most beautiful uses; he gave the world one of its great autobiographical documents; he produced a book unique in modern philosophy; he wrote one of the most original of English poems. He established the Oratory of St. Philip Neri in England; he advanced education by founding the Oratory School and by his work in Ireland; he performed the very greatest services to the English people in the cause of toleration and good will; he gave intellectual, moral, and social representation to the English Catholic group, and by so doing he raised the prestige of Catholics throughout the English-speaking world, and elsewhere too.

Because Newman did all this and more, the title of great is one that few will deny him. If it be a test of greatness for a man to leave a permanent impression upon his world, then again is Newman's claim beyond contest. This achievement was in every way positive and constructive, in the face of the negative and destructive work of so many of the great ones of the nineteenth century. It was in the field of religion, in contrast to the anti-religious genius of the modern world. It was in the service of genuine freedom, in opposition to a dominant liberalism, which he saw as leading inevitably to the defeat and enslavement found among men and nations today.

Despite the magnitude and character of his achievement, it is impossible to find in Newman the unique greatness of the saint and hero. The elements of pride, of self-complacence, and of self-pity that are seen working in him lessen his moral stature. Yet even so they add to the complexity of his nature and to the fascination of his story. They are parts of the essential New-man. His weaknesses unite with his strength, and his virtues with his defects, to form one of the most extraordinary of men. His portrait has never been drawn to satisfaction, nor has his full story ever been told. Perhaps in his case it is less possible to do this with anything approaching finality than it is with other men. Yet the task remains and awaits the psychologist equal to its demands. Certainly, of all the books that are yet to be written on Newman, there is especial need for a study that will penetrate more deeply into his being and reveal it more fully than have any that we have had thus far.

JOHN K. RYAN

The Catholic University of America

I

"MOST CONSOLING INTELLIGENCE FROM ENGLAND. . ."

"Most Consoling Intelligence From England. . ."

EDMOND DARVIL BENARD

It was about ten o'clock on the rainy evening of Oct. 8, 1845, when the Passionist Father, Dominic of the Mother of God, alighted from the coach at the Oxford "Angel." He was met by John Dobrée Dalgairns, whom he had received into the Catholic Church at Aston some days before, and by Ambrose St. John. Father Dominic, who was on his way to Belgium, had been invited by Dalgairns to stop over at Oxford; he might, Dalgairns had intimated, "find something to do there."

While the saintly Passionist missionary was descending damply from the top of the coach, Dalgairns told him the good news: John Henry Newman, that very afternoon, had finally expressed the wish to enter the Church. Father Dominic said simply, "God be praised." They entered the waiting chaise in silence and neither spoke again until they arrived at the tiny village of Littlemore, a few miles outside Oxford.

Hardly had Father Dominic entered the humble quarters occupied by Newman and his friends, and settled himself by the fire to dry his clothes, when Newman came into the room, threw himself at the feet of the missionary and asked to be received into the Catholic Church. He made his general confession the same night; and on the next day, Oct. 9, Father Dominic heard his profession of faith and baptized him *sub conditione*. In his forty-fifth year, John Henry Newman, onetime Fellow of Oriel College and Vicar of St. Mary's, had at last found his way home to the Church of the Fathers he revered.

It is perhaps difficult for Catholics of a century later to appreciate the full impact the conversion of Newman had upon the religious world. Here was a man who had been the intellectual pride of the establishment. His soul-searching sermons at St. Mary's had gained for him an unparalleled influence among the

3

students of Oxford. His writings had made him celebrated as a scholar and as a master of English prose wherever the language was read. He had been, in former years, a skillful and sometimes bitter opponent of Catholicism. With Pusey and Keble, he still enjoyed the confidence and love of a host of enthusiastic followers. It is true that for three years he had been in virtual retirement, and that his conversion was not unexpected; but the shock of it was not softened. "The thunderbolt has actually fallen upon us," wrote John Keble when he heard the news.[1] "Such a loss perhaps has not been experienced since the Reformation," was the comment of the *London Quarterly Review* in March, 1846.

The influence of Newman has expanded, not contracted, with the years, until his very real greatness has become a commonplace among Catholics. The Rev. W. J. Hegarty, C.C., writing in *The Irish Ecclesiastical Record* for March, 1945, calls the conversion of Newman "the most important event which has taken place in the Catholic Church in England since the accession of Queen Elizabeth in 1558 definitely ranked England among the Protestant states of Europe"; and he quotes Canon Barry's remark that "Newman's conversion undid, intellectually, the work of the Reformation."

Upon the occasion of the centennial of Newman's conversion a host of writers have paid tribute to his memory, examining his contributions to Catholic thought and spirituality from a variety of viewpoints and with the perspective of a hundred years to guide them. It is not without interest, also, to consider the reaction of the American Catholics of a century ago, when the news of Newman's conversion first crossed the Atlantic to the United States. In the yellowing pages of the American Catholic magazines and newspapers of the years 1845-47, the record of that conversion strikes us in all its freshness. They carry the reader away from the twentieth century back to the days when Newman's conversion was not yet an old story, when its interest was contemporary and its excitement still new.

The Catholic periodicals of the middle 1840's were obviously not much occupied with "spot news." The record of events

---

[1]*Letters and Correspondence of John Henry Newman,* edited by Anne Mozley (London: Longmans, Green and Co., 1890), II, 422.

traveled slowly, particularly from Europe to America. There was to be no successful Atlantic cable for almost twenty years, and even the company organized by Samuel Morse for the erection of a telegraph line between New York, Baltimore, and Washington was only a year old when Newman entered the Church. For news of Europe, the Catholic journals in the United States depended upon the British and continental papers arriving by ship, communications to the editors from abroad, and the accounts of travelers. The special treasury for Catholic news of Europe and the British Isles was the London *Tablet,* as the New York *Freeman's Journal* of May 3, 1845, testifies. The Catholic magazines were much given to reprinting long extracts from each other, which made for a certain uniformity among them (excepting, on some questions, that rugged individualist, *The Boston Pilot*).

The consistent impression given by the Catholic journals of the period is one of joyous confidence in the future of Catholicism, in America and in the world. There were at the time (to take the figures quoted by the Louisville *Catholic Advocate* in the issue of Dec. 20, 1845) only 1,071,800 Catholics in the entire country, ministered to by 709 priests. But they were an army with banners. There was a reliance on the ultimate triumph of the truth that led the Catholic periodicals to quote virulent attacks on the Church by Protestant writers and lecturers, sometimes without comment, and solely, it would seem, for comic relief. Some of the charges were funny indeed.

The great increase in conversions to Catholicism, especially in England under the influence of the Tractarian movement led by the Oxford divines, was faithfully reported to American Catholics by their journals. A reader of them would have a very good idea of the progress of the Oxford Movement. The weekly newspapers, as well as the monthly magazines, carried lists of the latest converts, giving names, dates, and places. For example, *The Catholic Cabinet,* published in St. Louis with the approbation of Bishop Peter Richard Kenrick, prints in the issue of Feb., 1845, "an exact list of the members of the University of Oxford known to have turned Roman Catholics during the last three years." *The Boston Pilot* of Dec. 27, 1845, in connection with a list of recent converts, remarks that "the Sectarian papers of the United States do not record these conversions. They fear that their hood-winked readers may be led to inquire into the truths of Catholicism, from seeing so many distinguished personages 'going to Rome.'" And the *Pilot* promises grimly: "We shall keep the people apprised of these conversions"

It was not only in published lists that the great interest of the day—conversions—was stressed; it was even reflected in the fiction appearing in the monthlies. *The United States Catholic Magazine* of Baltimore, which listed as a co-editor the Very Rev. M. J. Spalding, D.D., of Louisville, Ky., ran Mrs. Anna H. Dorsey's *The Student of Blenheim Forest, or, The Trials of a Convert*, through an unconscionable number of issues. The vicissitudes of Louis Clavering, the convert, were harrowing, to say the least. (An editorial note in the Louisville *Catholic Advocate* of Nov., 1845, remarks somewhat ambiguously: "We are glad to see the end of 'The Student of Blenheim Forest.'" The writer records the fact that "the editors of the magazine inform us that Mr. Murphy intends to present it to the public in book form," but he refrains—significantly or not, who can tell?—from adding any encouragement of his own.)

The Catholic journals did not hesitate to inform their readers of the "counter-offensive" launched by the Protestant periodicals of the day, which gave considerable space to supposed "conversions" from "Romanism" to Protestantism. In the Louisville *Catholic Advocate* for Nov. 8, 1845, there is reprinted a communication originally published in the London *Tablet*. It reads in part:

> Sir—The following statement came under my notice in the last number of the *Liverpool Mercury*:—"On Sunday week, *several* converts from the Church of Rome were publicly received into the communion of the Church of England, in St. Audeon's Church, Dublin." The frequency with which similar statements have been put forward during the last few years, emanating from the same source, and having reference to the same locality, has been, to me, a subject of no small surprise. . . . That they are false, I have the strongest reasons for believing—from my knowledge of the clergyman who is manager on these occasions—from my intimate acquaintance with the locality in which St.

Audeon's Church is situated—and from the advantages
I possessed, during many years' residence in Dublin,
of knowing much about the success of the "new lights"
in their "wonderful reformation". . . .

Nearly every Sunday witnesses the *show* of persons
brought up at St. Audeon's Church to be received into
the communion of the Church of England. Some of
these are *professing* Catholics, who have consciences
sufficiently pliable to allow them to receive money for
their hypocrisy, determined to be Catholics still when
the ceremony is over; but the greater number by far
ARE PROTESTANTS, from the distant parishes of the city,
and even from country parishes. Hundreds of these
good Protestants are "*received* into the Church of England" throughout the year, and of course have no
objection to be *received* as often as anything is to be
had for the reception. But scarcely ever does it occur,
that a single individual from the poor of St. Audeon's
or St. Nicholas' parishes is seen in these Sunday ex-
hibitions, and thus is the farce kept up, which swells
up a legion of converts in the yearly report, and opens
the pockets of those Christian ladies, who rush in such
eager crowds to rescue Ireland from the horrors of
Popery.

For the few years before his conversion, the attention of the
Catholic world (and of the Protestant, obviously) was fixed upon
John Henry Newman in his retirement at Littlemore. Which
way will Newman turn? was the question of the hour. Most
Protestants awaited his decision with foreboding; Catholics, and
many Anglicans, with hope. There were numerous prospective
converts in the Episcopal communion who waited for Newman
to lead the way. In *The Oxford Movement in America*, the Rev.
Clarence E. Walworth writes that in 1842-43 Arthur Carey and
James A. McMaster, his fellow students at the Protestant Episcopal seminary in New York, already looked longingly towards
the ancient faith, and were kept back only by "the example of
Newman, Oakeley, and others who were their acknowledged
masters."[2]

---

[2] Clarence E. Walworth, *The Oxford Movement in America; or, Glimpses
of Life in an Anglican Seminary* (New York: The Catholic Book Exchange,
1895), p. 15.

References to the probable conversion of Newman are ex-
tremely frequent in the American Catholic periodials for the first
ten months of 1845. In January, *The United States Catholic
Magazine* reprinted from the *London Episcopal Record* the
report that "we are now, in all probability, on the verge of a
considerable secession from our venerable establishment. The
fact, we believe to be that Mr. Newman would have gone over
to Rome a year ago, could he have carried Dr. Pusey with
him. . ." In the issue of July 10, 1845, an editorial in the Philadelphia *Catholic Herald* summed up the Protestant attitude towards the "rumored secession":

> THE TRACTARIANS.—We have nothing positive with
> regard to the intention of Mr. Newman and his friends.
> The late arrivals bring no confirmation of the rumored
> secessions to Rome. . . .
> In the meantime, the favorers and antagonists of the
> Tractarians estimate the rumored secession of Mr.
> Newman and his friends very differently. . . .
> The *N. Y. Churchman* says: "We shall be grieved in-
> deed for their sakes and for our own, that we may no
> longer be in communion with such men. . . . But when
> we consider the harsh treatment they have received,
> the interference their liberty of thought has met with,
> the manner in which their best services and most gener-
> ous offers have been slighted, the toleration and en-
> couragement given to all degrees of heresy and schism
> while their aspirations after Catholic truth are visited
> on them as deadly sins, and the violence of the Evan-
> gelical party as bitter in persecuting hate as its tenets
> are anti-Christian, we own that we cannot feel surprised
> if many are driven to take a step which some at least
> we feel will regret. . . ."
> Thus speak the friends of the Tractarians. Let us
> now hear what the evangelical doctors think of the mat-
> ter. The *Protestant Churchman* of June 28th, gives the
> following:
> ". . . .Again, the signs that the self-styled Catholic
> party in the Church are about to leave her, are becom-
> ing more positive and manifest. The policy of these
> men has doubtless been to remain in the Church so
> long as there was a fair prospect of effecting their
> objects more surely by that mode than by secession.
> The indications of the decadence of their influence has

been pressed home upon their attention so forcibly, by recent circumstances, that it is natural to suppose many of them deem the time for separation come. Hence the rumors of their contemplated secession now prevailing originated not by those opposed to them, but by their friends. . . ."

On July 26, *The Boston Pilot* reported: "The London Morning Herald states that Mr. Newman, the leader of the tractarian party at Oxford, is writing a book to justify his secession from the Church of England to that of Rome." (The London *Herald* was not mistaken. Newman was engaged in writing his famous *Essay on Development,* which was to be published shortly after he had entered the Church.) The Louisville *Catholic Advocate,* on Sept. 6, reproduced an article on the "progress of the Trac-tarians" which had appeared in the *Catholic Herald,* and which gives good indication of the manner in which Catholics awaited Newman's conversion:

If we may give entire credence to the *Protestant Churchman,* the secession of the Rev. John Henry New-man and his friends from the Church of England is *certain,* and beyond control of contingencies. A large number of his friends, some say forty; others, whose authority is deserving of much credit, say twice this number, intend to join their leader in his "retreat to Rome." The *Prot. Churchman,* who, by the way, is generally premature in sounding alarms, gives the Bishop of Chichester as his authority. The Bishop, in a recent letter on the Tractarian difficulties, takes it for granted that the end is at hand. "It is well known that Mr. Newman is preparing for secession." This authority is considered respectable. . . .

We know not if this rumor. . . .be more than one of the many premature reports of the conversion of the Tractarians. Until the announcement is made by Mr. Newman himself, we are inclined to receive such reports with distrust.

In a few days the truth of it may be known, and it be confirmed we shall look upon it as one of the victories of the church over English prejudice—mark of the happy influence of her truth and holiness, in drawing to her bosom men of piety and intelligence. *P. Church-man* need not fear that the Catholics will raise any "shouts or loud acclaims" on the occasion, or treat the "indignant but tearful farewell" of their sorrowing friends with disrespect. We shall look upon the conversion of these distinguished divines of the English University as the work of God, and not of man; to Him be all the honor and glory, and be it our part to put aside vain and foolish boasting. . . .

The rumors continued throughout October. Finally the "Caledonia," which had sailed on Oct. 19, ten days after Newman was received into the Church, docked in Boston with the news. Newman's conversion was no longer a mere probability; it was a fact. The Philadelphia *Catholic Herald* carried the account on Nov. 6, and *The Boston Pilot* on Nov. 8. The latter paper stated on the front page: "Mr. Newman has been received into the Roman Catholic Church. Several of the members of the University were received at the same time with Mr. Newman. These announcements have caused a great sensation at Oxford. No one seems to know where, and how it will end." The news brought by the "Caledonia" took a little longer to reach Louisville, but the *Catholic Advocate* had it on Nov. 15. *The United States Catholic Magazine,* a monthly, made the announcement in the December issue: "The last month has brought us the most consoling intelligence from England, where the power of truth is daily manifesting itself in the conversion of all classes of persons to the ancient church, the 'one fold under one shepherd'. . . . 'On the 9th October Father Dominick, the superior of the Passionists in England, received at Littlemore, near Oxford, after due examination, and in the usual form prescribed by the church, the renowned Rev. John Henry Newman, B.D., Fellow of Oriel College, Oxford, and late vicar of St. Mary's. . . .' "

Catholics all over the world heard the news with joy and satisfaction. The dependable London *Tablet* devoted to the event a thoughtful editorial that was picked up by the Philadelphia *Catholic Herald* (Nov. 27) and by the Louisville *Catholic Advocate* (Dec. 13). It read, in part:

> To use the current slang of the day, Mr. Newman's conversion is "a great fact." It has been prayed for, it has been written for; it has been wished; it has been dreaded. It has at length come. So far as a remote observer can presume, imperfectly at best, to judge of character, the Anglican Establishment has been de-

prived of the largest mind and the most penetrating intellect lately to be found, at least among her ecclesiastical children. The least part of what has occurred is that a man informed by profound genius has passed from heresy to the Church; has brought over to the camp of truth the stores of his profound learning, of his active and disciplined intelligence. . . .

Over him as over all who show themselves likeminded that Church will rejoice, as the Shepherd rejoices over the lost sheep, and the mother over the child that was lost and is found. But she will not boast nor exult over him. All human capacities, great and small, are her natural tributaries. They are her inalienable property, either cheerfully placed in her keeping or wrongfully withheld. She uses them; she purifies them; she gives them a sound and wholesome direction; she patronizes them; she gives them a new value; she rewards them infinitely for the petty services they render. But she does not need them, nor does her cause depend upon them. . . .

With the exception of a column and a half of verse, the entire first page of the *Catholic Advocate* was devoted to this editorial. In the same issue that carried the *Tablet* leader, the *Catholic Herald* ran an editorial note on "Mr. Newman": "This gentleman occupies a large space in the religious world at present. We can scarcely open a paper of any creed without meeting with his name therein, and his course praised or condemned. In the plenitude of our joy at the result of his labors, we may be charged with extravagance for the several places wherein he is alluded to in our columns today. The article on the subject of his Conversion, from the *Tablet,* is a most able one. . . .forming a high tribute to one who is regarded by a majority of his former clerical brethren as possessing the finest mind of the present day."

The Protestants who had looked with friendly eyes on the Tractarians were saddened by Newman's conversion, and realized the magnitude of their loss. *The Boston Pilot* for Nov. 22 reported: "The Episcopalian organ of this city, the *Witness,* thus alludes to the conversion to our faith of Mr. Newman:— 'A blow of equal magnitude, it must be allowed, has not befallen our Church, at least in this our day.'" In the Philadelphia *Cath-*

olic Herald issue of Nov. 27, from which we have already quoted, there was a communication, signed "Felix," which ran as follows:

> *Mr. Editor*:—Whilst there are some to abuse, there are others to defend this gentleman, in the course which he has thought proper to pursue. "Mr. Newman has left us," says a writer in the *Banner of the Cross,* of last Saturday week, "but I cannot sympathise with those who exult that he is gone. I suppose indeed, his withdrawl [*sic*] had become inevitable, and so it is best for all its parties that it should take place. But it fills me with sadness to think of it. We have lost one of the finest minds that the age has produced. His *piety* was a fit companion for his abilities. It belonged— (alas! that I should speak of him as if he was no more!)—it belonged to another and a better age."
>
> To another and a better age! What age? Shall we suppose: To an age when a Bernard, an Anselm, a Thomas, were living examples of piety, learning and humility:—to an age of Catholic devotion;—to an age of Catholic benevolence and charity;—to an age when England was Catholic, and undisturbed in her faith. . . . Tell me, is it to that age—for I know of none *better* since—is it to that age that Mr. Newman's piety and mind belong? Then has he come back to all that remains of that age—to its *Church!*

Of course the Protestant and secular journals rallied as time went on, and began to ascribe reasons (not complimentary) for Newman's conversion. The Philadelphia *Catholic Herald* for May 7, 1846, reprints an article from the *Liverpool Mail* which suggests that in Newman's conversion "the Romanists will have small cause to boast of anything beyond a numerical accession to their ranks"; one of the reasons being that "Mr. Newman is of a family whose high intellectuality has, in more than one instance, shown itself in combination with strange *eccentricity.*" And Newman himself, the same article relates on the basis of "well authenticated reports" is under the influence of "visions."

Newman was under the influence not of "visions," but of a Vision. His *Essay on Development,* which he left unfinished when he joined the Church, breaks off abruptly, and then is concluded with the famous paragraph which begins: "Such were the thoughts concerning the 'Blessed Vision of Peace,' of one whose long-continued petition had been that the Most Merciful would not despise the work of His own Hands, nor leave him to himself;—while yet his eyes were dim, and his breast laden, and he could but employ Reason in the things of Faith. . . ."[3]

The mention of the *Essay on Development* leads us to the final aspect of the American Catholic reaction to Newman's conversion. The *Essay* was published in 1845 in the United States as well as in England. And while the general impression among Catholics was very favorable, there was a sturdy dissent from Orestes Augustus Brownson, who had himself preceded Newman into the Church by less than a year.

The United States Catholic Magazine, in the issue of May, 1846, praised the *Essay on Development* in most decided terms. After commenting on the numerous conversions in England, the article continued:

> But in the foremost and greatest of these conversions the Catholic has in an especial manner reason to rejoice, and from it to anticipate an abundant harvest of good. Mr. Newman has brought with him to the Catholic Church his rare endowments, varied abilities, profound learning, and matured experience. They are from hence Catholic property, and will exert immense influence. The master-work before the reader, from his pen, is but a foretaste of what may be hereafter expected. All know with what solicitude the "Essay" was expected, and with how much avidity the volume has been received. We may judge somewhat of the sensation it has caused by the tone of the public journal and private circle. It has been since its appearance the topic of every tongue and almost of every pen. There have appeared already, or are announced, answers and replies without number, to withstand and counteract its influence. They can but avail in directing attention to the contents, and in impressing upon others the great example and precepts of its author.

In a footnote to this passage, the *Catholic Magazine* remarks that "the Puseyite organs of this country are continually pecking at the 'Essay'. . . . One is forcibly reminded by them of the heroes

---

[3] John Henry Cardinal Newman, *An Essay on the Development of Christian Doctrine* (London: Longmans, Green and Co., 1897), p. 445.

of *Lilliput*." The article also reminds "the men of this age of doubt or inquiry" that the conclusion that the Catholic Church is the true Church was reached "by one of the best minds of the age," after a "profound, serious, thorough, and sincere investigation of the claims of faith, as professed, taught, and practised in the most primitive ages of the Christian Church. . . ."

In the July, 1846, number of *Brownson's Quarterly Review*, however, there was launched against the *Essay* probably the strongest attack it has ever faced from a Catholic critic. Orestes Brownson considered it "essentially anticatholic and Protestant," and he criticized it minutely, point by point. The writer of the review in the May *United States Catholic Magazine* came indignantly to the defense of the *Essay* (and of his own evaluation of it) in the September number of that periodical, calling Brownson's critique "essentially unjust," but expressing himself as "willing to admit the writer quite sincere in his very peculiar view." Brownson returned to the attack in the Jan. 1847, issue of his *Quarterly Review*, calling the *Essay* "one of the most insidious attacks, though not so intended by its author, on religion, which we remember ever to have read, and that is saying much." In June, 1847, there appeared a scholarly defense of Newman and refutation of Brownson in the *Dublin Review*. Orestes Brownson was not impressed with the *Dublin* article. In the Oct., 1847, *Brownson's Quarterly Review*, he maintained that some of the statements in the *Dublin* made him "thrill with horror," and he remarked that their author "betrays an ignorance of the simple conditions of Catholic faith which we should not have marvelled at in a Protestant, but which in a Catholic is as astonishing as it is deplorable."

Since we have expressed elsewhere, and at some length, our conviction of the essential orthodoxy of Newman's theory of development, and considered Brownson's criticism of it, we shall not here discuss the theological merits of the controversy over the *Essay*.[4] Almost two decades later, in his *Quarterly Review* for Oct., 1864, Brownson admitted that his reviews of 1846 and

---

[4] Cf. Benard, *A Preface to Newman's Theology* (St. Louis and London: B. Herder Book Co., 1945), pp. 83-156; esp. pp. 97-105.

1847 were based on a misconception of what Newman really held.

There are a great many additional quotations which might have been made from the American Catholic periodicals of 1845-47, but we believe that those given are sufficient to indicate the reaction in the United States to the news of Newman's conversion. They demonstrate, at least, that the high estimation in which Newman's moral and intellectual attainments are held today, a century after his conversion, is not the mere result of publicity or legend, but a simple continuation of the regard that existed during Newman's own lifetime, and before he had even properly begun that work for the true faith which has put all English-speaking Catholics so deeply in his debt.

II

CARDINAL NEWMAN AND AMERICA

Cardinal Newman And America

EDWARD HAWKS

The conversion of John Henry Newman was not of direct interest to the great mass of people in this country. The religion prevailing in the United States was solidly Protestant. Those who knew anything about the event that rocked the established church of England on its foundations and drove the Oxford movement from its birthplace were complacent rather than surprised. They could see little difference between Prelacy and Popery, both of which, in their opinion, substituted a priesthood for the liberty of the Gospel. The only Americans who were directly interested were the Episcopalians and the Catholics, both feeble folk at that time.

The Catholics of 1845 had already lost conscious touch with England. Even in Maryland the relationship was genealogical. The fast-growing Church was almost wholly Irish and, as other immigrants poured in from every country in Europe, the saga of "The Ark and the Dove" passed into a hazy memory. Moreover, some Irish Catholics were suspicious of the Oxford men, and not without reason. Newman had written violent attacks on "Romanism," and as a staunch Tory he had openly opposed Daniel O'Connell. Yet this was to change quickly and within fifty years Newman Clubs were to be founded in American universities.

It is among the Episcopalians that we find reactions to the Tractarian movement and its climax. To understand the situation we must go back to the days before the revolution. The Church of England in this country was then a part of the diocese of London. In certain states, notably Virginia, it was supported by taxation. In New England it had for many years been proscribed. In Connecticut, however, owing to the conversion of the president and some members of the faculty of Yale to Episcopalianism earlier in the century, a strong native growth had

19

been developed. Elsewhere the lack of bishops, the irreligious spirit of the times, and above all the decay of dogmatic principles had left it without strength to face the shock of the revolution.

Strangely, it was in those parts of the country where its establishment had been strongest that it met with its greatest disaster. In Virginia it was deprived of all its property except the church buildings. Numbers of clergy, who had been faithful to George the Third, left the country, whilst others ceased to officiate. Most of the lay people were quite ready to unite with Presbyterianism and fashionable Unitarianism. The clergy who remained loyal to the Anglican traditions were only a handful. Their first efforts at reconstruction were faltering. They were willing to abandon the Nicene and Athanasian creeds and to cut one of the clauses out of the Apostles' creed. Thus the American Episcopalians were facing, at the beginning of the century, the same danger of infidelity that aroused the Oxford fathers thirty years later. In both cases the situation was met by an appeal to those distinctive features which separated the Anglican church from other Protestant bodies.

In 1832 the established church was in danger of dissolution. The reform bill had changed the character of the membership of the house of commons. The new parliament called upon the church to show cause why it should not be deprived of its privileges and be compelled to share its resources with other denominations. The Oxford movement was the answer to this threat. So loud was the answer that the establishment has been maintained to the present day. The claim was made that the church was of divine origin, and descended from the Apostles by episcopal succession. For this parliament cared nothing, but it did have to reckon with revived activities that baffled its schemes.

The Episcopal church in this country had made the same claim long before the Oxford movement. It offered itself to the country as the perfect primitive church. It occupied the path of virtue between the superstitions of Rome and the abnegations of Geneva. It appealed to the golden age of Anglicanism, which lay between the decay of Calvinism and the coming of William of Orange; the age of the Caroline divines, who had grounded their theology upon the writings of the Fathers of the early

Church rather than on the fulminations of the Protestant reformers.

The revival of Anglicanism in this country is bound up with the names of Seabury, Hobart, and Hopkins. The first saved it from Unitarianism; the second built up its institutional life, especially its educational facilities, and the third guided it through the dangers of the Tractarian controversy.

The Oxford fathers were well aware of the revival in America, and regarded Hobart as the ideal primitive bishop. Newman records the pleasure of meeting him at Oxford, where he was given a great welcome. He died before the Oxford movement achieved its stride. Catholics will remember that he was the dearest clerical friend of Mother Seton during her days of religious uncertainty.

When the *Tracts for the Times* began to reach America they were received with a certain condescension. At first it was thought that there was nothing novel in them, and there was surprise that they should arouse any opposition. The leaders in this country were strong High Churchmen, and the tracts were decidedly to their taste. But a new tendency was soon discovered. Bishop Hopkins sounded the alarm. He discovered three departures from the old High Church position.

The first departure was the refusal of the Oxford men to regard the other Protestant denominations as churches. The reference here is not so much to the nonconformists, or dissenters, in England, whom all good High Churchmen regarded as schismatics, but to the highly respectable Lutheran and Calvinistic churches on the continent of Europe. Their case was different. It was not their fault that they had no bishops. The Caroline divines did not scruple to communicate with them when abroad. They had worked out a theory that episcopacy was necessary where it could be had, but was not of the essence of church unity.

Bishop Hopkins had to face a different situation from that of his brethren in England. They could unchurch those who refused episcopacy; but he was living in a country where all but a handful of Christians abhorred bishops almost as much as they abhorred the pope. He contended that the Tractarians had introduced an idea that was practically unheard of. They regarded episcopacy as absolutely necessary; those who had no bishops had no sacraments and no membership in the church.

Another departure was the high sacramental doctrine concerning the eucharist. To Bishop Hopkins, who was a receptionist, the doctrine of the real presence as taught by the Oxford men was nothing less than transubstantiation. In this matter he is certainly unfair, and departs from the very divines he professes to follow. But we can see why. He realizes that the real presence demands a priesthood, and a priesthood demands a severance from the whole development of the reformation.

The third departure was the willingness of the Oxford men to accept the council of Trent as a possible settlement of religious belief. They denied that there was anything in Anglicanism which made it impossible for an Anglican to defend the decisions of the council as pious opinions. This gave mortal offense. Protestantism had flourished by its opposition to popery and its glorification of the reformers. The Oxford men were doing the exact reverse. They openly declared that it was their purpose to undo the reformation and to seek for eventual reunion with Rome.

The Oxford movement, both in England and in this country, has always been divided in its opinions about the Holy See. Newman wavered and eventually accepted Rome. Many of his followers adopted the anti-papal position and developed what is now known as the Anglo-Catholic party. In America the High Churchmen, who were led by Hopkins, practically stamped out the whole movement. They deposed one bishop and suspended two others. It was not until after the civil war that Anglo-Catholics, or ritualists, began to make headway again.

However, there were Episcopalians who opposed Hopkins. They followed Newman because they were attracted to the spiritual ideals of his leadership. In 1832 there were only 30,000 Anglican communicants, or one in every three hundred of the population in the United States. This handful spoke of their church as a model for Christendom to follow. It was far different in England. Here the call was for penitence, not boasting. The Oxford men fasted to the limit of endurance and practised severe discipline. They deplored the failure of their church. They saw its worldliness, its laxity, its defective teaching, and its subservience to the state. This return to asceticism made a strong appeal to noble hearts. It aroused interest in those who had been disciples of Hobart and in the students in those institutions which he had founded. The General Seminary in New York became the center of American Newmanism. The rift in the ranks of the Tractarians was extended to America, and a bitter struggle began.

Newman was a celibate by conviction, and so were the most notable of his followers who eventually became Catholics. Keble and Pusey were married men. The students at the General Seminary were attracted to the former, and several attempts were made to revive the religious life. The best known was made in Wisconsin, where three young clergymen founded Nashotah House near Milwaukee in the early forties. After several years of great privation they all succumbed to matrimony. Other attempts were equally unsuccessful.

After the publication of *Tract 90* and the retirement of Newman to Littlemore, Bishop Hopkins determined to cleanse the General Seminary from the "novelties which were disturbing the peace." An English student named Arthur Carey, who had been placed in his charge, was accused by his rector of maintaining false doctrine. He refused to condemn *Tract 90*. The bishop of New York ordained him to the diaconate of the Episcopal church over the public protests of his accusers. Carey, who was regarded almost as an angelic character, died soon afterwards and the case became famous. It cost the bishop his diocese, and the affair ended by numerous conversions to the Church and the temporary defeat of the Tractarian movement in America. Some of the converts rose to high positions in the Church, others joined the new Paulist congregation, and McMaster founded *The Freeman's Journal*.

When the Anglo-Catholic party revived after the civil war, it followed the anti-Roman trend that had become entrenched in England. But the influence of Newman was not dead. There were still Anglicans who realized that Rome must be the eventual goal of the Anglo-Catholic movement.

Amongst these was Dr. Henry R. Percival of Philadelphia. He was one of the few Anglican clergymen who had a thorough grasp of fundamental theology. Moreover, he was a convinced celibate. He died as an Anglican early in this century, admitting that he was uncertain of his ecclesiastical position. His disciples formed themselves into a religious congregation known as the Companions of the Holy Saviour. Most of these entered the Church under the leadership of their superior, William McGarvey, when the Episcopalian pulpits were opened to preachers of other Protestant bodies. Soon afterwards the founder of the Friars of the Atonement, Father Paul, and his lay associates made their submission. They brought into the Church the "Octave of Church Unity," which they had started as Anglicans.

The influence of Newman has never waned. It has destroyed the myths that had gathered around the English reformation. The names of Cranmer, Ridley, Latimer, Hooper, Jewel, and others, which were so sacred to the Episcopalians of one hundred years ago, have become almost unknown. The heroes are now St. John Fisher and St. Thomas More. It has also destroyed the internal unity of the Episcopal church and stunted its growth; today that church only claims one communicant in every hundred of the population. It has unified the nationalistic elements of the Church in this country by its appeal to history and the development of doctrine. It has given an ideal to fearless investigation of truth in scholarship, and it has broken down the barriers which separated the social relationships between Catholics and non-Catholics. Above all, it has prepared Catholics for the dire results of secularist education.

Of all the Oxford men, Newman alone remains, fresh and inspiring, with a message for our own times.

III

NEWMAN LETTERS IN THE BALTIMORE CATHEDRAL ARCHIVES

Newman Letters In The Baltimore Cathedral Archives

JOHN TRACY ELLIS

The centennial of the conversion of Cardinal Newman, celebrated on October 9, 1945, was the occasion of numerous expressions of appreciation of the great Oratorian on both sides of the Atlantic. At the very time of the centennial there were discovered in the Baltimore cathedral archives a number of letters of Newman to Francis Patrick Kenrick, archbishop of Baltimore, and one to James Roosevelt Bayley, at the time bishop of Newark. These were found too late to be included in the October issue of *The Catholic Historical Review,* but the editors felt it would be of interest to our readers to have them now.

They deal, for the most part, with the financial assistance given to Newman by the American hierarchy at the time of the Achilli trial. Giacinto Achilli was an apostate Dominican friar who had come to England in 1850 and had been engaged in giving lectures on the crimes of the Roman Inquisition. Cardinal Wiseman wrote an exposé of Achilli's crimes against morality in Italy in the *Dublin Review* for July, 1850. Newman was giving a series of lectures at the Corn Exchange in Birmingham with the idea of meeting the attack of Blanco White and other enemies of the Church in England and on July 28, 1851, he lectured on Achilli, using the materials assembled in the Wiseman article. Within a month Achilli sued for libel and when Cardinal Wiseman was appealed to for the documents upon which he rested his charges, he could not find them. There ensued one of the most painful and anxious episodes of Newman's life. The trial dragged on until January, 1853, when Newman was finally let off with a fine of £100, although the costs and expenses of the trial amounted to £12,000, which were met by his friends. The other major subject touched on in the letters related to Newman's projected translation of the Scriptures, a suggestion made by Cardinal Wiseman to Newman in August, 1857, but never carried out because of failure to secure support from the English hierarchy. The latter part of the letter of December 3, 1852, was published by Wilfrid Ward, *The Life of John Henry Cardinal Newman* (New York, 1912), I, 303, as well as the whole of the letter of July 8, 1860, *ibid.*, I, 427.

Thanks are due to the Right Reverend Joseph M. Nelligan, chancellor of the archdioceses of Baltimore and Washington, for permitting copies of these letters to be made.

Edgbaston, Birmingham, December 2, 1852 (*Private*)

To the Most Rev. Dr. Kenrick
    Archbishop of Baltimore

My dear Lord Archbishop.

You may fancy better than I can put into words the extreme gratification it was to me to receive from your Grace a copy of the Resolutions in my behalf passed by the American Prelates at Louisville.[1] That gratification was enhanced by the circumstances that they were condescendingly transmitted to me by one, who, while he is at the head of the Hierarchy of the United States, is known far and wide, and is in particular our own instructor and guide, in his theological works.

May I be allowed to add that I have reasons, peculiar to myself, for feeling a special satisfaction at the notice so kindly taken of me by the American Prelates. The most obvious and pressing burden indeed, of which they are aiding to relieve me, is of course my pecuniary obligations which would have weighed me down for life; but their charitable interest in me has an accidental value which encourages me much. As far as I know myself, my only earthly ambition is to gain the praise of my Fathers and Masters in the Church. Oftentimes it happens that such a reward is not good for a man; nor has he any right to be disappointed if it is withheld, but must lay the failure to the account of his own imperfections. However, when it pleases the loving

---

[1] The meeting in Louisville to which Newman refers was the consecration of the cathedral of the Assumption, which took place on October 3, 1852, and drew two archbishops and eight bishops to the city. Cf. J. L. Spalding, *The Life of the Most Rev. M. J. Spalding, D.D.* (New York: Catholic Publication Society, 1873), p. 148.

Providence of God to grant it to him, it is a source of consolation and strength, inferior only to that which comes supernaturally from Him Who is the source of grace and truth. This is the peculiar benefit which I thankfully recognize in the kind language in which your Grace and the other Prelates whose names you send me, speak of me. My own bankers are "the Birmingham Banking Company, Birmingham," and their London correspondents are "Messrs Jones and Lloyd Bankers, London." Contributions may be paid there, or to the account of "Lord Arundel and Surrey and the Chevalier Zulueta, at the London Joint Stock Bank 69 Pall Mall, London."

In the letter I inclose I have used the words "My Lords," "Your Lordships etc." I do not sufficiently know what is usual in the United States to feel confidence in my mode of publicly addressing the Bishops. May I leave it to your Grace's kindness to correct my error, if it be one.

Begging your Grace's blessing on me & mine, I am, My dear Lord,[2]

Edgbaston, Birmingham, December 3, 1852.

To the Most Rev. Dr. Kenrick
Archbishop of Baltimore

My dear Lord Archbishop.

I have received with feelings of the deepest veneration and gratitude the Resolutions which your Grace has condescended to transmit to me by his Lordship the Bishop of Louisville, professed by a large meeting of Catholic Prelates in that city; and I hope they will indulgently receive the few and imperfect words in which I attempt to express my sense of the great honour and kindness which those Resolutions have conferred upon me.

Did I need a fresh proof, in addition to the many which have already been showered upon me, how the loving Providence of God defeats evil and turns trial into joy and triumph, I should find it in the course and issue of the proceedings to which those Resolutions

---

[2] Baltimore Cathedral Archives, Special C Q-2. Hereafter these archives will be referred to as BCA. The signatures of both this letter and the one that follows have been cut away; both letters were written on mourning stationery.

relate. And did I look for an evidence of the unity of object and the world-encircling charity which are the characteristics of Catholicism, I should find an instance even more impressive than occurs in apostolic times, (as occupying a more extensive field and carried out amid the changes of human society,) in that vigilant paternal sollicitude which has fixed the eyes of an exalted Hierarchy, with the whole continent to engage them, upon one person, over the great ocean, who happens in a particular instance to have been made the sport of the common enemy of Christians in every land.

My Lord, I think I recollect the saying of a heathen sage, to the effect that the most perfect policy was that in which an injury done to the humblest citizen was felt as a blow dealt to the whole community; but how much nobler a conception do I see fulfilled today, when an individual whose claim on Catholics is not that of a citizen, but of a stranger, who has but come (as it were) to their hearth, and embraced their altars, and appealed to their hospitality, is raised by the hand and lifted out of his distress as if he had been, all his life long, of the number of the "cives sanctorum et domestici Dei."

But I have touched upon a higher theme. "Hospes eram, et collegistis ille." It is not I who am the real object of the bounty of Catholics; nor is gratitude, such as mine, its true reward. Let me venture to say it; they have been serving Him Who accepts, as done to Himself, mercies bestowed upon even the weakest of His disciples; and they have been securing a recompense from the just Judge, Who never suffers Himself to be outdone in the interchange of offices of love.

And now, My dear Lord Archbishop, it only remains to me to beg your blessing and the blessing of your Most Reverend and Right Reverend Brothers, and to subscribe myself.

With profound respect
    Your faithful and obedient servant in Xt.[3]

Edgbaston, Birmingham, March 18, 1853.
To the Most Rev. Dr. Kenrick
    Archbishop of Baltimore
My dear Lord.

How I wish it were given to me to thank you in

---

[3] BCA, Special C Q-1.

person & to ask for your blessing! That being impossible, I can but express in a few cold words on paper my great gratitude to you and all my American friends for the substantial marks of their sympathy, they have showed me. They have done quite *enough*, though your Grace's kindness has wished them to do more, for I trust the subscription has risen to the point required. The argument about the costs is still to come, unless we are fortunate enough to compromise the matter, but still, I trust, we are prepared for all contingencies. My friends, who have been so good to me, must help me to return thanks to the Source of all good, for having brought me through a great trial so safely.

There is a general undoubting feeling that our cause has been successful—and our opponents share it. The judges themselves seem to have been struck with the disappointed air of the counsel for the prosecution when the sentence was announced. There was apparently an expectation all over the court that I should suffer some considerable imprisonment—in which certainly I had participated up to the time of the sentence and when I left our London oratory in the morning, my dear brothers parted from me as if for prison.

However, I will not occupy your valuable time with more gossip, and repeating my acknowledgments and begging your Grace's blessing, I am, My dear Lord Archbishop,[4]

Edgbaston, St. Mark's Day, 1853.

To the Most Rev. Dr. Kenrick
Archbishop of Baltimore

My dear Lord Archbishop.

I have to acknowledge with many thanks your Grace's additional [next word illegible] & I beg to express my gratitude through you to my benefactors for their great liberality.

I have been lately quite overpowered with the Archbishop of New York's speech about me, which I see in the papers.

How can I ever praise sufficiently the Merciful Providence of God, Who has raised up for me such generous friends, and carried me through so great a trial! The blow intended for me has indirectly and accidently

---

[4] BCA, Special C Q-3.

fallen on our Bishop, Dr. Ullathorne, and Dr. Moore President of Oscott College. They had *ex officio* shares in a Welsh Bank which failed two years ago. The officers witnessing the liberality of Catholics to *me,* determined, as they expressed it, to "put the skrew on Catholics," for the benefit of the creditors, for *each* shareholder is legally answerable for the whole debt, which in this case is about £250,000! They demanded accordingly £1000 of the Bishop lately; & since he paid it, now they demand £3500 more, & so they will go on. The Bishop sees through it, & in consequence he and Dr. Moore are at this minute in Warwick Gaol! I have not seen them yet, since they did not go till the day before yesterday. They were in confinement in Birmingham before that. I have heard from the Bishop this morning. Their accommodations are *bad,* but he has been a missioner in Norfolk Island before now and does not mind it. They will both have to go through the Insolvent Court, & so disappoint their enemies.

Begging your Grace's blessing, I am, My dear Lord Archbishop,

Your faithful & obliged servant.

John H. Newman

P. S. I should have acknowledged the precise sum as being £91. 15. 6.[5]

The Oratory Birmingham, January 11, 1855.

To the Most Rev. Dr. Kenrick
Archbishop of Baltimore

My dear Lord.

What a sad disappointment to me that I have missed you! Had I known the time of your coming, I certainly would have had some arrangement which would have hindered such a piece of bad fortune. I have heard nothing of Dr. Hughes or any other American Prelate; so I hope they have not passed Dublin also since my absence.

The truth is, I had been four months away from this place, and my presence here was imperative. The

---

[5] BCA, Special C Q-4. The episode of Ullathorne and Moore in Warwick Gaol is explained in Cuthbert Butler, *The Life and Times of Bishop Ullathorne, 1806-1889* (London: Burns, Oates, and Washbourne, 1926), II, 171-74.

Holy Father has given me leave of absence, hence Dublin, but only for three years, and I must not be away from the Oratory longer time than Dublin actually requires—so that in the vacations I am bound to be here.[6]

We are getting on very well, I am glad to say. We have above 60 on the books for entrance—between 30 and 40 in lecture. In my own house I have eight—2 English, 2 Irish, 2 Scotch, and 2 French. I hope I shall one day add, 2 American.

We have watched with the greatest interest, as you may suppose, the late proceedings at Rome. They have issued in a most wonderful course, which employs the minds of Protestants almost as much as ours, tho in a different way.[7]

We were much pained to see by the papers, that the good priest who was tarred and feathered, has died in consequence of the ill usage.[8] Is he your first martyr? I think not. Begging your Grace's blessing,

I am, My dear Lord,
Yr faithful servt. in Xt.
John H. Newman
of the Oratory

P. S. I am sorry you should have occasion to notice errors in the American list of names.[9]

The Oratory, Birmingham, July 8, 1860.

To the Most Rev. Dr. Kenrick
Archbishop of Baltimore
My dear Lord Archbishop.

I have received from Mr. Shea a copy of the letter, which your Grace has been so good as to address to me through him on the subject of your translation of Scripture.

---

[6] At this time Newman was still very much preoccupied with his work as rector of the Catholic University of Ireland.

[7] Newman was here referring to the definition by Pius IX of the dogma of the Immaculate Conception on December 8, 1854.

[8] The reference is most likely to Father John Bapst, S.J., who was tarred and feathered, by a nativist mob at Ellsworth, Maine, on October 14, 1854. However, the press report of his death was false, as he lived to serve a term as president of Boston College after this incident.

[9] BCA, Special C Q-5.

I beg to congratulate you on the progress you are making towards the completion of your work, which is not the least of the benefits, of which the good Providence of God has made your Grace the instrument towards us. I earnestly trust & pray you may have leisure and health to bring it to a termination.

I did not know, what I find by your letter, that your Grace had been in some suspense as to the intention of the English Bishops with respect to it. For myself, as you seem to wish me to speak on the subject, I can only say, that I have been in the same suspense myself, and know nothing beyond the fact of the Bishop of Charleston's letter.[10] The Cardinal's many anxieties and engagements, and his late and present severe indisposition, doubtless are the cause of a silence which I am sorry you have felt to be an inconvenience.

Begging your Grace's blessing
    I am, My dear Lord Archbishop,
       with great respect,
        Your faithful servant in Xt.
         John H. Newman
         of the Oratory.[11]

    The Oratory, Birmingham, October 24, 1867.
To the Rt. Rev.
    The Bishop of Newark[12]

My dear Lord.

I am very sorry I was away when you did me the honour of a call. And nothing is left to me but to thank you for it, and to assure you of the value I set upon it.

It gratified me exceedingly to hear from Father Neville,[13] who saw your Lordship, that you spoke so well of my writings. The best human reward I can have for my endeavours to serve the Church, is the

---

[10] The bishop of Charleston at the time was Patrick N. Lynch (1817-1882).

[11] BCA, Special C Q-6.

[12] James Roosevelt Bayley (1814-1877) was bishop of Newark from 1853 to 1872 and archbishop of Baltimore from 1872 to 1877.

[13] William Paine Neville, a convert priest, who was the constant companion of Newman in these years.

testimony of such persons as yourself,—high as authorities, and weighty from their opportunities of judging,—given in favour of their usefulness. And since
those writings have not always been kindly received
on publication, I am proportionately relieved and encouraged on the other hand when persons, who ought
to know, tell me that on the whole they have done
good.

As to the Translation of Scripture, about which you
inquired of Fr. Neville, I would gladly have gone on
with it, had Cardinal Wiseman been warm about it.
But he was too busy to be strenuous about anything. He
was a man of large views, and full of resource and
suggestion—but he lived for the day—and every fresh
event seemed to wipe out from his mind those which
preceded it. As to the Translation, he wished to commit
to me the responsibility and liabilities of the whole
undertaking, and I felt the financial part of it was more
than I dare engage in.

I am, My dear Lord,
    begging your blessing for me & the Oratory,
    Your humble servt. in Xt.
        John H. Newman
        of the Oratory.[14]

---

[14] BCA, Special C Q-7. The editors of the *The Catholic Historical Review* are indebted for this letter to Sister M. Hildegarde Yeager, C.S.C.,
who discovered it in the Baltimore cathedral archives while doing research
on her forthcoming life of Archbishop Bayley.

IV

THE PSYCHOLOGY OF A CONVERSION

The Psychology Of A Conversion

DANIEL J. SAUNDERS

October 9, 1945, marked the centenary of the conversion of John Henry Newman. The remembrance of that great event occasioned a convention in England and many editorials and articles of recognition and appreciation throughout the world. It may also remind us, especially those of us who are interested in practical apologetics, that the letters which Newman wrote during the six years preceding his conversion still offer us the most amazing example in English of the tortuous psychological process that is possible before one enters the Catholic Church.

For us who discuss the competence of the human intellect in regard to religious truth, and who view the question of conversion in the abstract, it may be well to look again and again at the concrete story of Newman as history has left it for us.

The evidence he gives in his letters has the distinct advantage of being a record written, not while he was aglow with a recently acquired Catholicism, but while he was still in the process of conversion. The letters do not contain later reflections on the steps that he took; they record the feelings and reactions that went *pari passu* with each move that he made. They show the brilliance and the blindness, the effort and the heartbreak of six years, until the night when he wrote to his sister: "I must tell you what will pain you greatly, but will make it as short as you would wish me to do. This night Father Dominic, the Passionist, sleeps here. He does not know of my intention, but I shall ask him to receive me into what I believe to be the one Fold of the Redeemer."[1]

A review of those six years may be used as a startling paradigm of the intricate maze of difficulties that can be the in-

---

[1] *Letters and Correspondence of John Henry Newman*, edited by Anne Mozley, (London, Longmans, Green and Co., 1890), II, 418. Hereafter referred to as *Letters*.

gredients of the conversion even of an intellectual giant. It shows the keenness of the human intellect and also its blind spots, the claims of Catholicism on reason and the flight of reason from those claims, the urge toward truth and the strength of prejudice in rejecting truth. We know that a man can deliberately turn his mind from the Church. Newman did just that, but strangely enough, he felt that he was acting on principle. A man can blind himself to the truth and know it. Newman blinded himself and thought it the right thing to do. A man usually seeks for a reason to justify his actions. Newman, in all sincerity, sought for reasons; but some of them sound rather puerile to our ears today.

No one doubts the intellectual brilliance of Newman. Yet, at times, he is the perfect example of the saying, "Hearing you will hear, but not understand; and seeing you will see, and not perceive."[2] The sincerity and the sanctity of the man are apparent on every page he ever wrote. Yet that sincerity and sanctity go hand and hand with what looks almost like a deliberate rejection of light, even at the very moment when he is begging God to give him light. He studied and fasted and prayed, and yet when faced with facts that should have convinced him, he reacted against the conviction as one would to a temptation. He saw the Catholic Church as a *signum levatum in nationes*,[3] yet it was a sign which he contradicted, and when in conscience he could do that no more, he was in constant fear and doubt that what he saw so clearly might be just an illusion and a dream. All this we may read in his letters and, as we read, we cannot forget that the man who writes them is sincere, saintly, and intellectually gifted by God in a special way.

Doubt has been cast on the accuracy of Newman's own description of his conversion in the *Apologia*. Instead of being in the intellectual order, the conversion has been styled a *ressentiment,* an act of retaliation in which Newman disowned the

---

[2] *Matt.,* 13:14.

[3] Denzinger-Bannwart-Umberg, *Enchiridion Symbolorum* (Freiburg im Breisgau: Herder & Co., 1937), 1794.

church which had first disowned him.[4] De Sanctis calls it a love story,[5] and Bremond, who thought that "nearly all the books written on him swarm with misunderstandings,"[6] calls the history of the conversion "the long distress of a seeker after signs."[7] "The discussions of the intelligence, the sympathies of the heart count for nothing in a matter in which salvation is concerned."[8]

Such statements give us all the more incentive to look again at what Newman himself has to say of the process while he is actually experiencing it.

Newman himself, to my mind, gives us a key to the solution of his difficulties when he writes in 1845, while still outside the Church: "If intellect were to settle the matter, I should not be now where I am. But other considerations come in, and distress me."[9] Even as early as 1839 he had sufficient proof for the intellect; for it was then that he realized that he was in "loco hereticorum."[10] That realization, however, was not enough. Truth, to be effective, must do more than convince the intellect; it has to exhibit some real attraction for the will. And, in the case of Newman, there was absolutely no attraction for the will in the proposition which he faced.

When Newman faced that proposition, he was weighed down under the burden of deep-seated prejudice, a real dislike for Rome, a childlike confidence in Anglican teachers, and a tender love for the church he had tried to defend. It was against all this that his intellectual conviction had to struggle.

---

[4] F. Cross, *John Henry Newman* (London: Philip Allan, 1933), pp. 142-43.

[5] S. de Sanctis, *Religious Conversion* (New York, Harcourt, Brace, 1927), p. 110.

[6] H. Bremond, *The Mystery of Newman*, translated by H. Corrance (London: Williams and Norgate, 1907), p. 10.

[7] *Ibid.*, p. 306.   [8] *Loc. cit.*

[9] W. Ward, *The Life of John Henry Cardinal Newman* (London: Longmans, Green and Co., 1927), I, 81 (letter to Wilberforce, April 27, 1845).

[10] *Correspondence of John Henry Newman with John Keble and Others, 1839-1845*, edited at the Birmingham Oratory (London: Longmans, Green and Co., 1917), p. 20 (letter to a friend, October 30, 1844). Hereafter referred to as *Correspondence*.

The first blow hit him at a time when he was supremely confident of his position as a controversialist in the Anglican church.[11] He had begun to read the Monophysite controversy during the summer, and the reading had disturbed his peace of mind. Then, in August, a friend called his attention to Dr. Wiseman's article in the *Dublin Review,* particularly to the principle in it: *Securus judicat orbis terrarum.*[12] How great an impression this made on him is apparent from the number of places in his correspondence where he mentions it: to Keble, to Coleridge, to a friend, in a fragment, to Manning,[13] to Mozley,[14] and to others. The letter closest to the event is written to F. Rogers on September 22, 1839:

> Since I wrote to you, I have had the first real hit from Romanism which has happened to me. R. W., who has been passing through, directed my attention to Dr. Wiseman's article in the new *Dublin.* I must confess it has given me a stomach-ache. You see the whole history of the Monophysites has been a sort of alternative. And now comes this dose at the end of it. It does certainly come upon one that we are not at the bottom of things. At this moment we have sprung a leak; and the worst of it is that those sharp fellows, Ward, Stanley, and Co., will not let one go to sleep on it. . . .
>
> It is no laughing matter. I will not blink the question, so be it; but you don't suppose that I am a madcap to take up notions suddenly—only there is an uncomfortable vista opened which was closed before.[15]

He admitted to Keble later that an attentive consideration of the Donatist heresy had made him "quite excited." "It broke in upon me that we were in a state of schism."[16] During this excitement he took Wilberforce into his confidence. "His companion expressed the hope that Newman might die before taking such a step. He replied that he had thought, if ever the time should come when he was in serious danger, of asking his

---

[11] *Apologia Pro Vita Sua* (London: Longmans, Green and Co., 1900), p. 93.

[12] *Correspondence,* pp. 1-16.   [13] *Ibid.,* pp. 219, 316, 345, 20, 18, 276.

[14] *Letters,* II, 384.   [15] *Ibid.,* p. 256.

[16] *Correspondence,* p. 219.

friends to pray that if it was not indeed the will of God, he might be taken away."[17]

In a fragment written in October, 1844, he describes his reaction to the realization that broke in on him that he was *in loco hereticorum*:

> I did not dare to trust my impression and resisted it. I trust I did so on principle; certainly I have long thought it a duty to resist such impressions—if true they will return (St. Theresa). I collected myself and wrote a paper against the article in the *Dublin Review*. This paper quieted me for two years, till the autumn of 1841.[18]

There are some important truths in this bit of self-revelation. First, although faced with the truth, Newman's almost instinctive reaction was to reject it because it was so directly opposed to all that he had known and loved. This he does in all sincerity, basing his action on principle—a fact that we might easily disregard if we were to consider truth and its acceptance or rejection merely in the abstract. Secondly, it is clear that, at this particular stage of his career, an individual intellectual conviction was not enough to move Newman. Wiseman's article might be sufficient for the intellect, but it fell far short of contending successfully with the weight of prejudice, emotion, and sentiment, and, in general, with Newman's attachment for what he was later to call the "dying or dead system in which we have lived all our days."[19]

The article did, however, open an agonizing conflict between the intellect that could not resist truth and the will that did not want it. Moreover, it left Newman, as he was later to describe himself, a pure Protestant. He had nothing positive except a strong desire to "speak sharply against what I considered the practical corruptions of the Church of Rome."[20]

In 1841, three blows broke him, as he tells us in the *Apologia*:

> I had got but a little way in my work [the translation of St. Athanasius], when my trouble returned on me. The ghost had come a second time. In the Arian

---

[17] *Letters*, II, 257. [18] *Correspondence*, p. 18.
[19] *Ibid.*, p. 329. [20] *Ibid.*, p. 23.

> history I found the very same phenomenon, in a far
> bolder shape, which I found in the Monophysite. . . .
> I saw clearly, that in the history of Arianism, the pure
> Arians were the Protestants, the semi-Arians were the
> Anglicans, and that Rome now was what it was then.[21]

Added to this second vivid impression on his intellect were
the two practical difficulties with the Anglicans—the charges of
the bishops and the Jerusalem bishopric, "inflicting on my
imagination what my reason had been unable to withstand some
years before that."[22] Yet, despite this impression on intellect
and imagination, there is no indication that he unburdened his
soul to anyone, as he had two years before when faced with the
Donatist controversy. Nor is there any indication that the impression led him any nearer to Rome. As a matter of fact the
contrary seems to be true. He writes to Hope in October, 1841:

> Your account of the Jerusalem matter is fearful—the
> more I think of it the more I am dismayed. On me it
> falls very hard—here I am laboring with all my might
> to keep men from Rome, and as if I had not enough
> trouble, a new element of separation is introduced. . . .
> If people are driving me quite against my feeling out of
> the Church of England, they shall know that they are
> doing so.[23]

Were we to consider merely the intellect of the man we would
certainly think such a reaction strange. For him Rome is right,
and Anglicanism is heresy; yet he is "laboring with all my might
to keep men from Rome." The only reason for such zeal is the
principle which he had adopted of resisting unwelcome intellectual convictions as merely temptations. On that principle he
felt that he personally should not leave his church and, for the
same reason, should hold all others back with him.

Such action, sincere though it was, took its toll of Newman.
Perhaps some indication of the disturbance in his soul may be
found in a complaint he makes to an unknown correspondent
in 1843: "People cannot understand a state of doubt, of misgiving, of being unequal to responsibilities, etc., but they conclude either that you have a clear view one way or the other."[24]

---

[21] *Apologia*, p. 139.　　[22] *Correspondence*, p. 327.
[23] *Ibid.*, p. 145.　　[24] *Ibid.*, p. 268.

His view, at the time, was certainly not clear; it could not be clear under the circumstances. He gives an analysis of himself to Keble in 1843:

> I have enough consciousness in me of insincerity and double dealing which I know you abhor, to doubt about the correctness of what I shall tell you about myself. I really cannot say whether I am stating my existing feelings, motives and view fairly, and whether my memory will play me false. I cannot hope but I shall seem inconsistent to you—and whether I am or have been I cannot say. I will but observe that it is very difficult to realise one's own views in certain cases, at the time of acting, which is implied in culpable inconsistence; and difficult again when conscious of them to discriminate between passing thought and permanent impressions, particularly when they are unwelcome.[25]

Such vagueness, uneasiness, doubt, and difficulty were the natural consequences of the constant internal battle between the intellect and the will. Regardless of how much the intellect was impressed by the reading of the Monophysite and Donatist heresy, the will could still make Newman wonder whether this was just a "passing thought or a permanent impression." So strongly did the will cling to its former position that he could write in 1841: "I am in full dismay lest a secession to the Church of Rome is in full prospect (years hence perhaps) on the part of men who are least suspected."[26]

In December of the same year we find him solicitous for a friend:

> R. W. makes me think that your mind is getting unsettled on the subject of Rome. I think you will give me enough credit, carissime, of not undervaluing the feeling that draws one that way—and yet I am (I trust) quite clear about my duty to remain where I am. . . . I am content to be Moses in the desert—or with Elijah excommunicated from the Temple.[27]

For a full appreciation of this last statement we must read his sermon on "Elijah the Prophet of the Latter Days," which he

---

[25] *Ibid.*, p. 218.   [26] *Ibid.*, p. 148.

[27] *Ibid.*, p. 161.

delivered in the same month. It is a pitiable sermon with its admission that Newman was "cut off from the great body of the Church,"[28] and with its exhortation to "think it enough, with the Prophets of old, to be patient, to pray, and to wait."[29]

This resolution to remain where he was, "with Elijah excommunicated from the Temple," had to have some justification. We find that justification in a letter to Dr. Jelf:

> As to the present authoritative teaching of Rome, to judge by what we see in Public, I think it goes very far indeed to substitute another Gospel for the true one. Instead of setting before the soul the Holy Trinity and hell and heaven; it does seem to me as a popular system, to preach the Blessed Virgin and the Saints, and Purgatory. If ever there was a system which required reformation, it is that of Rome at this day.[30]

While we realize that Newman had tremendous intellectual power and that he was honestly searching for the truth, we have to note here that this justification for remaining where he was is prejudice pure and simple. He himself later admitted that his viewpoint was based simply on ignorance.[31] While his desire for the truth would take him to Littlemore to seclusion and penance and prayer, even to the Spiritual Exercises of St. Ignatius, it would not take him to the study of the doctrines of Catholicism to verify the statements he makes about the position of the Roman Church. He is content "to judge by what we see in Public." As he was to write to a friend in 1844:

> I hardly ever, even abroad, was at their services. I was scarcely for an hour in the same room with a Roman Catholic in my life. I have had no correspondence with anyone. I know absolutely nothing of them except that external aspect that is so uninviting. In the *Tablet* and *Dublin Review*, in radical combinations and liberal meetings, this is how I know them.[32]

---

[28] *Sermons on Subjects of the Day* (London: Longmans, Green and Co., 1909), p. 371.

[29] *Ibid.*, p. 378.   [30] *Correspondence*, pp. 166-67.

[31] *Apologia*, p. 195.   [32] *Correspondence*, p. 345.

On such knowledge Newman could condemn Rome and feel justified in remaining where he was and in attempting to keep all others with him.

At the beginning of 1843 we note a change in his position. Not that he was beginning to love Rome more, but rather that he felt he could attack its position less. He had been uncomfortably conscious all along that whatever influence he had exerted on men had been in the direction of Rome. "There was a time when I tried to balance this by strong statements against Rome, which I suppose to a certain extent effected my object. But now, when I feel I can do this no more, how greatly is the embarrassment of my position increased."[33]

What was it that brought about this change in his position? Was it the few books he had received from Dr. Russell that gave him the true Catholic doctrine on some of the points that he had misunderstood? Was it the result of prayer and meditation at Littlemore? Whatever it was, he quietly retracted the strongest of his charges against Catholicism in a letter to the *Conservative Journal*. Concerning that letter he writes an honest and humble note to Hope: "My conscience goaded me some two months since to an act which comes into effect, I believe, in the *Conservative Journal* next Saturday—viz. to eat a few dirty words of mine."[34]

Finally in May, 1843, we find the beginning of the capitulation. He writes to Keble:

> The most kind tone of your letter has strongly urged me to tell you something which has at last been forced upon my full consciousness.
> There is something about myself which is no longer a secret to me—and if not to me, surely it ought not to be so to someone else; and I think the other person should be you, whose advice I always wished to follow.

We may interrupt the letter here to note that "what has at last been forced upon his full consciousness" is by no means something clear and definite. Nor is it a thought that brings peace, or security, or any sense of finality. Newman's honest effort at self-analysis merely brings him face to face with the

---

[33] *Ibid.*, pp. 210-11.   [34] *Letters*, II, 363.

same stumbling block that had been perpetually halting his progress for the past four years.

> Some thoughts are like hideous dreams, and we wake from them, and think they will never return; and though they do return, we cannot be sure still that they are more than vague fancies; and till one is so sure that they are not, as to be afraid of concealing within what is at variance with one's professions, one does not like, or rather it is wrong to mention them to another.[35]

This revelation to a friend gives us as clear an insight into the working and confusion and unsettlement and sincerity and honesty of the mind of Newman during these six years as we can find anywhere. It has at last been forced upon his full consciousness, but the impression that has been lodged there has all the horror of a "hideous dream." In a subsequent letter he tells Keble what the "hideous dream" actually is. It is "to begin to suspect oneself external to the Catholic Church, having publicly, earnestly, frequently, insisted on the ordinary necessity of being in it."[36]

In a separate paper, inclosed in the letter, is a short history of Newman's position from 1839 to 1843. He tells of the reading of the Monophysite and Donatist controversy; then, he says:

> It broke in upon me that we were in a state of schism. . . . To conquer this feeling I wrote my article on the Catholicity of the English Church, as I have written other things since. For a while my mind was quieted. . . . At present, I fear, as far as I can realise my own conviction, I consider the Roman Catholic Communion the Church of the Apostles, and what grace is among us (which, through God's mercy, is not little) is extraordinary, and the overflowings of His Dispensation.[37]

We might think that after this open profession, not only that his church was in schism but also that the Roman Catholic communion was the Church of the Apostles, the troubles of Newman would cease and that he would seek entrance into the Catholic Church. Yet we find him telling Keble in August that one reason for publishing his volume *Sermons on Subjects of the Day* was that it "would be a sort of guarantee to people that

---

[35] *Correspondence*, p. 218.   [36] *Ibid.*, p. 226.   [37] *Ibid.*, p. 219.

my resigning St. Mary's (to which I am more and more strongly
drawn) did not involve an ulterior step—for no one could suppose that I should be publishing to-day, and leaving the Church
tomorrow."[38]   And, a few days later, his real attitude is manifest
in another letter: "I have just had a letter from Lockhart, one
of my inmates, who has been away for three weeks, saying that
he is on the point of joining the Church of Rome and is in
retreat under Dr. Gentili. . . . You may fancy how sick this
makes me."[39]

As usual, his determination not to move finds some sort of
justification. This time it is an appeal to the "ordinary way of
Providence," which acts "both as a precept and a mercy, that
men should not make great changes by themselves, or on private
judgment, but should change with the body in which they find
themselves, or at least in company."[40] Newman makes a good
deal of that reason at this particular time. Even in the following January, when he is still debating whether to publish his
Sermons on Subjects of the Day, he tells Keble that he wants
to make the action of the crowd his norm for action. He wishes
to go "not by my own judgment, but by something external, like
the pillar of cloud in the desert. Such is the united movement
of many." As for the volume of sermons, "if it were permanently
to stop people, this would have a great influence on me. I should
think there was something real in them. What I fear is that
they are only ingenious."[41]

There are four sermons in this volume which, more than the
others, might stop people from going to Rome. And it is the
same four sermons that give Newman his scruples about publishing. They are entitled "Invisible Presence of Christ," "Outward
and Inward Notes of the Church," "Grounds for Steadfastness in
our Religious Profession," and "Elijah the Prophet of the Latter
Days." They have for their general subject matter the "safety
of continuance in our communion."[42] He says of them: "the
only objection to publishing, I suppose, would be from fear of

---

[38] *Ibid.,* p. 246.   [39] *Ibid.,* p. 248.
[40] *Ibid.,* p. 253.   [41] *Ibid.,* p. 300.
[42] *Sermons on Subjects of the Day,* p. 308.

being or seeming insincere."[43]   He develops that idea in a letter to Keble:

> I felt the argument of the Four Sermons when I wrote
> them—I feel it now (tho' not so strongly, I suppose)—
> I think it is mainly (whether correctly analysed in them
> and drawn out, or not) what reconciles me to our posi-
> tion. But I don't feel confident, judging of myself by
> former changes, that I shall think it a good argument
> five years hence. Now, is it fair, I think it is, to put for-
> ward the argument under the circumstances? I think
> it *is* fair to stop people in a headlong movement, (if it
> be possible)—to give them time to think—to give the
> English cause the advantage of this argument—and to
> see what comes of it, as to myself, so to others. A man
> only said to me to-day, 'You have not an idea of the
> effect of those Sermons when you preach them.' How-
> ever, you shall judge whether it is trifling with so solemn
> a thing as truth.[44]

Finally, it was decided to publish the sermons but with a
note attached that "the four following sermons, on the safety
of continuance in our communion, are not addressed, (1) either
to those who happily are without doubts on the subject, (2) or
to those who have no right to be in doubt about it."[45]

While he is waiting for the action of the group to determine
his manner of action, and hoping that these sermons, which he
fears are only ingenious, might influence the group, he gives
an interesting bit of advice to an unknown correspondent in
regard to joining the Church of Rome. He mentions the case
of one who went to Rome and then returned to his own sect
as a warning that should be taken against sudden moves. He
writes: "Our Lord tells us to count the cost, how can you tell
whether it is His voice, or that of a deceiving spirit. It is a
rule in spiritual matters to reject a suggestion at first to anything extraordinary, from the certainty that if it is from heaven
it will return."[46]

He then tells the man to put himself on probation and to
resolve not to move for three years. This injunction is followed

---

[43] *Correspondence*, p. 248.   [44] *Ibid.*, p. 260.

[45] *Sermons on Subjects of the Day*, p. 308.

[46] *Correspondence*, p. 269.

by a very strange exception: the man may conform at once if he
is in imminent prospect of death. Apart from that exception,
he should endeavor to put the thought of Rome out of his head
as effectively as he can, and give himself directly to spiritual
duties. If, at the end of six months, the thoughts still return,
the process is to be repeated, and so for three years. "I cannot
understand how one can have any fear lest it be resisting
grace."[47]

Such advice is but a repetition of Newman's own method of
proceeding. He had already admitted as much in a letter to
Faber:

> Ought not, moreover, a certain period of probation be
> given oneself, before so awful a change as I am allud-
> ing to? e.g., I have sometimes thought that, were I
> tempted to go to Rome, I should for three years pray,
> and get my friends to pray, that I might rather die than
> go, if going were wrong.[48]

To have a correct picture of the confusion in Newman's soul
at this time, the preceding letter must be contrasted with a confession he makes to Manning only a few weeks later. Placed
side by side, the two letters will show how the will of a man can
still dominate even though the strongest intellectual convictions
are present in the soul:

> I must tell you then frankly, unless I combat argu-
> ments which to me, alas, are shadows, that it is from
> no disappointment, irritation, or impatience, that I have,
> whether rightly or wrongly, resigned St. Mary's—but
> because I think the Church of Rome the Catholic
> Church, and ours not part of the Catholic Church, be-
> cause not in communion with Rome, and I felt I could
> not honestly be a teacher in it any longer.[49]

In January, 1844, there is evidence that the intellect is finally
beginning to exert pressure on Newman. He begins to feel that
the reasons which had guided him and the principles on which
he had based his actions now no longer have the persuasiveness
they once had. He reaches the position where he has to say

[47] *Ibid.*, p. 270.   [48] *Ibid.*, pp. 253-54.
[49] *Ibid.*, p. 276.

very pathetically: "Whatever is truth and whatever is not, I
do not feel called to do anything but go on where I am."[50]
The old desire to resist the appeal to Rome still holds him;
he still would like to consider it a duty to resist; but, now, "I
cannot feel the question of duty as strongly as it is sometimes
put."[51] He now begins to think that perhaps he had overworked the principle taken from St. Teresa about resisting impressions: "How could a Jew, formerly or now, ever become a
Christian, if he must at all hazards resist convictions and for
ever? How could a Nestorian or Monophysite join the Catholic
Church but by a similar undutifulness?"[52]

The pros and cons of this constant debate made Newman act
like a weary man, weary of argument. No wonder he began
to look for a norm of action other than his own private judgment. No wonder he looked for the movement of the group to
determine his own attitude. But this also was a subterfuge. During all this period he had certainly given no encouragement to
his reason and the dictates of his reason, but it finally began to
dawn on him that this anomaly could not last forever. In
March, 1844, he writes to Hope:

> If a person is convinced in his reason that her [the
> Anglican Church's] claims to Catholicity are untenable,
> but fears to trust his reason, such events, when they
> come upon him again and again, seem to do just what
> is wanting, corroborate his reason experimentally. They
> force upon his imagination and familiarise his moral
> perception with the conclusions of his intellect. Prop-
> ositions become facts.[53]

On June 8, 1844, he writes a momentous letter to Keble, in
which there is a decided change in his attitude toward friends
who had felt the appeal of Rome. He tells Keble of his habitual
conviction that is "growing more urgent and imperative continually, that the Roman Communion is the only true Church";
he speaks of how he had tried to resist that impression and of
how he wrote against it; and he adds: "I am not aware in what
respect I have indulged it. I have attempted to live a stricter

---

[50] *Ibid.*, p. 300.   [51] *Loc. cit.*
[52] *Loc. cit.*   [53] *Ibid.*, p. 311.

life. . . . And I have made great efforts to keep others from moving in the direction of Rome also."[54] Then, for the first time,
he feels compunction for the fact that his efforts may have
caused souls to die outside the Catholic Church when they
really had a call to belong to it.

Strangely enough, this is the only evidence in his letters that
such a thought had dawned on him. Yet, even here, he mentions it only to pass on to thoughts of the struggle within his
own soul which is attracting all his attention. Now that struggle is almost at the end. "Surely time enough has been allowed
for wavering and preparation—I have fought against these feelings in myself and others long enough. . . . The time for argument has passed."[55]

Having said so much, he has by no means settled the problem
of his soul. The will has one more weapon that will keep him
unsettled and in turmoil:

> Am I in a delusion, given over to believe a lie? Am
> I deceiving myself and thinking myself convinced when
> I am not? Does any subtle feeling or temptation,
> which I cannot detect, govern me and bias my judg-
> ment? But is it possible that Divine Mercy should not
> wish me, if so, to discover and escape it? Has He led
> me thus far to destroy me in the wilderness?"[56]

That summer must have been a time of great interior trial for
him. He tells Badeley in September: "I have acted like persons
who pinch themselves to be sure that they are not asleep or
dreaming. That I had only one view was certain, but then, was
it a delusion?"[57] He still does not think that his original plan
of repelling the conviction was wrong; but now he adds: "Nor
does it seem to be wrong after many years of patient waiting,
to begin to listen to it."[58]

A short time later, to a friend who tried to explain away the
attraction of Rome, Newman gives a rather accurate outline
of the policy he had been following through the years. It is also
the perfect answer to the explanation of the correspondent.

---

[54] *Ibid.*, p. 316.   [55] *Ibid.*, p. 317.   [56] *Ibid.*, p. 318.
[57] *Ibid.*, p. 329.   [58] *Loc. cit.*

> We are naturally friends, for we are children of this dying or dead system in which we have lived all our days. We cannot, we will not, believe what the real state of the case is. We cannot be persuaded to open our eyes. Every ominous fact admits of an explanation, and we take refuge in it.[59]

That could be taken as a fairly accurate description of the state of Newman's mind during the preceding five years. He could not, he would not, believe what the real state of the case was. Whenever an ominous fact became apparent, he sought for some possible explanation, and took refuge in it. First, England was in schism, but there was no thought of turning to Rome. In fact, since such impressions were to be rejected, he attacked Rome and did what he could to prevent others from going in that direction. But he was an honest man. And when he saw again in his reading of Arianism the same ghost that had risen to bother him before; when, at the same time, the affair of the Jerusalem bishopric hit his imagination with the same force that the truth of Rome impressed itself on his intellect, then he had to find another explanation and take refuge in it. This time it consisted in the fact that the practices of Rome were certainly corrupt, and also that he still had an obligation to remain where he was even though in schism. When these principles and reasons lost more and more of their force, he turned to an external norm of action, the movement of the crowd. And, when even that failed, he was left with only one final refuge: Is it not at least possible that I am deceiving myself, that what I am beginning to believe may be a lie?

We have mentioned how little he had studied Catholic practices during this time. His knowledge of Catholic individuals is just as meager. In a letter to Coleridge he writes: "What possible reason for 'preference' can I have for the Roman Church above our own?" He then tells him how little he knows of Catholics, and adds: "My habits, tastes, feelings are as different as can well be conceived from theirs, as they show outwardly." His reason for thinking he should become a Catholic then follows:

---

[59] *Ibid.*, pp. 329-30.

> No—as far as I know myself the one single over-powering feeling is that our Church is in schism—and that there is no salvation for one who is convinced of this. . . . This time three years the conviction came on me again, and now for that long time it has been clear and unbroken under all change of circumstance, peace, and spirits. Through this time my own question has been: 'Is this a delusion?' And I have waited, not because my conviction was not clear, but because I doubted whether it was a duty to trust it. I am still waiting on that consideration.[60]

On November 21, 1844, he tells Keble of some letters which he had received from Manning, Gladstone, and others; "but they have not operated ever so little in shaking the deep confidence I have at present that Christianity and the Roman Catholic system are convertible terms." But then he looks to the members of the Roman system and adds:

> I scarcely ever was present at a Roman service even abroad. I knew no Roman Catholics. I have no sympathies towards them as an existing body. (I should observe, however, that I have certainly been touched by hearing some were praying for me.) I am setting my face absolutely towards the wilderness.[61]

With the prospect of setting his face towards the wilderness, he can give only a very inadequate description of his motives, but he does picture very accurately the disturbance of his soul:

> You must not suppose, I am fancying that I know *why* or on *what*, on what motive, I am acting. I cannot. I do not feel love, or faith. I feel myself very unreal. I can only say negatively, what I think does *not* influence me. But I cannot analyse my mind, and, I suppose, should do no good if I tried. . . . My sole ascertainable reason for moving is a feeling of indefinite *risk* to my soul in staying. This, I seem to ascertain in the following manner. I don't think I *could* die in our communion. Then the question comes upon me, is not death the test? shall one bear to live where die one cannot? I am kept first from deference to my friends—next by the fear of some dreadful delusion being over me.[62]

---

[60] *Ibid.*, p. 345.   [61] *Ibid.*, p. 351.   [62] *Ibid.*, p. 352.

This fear of delusion was particularly strong in Newman, so strong that it seems to be the real reason that kept him from the Church for almost a year. Three days after the preceding letter, he writes to his sister: "Unless something occurs which I cannot anticipate I have no intention of any early step even now." The reason for the delay is also given to his sister in a letter of December 22, 1844:

> My motive simply is that I believe the Roman Church to be true, and I have come to this belief without assignable fault on my part. Far indeed am I from saying "without fault" absolutely, but I say without fault that can be detected and assigned. Were I sure that it was without fault absolutely, I should not hesitate to move tomorrow.[63]

This determination to move on the next day if it were clear to him that his conviction was absolutely correct does not mean that Newman looked forward to it with any sensible joy. In fact, quite the opposite was true. He knew and loved Anglicans and England, while the Church that he found to be true was neither Anglican nor restricted in any sense to England. On December 29 he writes to Keble: "No one can have a more unfavorable view of the present state of the Roman Catholics— so much so, that any who join them would be like the Cistercians of Fountains, living under trees till their house was built."[64]

With the beginning of 1845 he had started on the *Essay on the Development of Christian Doctrine.* In March of that same year his sister had asked in an anxious communication: "O dear John, can you have thought long enough before deciding on a step, which, with its probable effects, must plunge so many into confusion and dismay?" In answer to that letter, he writes:

> If I went by what I wished, I should complete my seven years of waiting. Surely more than this, or as much, cannot be expected of me—cannot be right in me to give at my age. . . . Is it not like death-bed repentance to put off what one feels one ought to do?
> As to my convictions, I can but say what I have told you already, that I cannot at all make out *why* I should determine on moving, except as thinking I should offend

---

[63] *Letters,* II, 398, 403.   [64] *Correspondence,* p. 369.

God by not doing so.   I cannot make out what I am
at except on this supposition.[65]

He then tells her all that is to be sacrificed in the step he is
taking.   He is giving up a maintenance which involved no
particular duties and was adequate for his wants.   He is risking
a rather large income from his volumes of sermons.   He is deliberately sacrificing the good name he has with many, and not
only fulfilling the worst wishes of his enemies but also giving
them their most coveted triumph.   He is distressing those whom
he loves, and unsettling all whom he has instructed.   "I am
going to those whom I do not know, and of whom I expect little.
I am making myself an outcast, and that at my age.   Oh, what
can it be but stern necessity which causes this?"[66]

If we place on one side of a scale the confession of this letter,
and on the other the conviction that has been in his mind through
the years, it is not too difficult to understand why he continues
to fight with the possibility that his call to Rome might be just
a delusion.   Even through the month of April the difficulty is
still calling for an answer:

> I say to myself, if I am under a delusion, what have
> I done, what grave sin have I committed, to bring such
> a judgment on me?   O that it may be revealed to me,
> and the delusion broken.   But I go on month after
> month, year after year, without change of feeling except
> in one direction; not floating up and down, but driving
> one way. . . . What complicated distress!   I suppose it
> will be less when the worst is over.[67]

The same distress is found in a letter written to Wilberforce
on April 27, after he had read the autobiography of Blanco
White, a former associate of Newman who had become a pan-
theist before he died.

> I see Blanco White going wrong yet sincere—Arnold
> going wrong yet sincere. . . . They did not know the
> fault, and so it comes to me, How do I know that I
> too have not my weak points which occasion me to think
> as I think?   How can I be sure I have not committed
> sins which bring this unsettled state of mind on me as

---

[65] *Letters,* II, 410-11.   [66] *Ibid.,* p. 411.
[67] *Ibid.,* pp. 415-16.

a judgment? This is what is so very harassing, as you may suppose.[68]

From that point until the momentous day in October when he asked for admission into the Church, Newman wrote comparatively few letters. And, in the letters written, little evidence is given of his spiritual progress. He mentions only two things of importance—the joy and contentment of a friend who had become a Catholic before him, and also his own intense efforts to complete his work on the development of Christian doctrine. He tells us in the *Apologia*: "As I advanced, my difficulties so cleared away that I ceased to speak of "the Roman Catholics," and boldly called them Catholics. Before I got to the end, I resolved to be received, and the book remains in the state in which it was then, unfinished."[69]

One final letter, written on the day of his reception into the Church, shows the state of his mind as he approached the priest: "May I have only one-tenth part as much faith as I have intellectual conviction where the truth lies? I do not suppose any one can have had such combined reasons pouring in upon him that he is doing right."[70]

Let us go back to the first statement we have quoted from the letters of Newman: "If intellect were to settle the matter, I would not be where I now am. But other things come in and distress me." From an examination of the letters it seems clear that these words give the sum and substance of the years of distress and conflict before Newman became a Catholic. The history of Newman's conversion is not a "love story," nor can it be reduced to some form of *ressentiment*. It is rather the story of the effort of the intellect to assume its proper place and function in the soul of a man—the effort to reach a position where it actually did settle the matter.

It has been said very accurately that, although supernatural grace is not absolutely necessary before a man gives a natural assent to what the faith teaches, nevertheless men will not give even a natural assent in many instances unless God gives a spe-

---

[68] Ward, *op. cit.*, I, 81.   [69] *Op. cit.*, p. 234.

[70] J. Oldcastle, *Catholic Life and Letters of Cardinal Newman* (London: Burns, Oates, 1909), p. 11.

cial illumination for the intellect and a special attraction and allurement for the will.[71] The reason for this is not that there is something in the motives of credibility that is too sublime for the intellect to grasp; there is nothing hidden away in them that the intellect cannot see. The motives of credibility for the Catholic Church are very much on the same plane as the proofs of revelation mentioned in the Vatican council which are *omnium intelligentiae accommodata.*[72] If they are not accepted when presented, the difficulty comes, not from the truth, but from all that seems to be implied in accepting the truth.

We must, it is true, make a distinction between conviction and conversion. But, in Newman's mind, the acceptance of the intellectual conviction was tantamount to taking steps that would ultimately lead to conversion. For him those steps meant a severe change in his way of life, the estrangement of his friends, the misunderstanding of those whom he loved, in fact, all those heartbreaking things which he mentions in the letter to his sister. Until all that is in some way counterbalanced, it is practically morally impossible for him to accept the dictates of his reason.[73]

Molina tells us that in many instances the conviction of the truth of the faith will not be accepted unless God gives a special illumination of the intellect and an attraction for the will. Here we are not investigating the influence of medicinal graces in Newman's conversion. Grace is not readily susceptible of analysis. What we can investigate, however, is the working of the intellect in conceiving the truth, and the rejection of the will which found that the truth was too "hideous" to accept. For the first five years after Newman had been stunned by the words, *Securus judicat orbis terrarum,* few things occurred in

---

[71] Molina, *Concordia Liberi Arbitrii* (Paris: P. Lethielleux, 1876), q. 14, a. 13, disp. 7.

[72] Denzinger-Bannwart-Umberg, *op. cit.,* 1790.

[73] L. Billot, S.J. *De Virtutibus Infusis* (Rome: Universitas Gregoriana, 1901), pp. 76-77.

his life to make the truth less hideous. What little he saw of Catholicism offered little solace to a will that was absolutely attached to life as he then led it. During those years, reasons of every description were advanced as places of refuge from the truth that stared him in the face. But, one by one, those reasons fell before the careful, sincere scrutiny of the intellect, and they had to be abandoned, as they came, one by one. Finally, Newman had to admit that he had no reason at all for his position.

Meanwhile the intellect had forced him to stop his attacks on Rome, and also to retract the most vicious of his former charges. Next came the realization that he had no reason for attempting to keep others from Rome, and, finally, that he had no solid reason for his own personal desire to remain where he was. He still felt the duty to remain; but he could find no reason to substantiate it. Unfortunately, his meager knowledge of Catholicism and Catholics did not help to lessen the anguish or to create better dispositions. He was facing the wilderness.

Only one uneasy refuge was left him—the fear of delusion. There was nothing abnormal about that fear; it stemmed from a deep love of the religion of his youth, from which he was about to sever himself, a real love of his friends to whom he would have to say a final farewell, and a forward glance at Rome, of which he knew little and from which he expected little in the way of sensible consolation.

What was it that drove away this fear of delusion? Bremond thought that a "bundle of coincidences took the place of a miracle,"[74] and gave him "that supreme sign which put an end to his last doubts."[75] These coincidences he finds in a letter which Newman wrote to his friends telling of Father Dominic and the strange way in which he happened to be in England. I am not too impressed by these coincidences. To my mind, the happiness and contentment of Lockhart, who had been converted and had entered a religious community,[76] could have been just as effective in dispelling Newman's fear.

---

[74] *Op. cit.*, p. 310. [75] *Ibid.*, p. 311.
[76] *Correspondence*, p. 378.

Whatever it was, there is no doubt that Newman's religious Odyssey finally brought him to the point where the intellect actually did "settle the matter." As he said himself: "May I have only one-tenth part as much faith as I have intellectual conviction where the truth lies." In that frame of mind he entered the Catholic Church.

V

THE TONE OF THE CENTRE

The Tone Of The Centre

JOSEPH J. REILLY

The key to Newman as man and writer is his realization that there were "two and two only luminously self-evident beings," himself and God. To most of us, even though reasonably free from egotism, our own personal self, with its desires, sorrows, joys, and pains, is everlastingly present, often to our shame or annoyance. Though our senses fail us, our consciousness remains and incessantly returns upon itself. Each of us is to himself the one, inescapable, demonstrable reality of whose existence we never for a moment doubt. That Newman should have been as luminously aware of God as that, so intimately, indubitably, completely and constantly aware, sets him aside at once and forever.

Such certitude, coming as if with the force and convincingness of a revelation, explains many things: why his faith never wavered, why he awakened in the hearts and minds of his listeners at St. Mary's a personal conviction of the living God, why he was consumed to know the divine will and to follow its dictates.

What impressed Newman most in the England of his day was the rise of what he called "liberalism," by which he meant the sum of those influences in contemporary life that tended to undermine the bases of revealed religion. He saw in liberalism her connatural foe; hence, as an Anglican, he resisted it with all his strength and, as a Catholic, with renewed determination, more effective weapons, and a more fully ripened genius.

Herein we find the unity of his life and writings. His aim never varied. Like Wordsworth, he believed himself "a dedicated spirit" charged with a unique duty to perform "else sinning greatly," for the accomplishment of which all his endowments had been given. To this end he consecrated his life, devoting endless days to thought and study and, like Carlyle, to the agony

65

of composition, struggling to present to the mind of his reader the conclusions at which he had arrived and to do so with a precision which left no word of his meaning to chance and with a beauty which comported with the truth he uttered.

If his aim seems narrow, it is only because we fail to understand the immense importance he attached to it. If there is no revelation, nothing supernatural about religion, if Christ is not God and God is not the supreme reality, then Arnold was right when he wrote that the life of man

> Though bearable, seems hardly worth
> This pomp of worlds, this pain of birth.

The religion of Carlyle, of Arnold, and fitfully, of Ruskin, seemed to Newman as unsubstantial as a cloud.

Regret has often been expressed that Newman seemed indifferent to social reform in the sense in which it engaged the attention of Carlyle, Ruskin, and Cardinal Manning. When Newman voluntarily went to the cholera-ridden town of Bilston in September, 1849, to help the overworked resident priest, he gave eloquent evidence of his interest in the unfortunate, and his letters of advice and consolation written to simple folk who knew him only by name are equally significant. The charge of indifference, moreover, disregards several important facts: first, that Newman's efforts were directed, as already pointed out, "to withstand and baffle the fierce energy of passion and the all-corroding, all-dissolving skepticism of the intellect in religious inquiries"; secondly, that to achieve this purpose required extraordinary gifts of patience, psychological insight, tact, scholarship, ability to recognize even the subtler protean forms which "liberalism" assumed, and mastery of the arts of clarification and persuasion; thirdly, that only one Catholic in the English-speaking world possessed the qualities and special talents needed for the task and the genius to transform them into an energizing spiritual and intellectual force.

Newman was that man. Others with different gifts might well devote them to effecting reforms in government policy, or to curing the evils begotten of the industrial revolution. To blame Newman for accepting his unique destiny is to blame Virgil for not being Caesar, or Plato for not being Euripides.

Those whose views are at variance with Newman's call him
a reactionary, courteously like Arnold or derisively like Carlyle.
To those who understand and sympathize with his primary aim,
he was the greatest apostle of reform in the Victorian age. It
was he who, as an Anglican, awoke the Anglican church to her
true mission and, as a Catholic, inspired his coreligionists with
a fresh confidence and a new sense of moral and intellectual
energy. It was he who set before them a plan for a Catholic
university in which the rightful spheres of science and letters
were established and the "Science of God" vindicated as an
essential part of the curriculum, and who in a series of candid
and brilliant lectures won a great victory over the intolerance
which had plagued them for generations. Is it too much to say
that what Newman achieved by *The Idea of a University* and *The
Present Position of Catholics in England* was, and still remains,
a major contribution to what in the broad sense is social reform?

The term "prophet" is often applied to three great Victorian
prose-masters, Carlyle, Ruskin, and Arnold. The prophet is the
conscience of contemporary society, the symbol and reminder
of its moral life. He speaks out of the fulness of his heart and
the strength of his own mind and with the power of great convictions. He condemns the shortcomings of his day with a
noble indignation and, with a sense of his mission strong upon
him, points the way toward wisdom and justice as the only means
of achieving the good life. He speaks as one having authority
and it is to man's higher nature that he appeals and the sacred
name of duty that he invokes.

Most men recognize three primary obligations, one to the
individual himself, one to his fellow man, and one to God. While
it is clear that Carlyle, Ruskin, and Arnold recognized these three
obligations, each gave particular consideration to the one he
believed to be most neglected by his generation.

First in the eyes of Carlyle and Ruskin came a man's obligations to others; in those of Arnold, his obligations to himself
first, and after that to his fellows. A fourth great Victorian, the
peer of these as a master of prose and their superior in intellect,
was primarily concerned with man's obligation to God. This
fourth prophet was Newman. The sense of an obligation to

speak out, of a mission to perform, and the voice of authority which marks the true prophet are unmistakable before *Tract 90* and after October 9, 1845. There is a striking difference, however, between Newman and the others: he alone gives the impression of doubting his personal infallibility, of relying upon an authority greater than his own.

Newman's self-dedication to the cause of revealed religion made all his works in a certain sense controversial, for in asserting and defending the claims of faith he had always in mind the presence of those who questioned, doubted, or denied. As a foe of inexactness of thought and word he used to say that few arguments would occur if only (to use a legal phrase) the minds of the opponents met. This explains why he never failed to state the opposite side of the case no matter how strongly it seemed to tell against his own. He had no joy in controversy for its own sake; thus it was not his aim to breed a generation of Catholic controversialists but of Catholics whose faith was so intelligent and so strong that it could withstand "not only the hammer blows of rationalism in the 'fifties but its big guns in the 'eighties."

Despite his dedication to one great purpose and his understanding of the strength of the opposing forces, Newman was never narrow, never vehement, never ill-natured. Arnold, finding these flaws in Carlyle and Ruskin, points by contrast to Newman who has graciousness, who does not make war but persuades, who has urbanity, "the tone of the city, of the centre, the tone which always aims at a spiritual and intellectual effect, and. . . .never disjoins banter. . . .from politeness, from felicity."

It is not extravagant to say that Newman had a passion for lucidity. It sprang partly from his eagerness to convey exactly to other minds the thoughts of his own, even to the emotional and imaginative coloring that invested them and modified their meaning; partly from his instinctive distrust of, and impatience with, hazy thinking and inexplicit expression. "Mistiness is the mother of wisdom," was his ironic comment on a form of intellectual gullibility current in his time—and current still. All he learned from his studies, his personal experiences, or his association with others provided examples and analogies which he transformed into instruments of clarification rarely matched in English literature.

Among the most striking aspects of Newman's genius was his power to probe into the inner workings of men's minds. Only Browning in his century could compare with him. A case book in religious psychology could be made from his sermons alone, and increased enormously from his other writings. He knows all the temptations against faith, all the curious forms which pride assumes to corrupt us, the intoxicating sense of freedom which animates the man who casts religion aside. Newman does not stop with the individual. He has a startling insight into the workings of mob psychology and equal insight into what he calls "the popular mind." Thus he knows the right approach to an England which for nearly twenty years had believed that his conversion was tainted by intellectual dishonesty, which for generations had persecuted its Catholic citizens, and which, under the spur of Gladstone's allegations against the dogma of papal infallibility, was prepared to believe that no English Catholic could be loyal to his sovereign.

Newman's style has been universally praised for a hundred years. It is as definitely his as his personality and serves every use from the homeliest to the most sublime. He can describe the Saviour's anguish in Gethsemane in words of poignant beauty and, with no loss of dignity, the frantic efforts of a bird seeking freedom by flinging itself against a closed window. He can describe Attica, "a confined triangle," as it appears to the unimaginative eye of a traveling salesman, and a moment later he can depict in words of unforgettable loveliness what the salesman failed to see:

> the dark violet billows with their white edges down below; those graceful, fan-like jets of silver upon the rocks, which slowly rise aloft like water-spirits from the deep, then shiver, and break, and spread, and shroud themselves, and disappear, in a soft mist of foam.

Newman's significance today is what it always has been— fundamentally spiritual and hence as changeless as the great problems with which he dealt. He teaches that duty is personal, inalienable, sacred. The current notion that it is a vague

relationship between the individual and the community would
be to him unthinkable. He teaches that higher education should
be a process of intellectual development worth securing for its
own sake; that when it brings to full flower a man's loftiest social and personal qualities it is in the best sense utilitarian; that
if it is to be true to its noblest obligations there must be at the
heart of it a philosophy which so deals with the universal issues
of human destiny that the dignity of man and the meaning of
life are made manifest. Newman was the greatest apostle of
religious tolerance in English literature. He considered it an
essential mark of a gentleman, an unfailing evidence of culture, one of the purest aims and essential achievements of a
civilized society. Finally, he never wearies of reminding us
that beyond the limitations of human insight and experience
dwell those unseen realities which shall outlast the kingdoms
of the world and whose splendor the mind of man has only
fitfully conceived.

One last word. Let us be done with the notion that Newman
was "born out of his due time," that he looked back with long-
ing eyes to the middle ages, and that temperamentally he was
of them. Nothing could be farther from the truth. Newman
was a modern who saw with keener vision than any of his contemporaries the implications of the new phase of the undying
war against revealed religion; a modern who scorned to ask
why he was born "to set the crooked straight," but gave to the
defense talents that seem to have been formed and bestowed
for that special purpose; a modern, finally, whose personality
flowered under stress and whose genius was quickened by the
challenges of his day. It was this Newman, the true Newman,
who said, "I write for the future."

VI

MAKER AND THINKER

Maker And Thinker

JOHN K. RYAN

Newman's greatness as a prose writer has had a twofold effect upon his reputation as a poet. It has over-shadowed his work in verse, so that as a poet he is remembered almost solely as the author of *The Dream of Gerontius* and of a famous hymn. At the same time, it is as the work of the writer of *The Grammar of Assent, The Idea of a University, The Development of Doctrine,* the *Apologia Pro Vita Sua,* the sermons, and the rest that the poems will continue to be read and prized. If he had not achieved such greatness as a master of English prose, it is doubtful if his memory as a poet would have long survived. Even the best of hymns have a way of becoming anonymous. Nor is Newman's verse so striking in quality or so large in bulk as to secure it an outstanding place amid the profusion of riches that is England's Parnassus. Yet when considered as a part of his whole literary production and in its own right and character as poetry, his volume of verse provides a rewarding study.

Newman's practice of giving the place and date of composition of his poems necessarily throws light upon his career as a poet. He began to write verse early in life, and the first of his collected poems was written in September, 1818, when he was seventeen years old. Of the 183 titles in the 1888 edition of the collected poems,[1] only a small number were written in the decade between 1821 and 1831. The most productive period of his life as a poet lay between November, 1832, and June, 1833. On December 7, 1832, in company with his friend Hurrell Froude, Newman sailed from Falmouth on a voyage to the Mediterranean. The long days at sea, the reading of Sacred Scripture, visits to Rome, Palermo, Corfu, Malta, and

---

[1] John Henry Cardinal Newman, *Verses on Various Occasions* (London: Longmans, Green and Co., 1888).

other places, experiences with foreign ways, and his own plans
and difficulties provided Newman with the occasion and stimula-
tion to write the bulk of the poems that he published in *Lyra
Apostolica*.[2] They were, in fact, more than half of what he
published throughout his entire life.

In Newman's life the years following 1833 were too crowded
with other things to permit a steady concern with poetry.
In 1834 he wrote five poems, all headed "From St. Gregory
Nazianzen." Only two of his collected poems are dated 1835.
In the years 1836-38 he made metrical translations of thirty-
three hymns from the Roman breviary, and in 1842, at the
request of Sir Francis Palgrave, of two hymns from the Parisian
breviary. While living at Littlemore in 1844, the year preceding his conversion, Newman wrote one poem, "Ethelwald,"
headed "From St. Bede's Metrical History of St. Cuthbert."
In the following twenty years he composed little in verse.
Two poems are dated 1849; six, 1850; two, 1853; two, 1856;
three, 1857; one, 1858; two, 1862. Yet the most considerable
of all his works in poetry was still to appear. *The Dream of
Gerontius* is dated "The Oratory, January, 1865." Seventeen
of the poems appearing in *Lyra Apostolica* were left out of
the 1868 edition of *Verses on Various Occasions*, but five of
these were later revised and restored in the edition of 1874.
An appendix to this volume contains two undated Latin hymns
in honor of St. Philip Neri. To the 1888 edition a second appendix was added containing three Latin prologues to plays
given at the Oratory School—*Phormio*, *Pincerna*, and *Andria*—

---

[2] *Lyra Apostolica* is a volume of 179 poems, first published in 1836. Of the
poems Newman wrote 109; John Keble, forty-six; Isaac Williams, nine;
Richard Hurrell Froude, eight; John William Bowden, six; and Robert
Isaac Wilberforce, one.

In a postscript to a new edition put out in 1879, Newman wrote of the
verses: "They were contemporaneous, on their first appearance in 1833,
with the 'Tracts for the Times,' and 'The Church of the Fathers,' being
contributions month by month. . . .to the 'British Magazine'. . . .The
'Lyra Apostolica,' on the whole, took the ethical side of Christianity; the
Tracts, the theological and controversial; while the 'Church of the Fathers'
was mainly historical." Newman took a modest view of the poetic character of his own contributions to the volume.

together with a translation into English verse of the "Prologus in Phormionem."[3]

The derivative character of much of Newman's verse is apparent. Out of 183 collected poems, forty-four are translations or adaptations. Among the earliest of his published poems is a paraphrase of the sixty-fourth chapter of Isaias, and passages in *The Dream of Gerontius* are based on the Church's commendation of the dying. Numerous verses are occasioned by the author's reading of Sacred Scripture; from a biblical figure, such as Moses, Jonah, or St. Paul, a lesson is drawn for himself or his age. Other verses are occasioned by scenes in his travels. Two poems, "The Elements" and "Judaism," are exercises in the antique form of the tragic chorus. Some of the earliest poems—and a few of them are not the least interesting of all—were written at the request of friends. Others celebrate seasons or feast days in the Church, or express religious doctrines and practices.

It is in this derivative character of Newman's poetry that a main defect is found. Few modern men of letters have come triumphantly through such struggles as were his. Yet although he was a man of emotional as well as of intellectual depth and power, Newman seems to have been stirred too seldom in his younger days in such manner as to pour forth his feelings in spontaneous and passionate poetry. Hence much of his verse gives the impression of being that of a man cultivated, religious, sensitive, but controlled and disciplined. He travels, observes, reads, thinks, and prays. He expresses in writing some of his reflections upon men and things and upon his own interior struggles, but in part at least these reflections could have been put down in prose as well as in verse.

This lack of spontaneity and passion necessarily makes itself felt in the form as well as in the content of his verse, although the two are not in fact entirely separable. In most of his poems conventional forms are used. There is a lack of freshness of

---

[3] Only the poems in the collected edition are considered in this study. Newman published at various times a number of poems that he never included in *Verses on Various Occasions*. Among these is his well-known translation of the *Anima Christi*.

phrase. The clichés of poetic diction and academic contrivance are frequent. We read of "the sun's smile benign," of "garb austere, and dauntless mien," of "rash scholar mine," of "heaven's majestic dome," of "beauty surpassing," of "humble heart and true," of "thy bashful face" and of "that guileless face and form." Pedestrian lines appear, such as "He deemed a safe, refined pursuit," "Nor raiment soft, nor empire's golden rod," and " 'Woe's me!' the peaceful prophet cried."

Of Jonah it is said:

> Deep in his meditative bower,
>   The tranquil seer reclined;
> Numbering the creepers of an hour,
>   The gourds which o'er him twined.

Of Isaac:

> Many the guileless years the Patriarch spent,
>   Bless'd in the wife a father's foresight chose.

Of Moses:

> Moses, the patriot fierce, became
>   The meekest man on earth,
> To show us how love's quick'ning flame
>   Can give our souls new birth.

But most awkward of all:

> Plants in the garden
>   See best the Sun's glory;
> They miss the green sward in
>   A conservatory.

To quote such things is to say the worst of Newman as a poet, but it is not to say everything or the most important things. One has only to read the pages of *Lyra Apostolica* and *Verses on Various Occasions* to become aware not only of things that are cold and severe, but also of much that reveals a genuine poetic power along with much else in the mind and heart of Newman. There are fine, thoughtful sonnets such as "Messina," "Corcyra," "Memory," "Angelic Guidance," and "Home." There are tender verses such as "Epiphany-Eve," "Valentine to a Little Girl," and "The Pilgrim Queen." There are others filled with complete honesty and simple faith, such as "Temptation" and "The Sign of the Cross." There are some memorable phrases, such as "brute mischiefs," "red dooming hour," and "vesture-skirts of light," and there are poems where the thought is summed up in compact and impressive form. In one of the later poems, "Heathen Greece,"[4] are found lines unlike any others that Newman wrote and not unworthy, in the picture they paint, of a place in Poe's "The City in the Sea."

> What the low beach and silent gloom,
> And chilling mists of that dull river,
> Along whose banks the thin ghosts shiver,—
> The thin wan ghosts that once were men,—

Different in another way is the little group of light verses that Newman wrote as a young man, some of which he preserved and republished. They include "Opusculum," "Seeds in the Air," and "Monks," all to be found in *Verses on Various Occasions,* and the delightful "To Chat—A Rhyming Letter," published in Ward's biography of Newman.[5] Like Lewis Carroll and A. E. Housman, Newman could descend from high themes and the concerns of scholarship to trivial things and playful moods. His humorous verse likewise illustrates another aspect of his genius. In poetry as well as in prose Newman was both the original and the versatile craftsman. He possessed an extraordinary command over verse-forms, although he did not always choose to exercise it. It is not too much to say that few English poets have shown so successful a use of such greatly differing types of line and stanza.

Growing to manhood where and when he did, Newman could hardly escape having a love of nature. It was the age of Wordsworth, Coleridge, and Southey, of Blake, of Shelley and Keats, and of Scott and Byron. So different from all of these, Newman yet had something of them in him, as is seen from the feeling for nature that is expressed in a few early poems, notably "Snapdragon" and "The Trance of Life." Something more

----

[4] This poem originally appeared as a song by Callista, the Greek girl, in Newman's story of the same name. Cf. *Callista, A Tale of the Third Century* (London: Longmans, Green, and Co., 1889), Chapter X.

[5] Wilfrid Ward, *The Life of Cardinal Newman* (London: Longmans, Green, and Co., 1912), II, 318.

is revealed in the lines called "The Pilgrim," written at Darting-
ton in the summer of 1831:

> There stray'd awhile, amid the woods of Dart,
>   One who could love them, but who durst not love.
> A vow had bound him, ne'er to give his heart
>   To streamlet bright, or soft secluded grove.
> 'Twas a hard humbling task, onwards to move
> His easy-captured eyes from each fair spot,
>   With unattach'd and lonely step to rove
> O'er happy meads, which soon its print forgot:—
> Yet kept he safe his pledge, prizing his pilgrim-lot.

Here is seen as genuine a love of nature as that of the roman-
tic poets, but it has been offered up for something higher. This
work to which young Newman has dedicated himself, and for
which he was to do many a "hard humbling task," is the life
of service to the truth in religion. Undoubtedly there was in
that service both loss and gain for him. The revealing lines
tell clearly how Newman had weighed what he must give
up in order to do hard and great things. How great a com-
pensation was finally to be his he could not then divine.

This high religious motive, with its attendant high spiritual
view of men and of life, is constantly felt in Newman's most
significant poetry. He could look around him in the England
of his day, the "Tyre of the West, and glorying in the name,"
and see wherein its troubles and its dangers lay. He pleads
with his native land not to put its trust in might alone, for
since the time of Babel "High towers have been man's crime,"
and "Strongholds have been man's snare." England's temptation and sin are described in the fine sonnet, "The Progress of
Unbelief."

> Now is the Autumn of the Tree of Life;
>   Its leaves are shed upon the unthankful earth,
> Which lets them whirl, a prey to the winds' strife,
>   Heartless to store them for the months of dearth.
>   Men close the door, and dress the cheerful hearth,
> Self-trusting still; and in his comely gear
> Of precept and of rite, a household Baal rear.
> But I will out amid the sleet, and view
>   Each shrivelling stalk and silent-falling leaf.
> Truth after truth, of choicest scent and hue,

Fades, and in fading stirs the Angels' grief,
Unanswer'd here; for she, once pattern chief
Of faith, my Country, now gross-hearted grown,
Waits but to burn the stem before her idol's throne.

To work against this progressive unbelief Newman saw to
be his duty. For it he sacrificed home and family and much
else. In "The Pillar of the Cloud" is found his most famous
prayer for light and help "amid the encircling gloom," but
in other verses, less known but of equal or greater merit, he
gives further expression of his plans and hopes. He sees that
"trials and crimes" will come and that the future will hold "the
same bad round" as the past. Yet this is

Not by some fated law, which need appal
Our faith, or binds our deeds as with a chain.

It is because of "men's separate crimes" that "rough deeds must
be." This being so, he adjures his comrades to learn well their
parts, to plough once more the earth, and to "scatter wide the
seed." In "Pusillanimity" he calls to mind the example of John
the Baptist and thinks of the task they are engaged in.

And so on us at whiles it falls, to claim
    Powers that we dread, or dare some forward part,
Nor must we shrink as cravens from the blame
    Of Pride, in common eyes, or purpose deep;
But with pure thoughts look up to God, and keep
    Our secret in our heart.

So too, a few days after he had written "Lead, Kindly Light,"
Newman could write "Semita Justorum." Looking in the same
clear-eyed and confident way both in upon himself and up to
God, he was able to draw from the past something of what the
future held.

When I look back upon my former race,
    Seasons I see, at which the Inward Ray
    More brightly burn'd, or guided some new way;
Truth, in its wealthier scene and nobler space
Given for my eye to range, and feet to trace.
    And next I mark, 'twas trial did convey,
    Or grief, or pain, or strange eventful day,
To my tormented soul such larger grace.
So now, whene'er, in journeying on, I feel

The shadow of the Providential Hand,
Deep breathless stirrings shoot across my breast,
Searching to know what He will now reveal,
What sin uncloak, what stricter rule command,
And girding me to work His full behest.

Such gifts of grace and faith could enable Newman to look still farther ahead. It is thus that he gained strength to rise above the arguments of doubters and defeatists. In "The Age to Come" he again gazes into the future:

When I would search the truths that in me burn,
And mould them into rule and argument,
A hundred reasoners cried,—"Hast thou to learn
Those dreams are scattered now, those fires are spent?"
And, did I mount to simpler thoughts, and try
Some theme of peace, 'twas still the same reply.

Perplex'd I hoped my heart was pure of guile,
But judged me weak in wit, to disagree;
But now, I see that men are mad awhile,
And joy the Age to come will think with me:—
'Tis the old history—Truth without a home,
Despised and slain, then rising from the tomb.

The Dream of Gerontius is unique among Newman's poems and in a way among all poems. It is uniquely ambitious because of all the poems that have been written about death and life after death, none has been quite so daringly explicit as this one in its use of revelation and of metaphysics and in its psychological analysis. A drama in five scenes and with a varied cast of characters, the poem opens with an old man at the point of death. He utters his last prayers; friends at his bedside repeat the litanies; the priest gives the last blessing. Then the soul of Gerontius finds itself in another world where it is met by its Guardian Angel who takes it before the throne of God for judgment. Demons hiss and mutter with an impotent malice. Choirs of angels sing hymns of praise to the Almighty. The great angel that was present at Christ's agony in the garden speaks to Him in behalf of Gerontius, whose soul is then sent to purgatory for an allotted time. The poor souls send up a chant of praise, and the poem ends with the beautiful parting song of the Guardian Angel.

In *The Dream of Gerontius* Newman has been completely successful in his daring and difficult task. He has not fallen into the temptation of painting banal pictures of another world. The soul of Gerontius has left this world of time and sense and has entered one that is completely different. It has been Newman's art to present this spirit-world in its true character as timeless and immaterial and yet real. Throughout the 900 lines of the poem there is unity in the midst of great variety. Each of the varied characters speaks in its own personal way. The living, the Guardian Angel, the Angel of the Agony, the five choirs of angelicals, the demons, the souls in purgatory, and Gerontius himself, all have their authentic voices and to each the verse-form used is admirably suited. The demons, "hungry and wild" in hell, with their "fierce hubbub" and "sullen howl," are shown convincingly in their own words and by brief description.

> It is the restless panting of their being;
> Like beasts of prey, who, caged within their bars,
> In a deep hideous purring have their life,
> And an incessant pacing to and fro.

Convincing too are the prayers of the Angel of the Agony and the strong biblical words sent up by the souls in purgatory.

Newman's use of metaphysics and theology in his description of the disembodied soul is sure and impressive. When the soul of Gerontius passes out of the body, it feels light and free, as if it were itself for the first time. In the deep stillness it hears "no more the busy beat of time." It knows only itself. It seems to be still in the body and yet it is unable to speak or move and thus assure itself that it possesses a body. Of one thing Gerontius is sure, that the vast material universe is quitting him, or else he is quitting it. Either he or the universe is rushing away "on the wings of light," so that "we e'en now are million miles apart." Yet there is another possibility:

> Or am I traversing infinity
> By endless subdivision, hurrying back
> From finite towards infinitesimal,
> Thus dying out of the expansive world?

Not even a moment in men's time divided "into its million-million-millionth part" has passed since Gerontius died. The

way in which spirits measure "the less and greater in the flow
of time" is different from ours. Time is no longer measured
by the sun and moon and stars, by recurring seasons, or by
clocks. It is measured "by the living thought alone." Hence
it grows or wanes by the intensity of individual thought. For
spirits, "time is not a common property," but each mind "is
standard of his own chronology."

After death Gerontius still seems to hear, taste, and touch,
but he lacks that "princely sense" of sight "which binds ideas
in one, and makes them live." It is explained to him by his
Guardian Angel that he now lacks all sense:

> A disembodied soul, thou hast by right
> No converse with aught else beside thyself.

Lest this stern solitude prove too much for it, the soul is given
perceptions which seem to come through bodily sense organs.
It is wrapped and swathed in dreams, "dreams that are true,
yet enigmatical." It is like the man who has lost a hand or
foot and yet seems to suffer pain in the missing member. So
also the soul. Although it has lost the entire body, it still per-
ceives in terms of space and time, of pain and pleasure, and of
sensations of odor, taste, touch, and hearing. It is "as ice
which blisters may be said to burn." Yet blind will the soul
remain until the Beatific Vision comes.

> For e'en thy purgatory, which comes like fire,   .
> Is fire without its light.

When his Guardian Angel takes Gerontius' soul in hand and
speaks to him, Gerontius is sure that he is no longer in the
body. On earth he could not have heard so musical a voice
without worshiping it as a God. Now he has no fear either of
falling into sin or of being "clasp'd by such a saintliness." He
is confirmed in grace, in the language of theology; or, as the
angel explains it, he cannot now "cherish a wish which ought
not to be wish'd." Nor does Gerontius fear to meet God and to
be judged. The reason for this confidence, so the angel tells
him, is because he feared death and judgment while he was on
earth. In doing so he had "forestall'd the agony," even as the
judgment of each individual soul anticipates the general judgment on the last day.

All in all, it may be said that *The Dream of Gerontius* is perfect in its kind as well as unique. Here Newman has given in poetry of a high order as exact an expression as may be hoped for of deeply mysterious doctrines. The doctrines of judgment and reward and punishment after death are difficult to treat even in the abstract language of theology. The difficulty becomes immeasurably greater when they are transferred to the concrete realm of poetry. Yet from the first solemn scene about the bed of the dying man, through the passage of the soul of the Judgment Seat, and on to the close in purgatory, there is no faltering in the sureness with which Newman writes and no loss in the light that he throws upon his subject. Neither the believer nor the unbeliever can fail to learn from this poem, or, one hopes, to be moved by it.

Among Newman's shorter poems there is one that sums up better than any other his view of the world and of man. In "Substance and Shadow" he expresses a Christian Platonism in terms as clear and lofty as that doctrine has ever received. The sonnet is nobly phrased and built. Written early in Newman's life, it is a compound of ancient as well as of original wisdom. Today, when so many men have taken to worshiping "an idol substance," when so many other men fear that this world has the power to wound even though they know that it cannot save, and when it is denied or forgotten that man is of immortal seed and high destiny, "Substance and Shadow" speaks even more clearly and compellingly than it did a century ago.

> They do but grope in learning's pedant round,
>   Who on the fantasies of sense bestow
>   An idol substance, bidding us bow low
> Before those shades of being which are found,
> Stirring or still, on man's brief trial-ground;
>   As if such shapes and moods, which come and go,
>   Had aught of Truth or Life in their poor show,
> To sway or judge, and skill to sane or wound.
> Son of immortal seed, high-destined Man!
> Know thy dread gift,—a creature, yet a cause:
> Each mind is its own centre, and it draws
> Home to itself, and moulds in its thought's span

> All outward things, the vassals of its will,
> Aided by Heaven, by earth unthwarted still.

The final feeling to which Newman's poetry brings its reader is one of admiration. A great man and a great mind, the greatness of Newman's thought and character is not absent from the sum total of his poetry, even though he did not attain to greatness as a poet. He is like Wordsworth in that he is to be judged by the best that he wrote, not by the poorest and most awkward. The best includes such sonnets as "Substance and Shadow," "The Progress of Unbelief," "Messina," "Angelic Guidance," and "Memory," all of which can stand high in a literature rich in sonnets. It includes *The Dream of Gerontius* and "The Pillar of the Cloud." It includes a series of poems that always win respect because of the complete candor and humility with which the deepest concerns and troubles of a heart and mind are laid bare. To find these last things among any poet's work is no small matter, for they are not often found in the work of others who were equipped with far greater poetic gifts than Newman was.

Yet this feeling of admiration contains something further. It is perception of the fact that Newman could have made a much greater name for himself in poetry if he had so willed. To be a poet is not alone a matter of willing, but given the other requisites, the will too has its part in achievements in the realm of poetry as well as in other realms. Both from what Newman did in literature and from what he did not do, it may be drawn that poetry too was among the goods he put away order to keep that pilgrim-lot which was his "amid the woods of Dart" and which he prized above all else in life. It was this dedication, this steadfast, solitary search for the truth, at no matter what cost and sacrifice, that at length brought Newman to a higher greatness than that of one who is a singer but no more.

VII

"THE SALVATION OF THE HEARER. . ."

"The Salvation Of The Hearer. . ."

Eugene M. Burke

For the conscientious priest the problem of sermon work is a perennial source of unrest. Not only does it crop up week after week, but it is as many-sided as it is constant. There are, for example, the basic practical difficulties that attend most parochial preaching. Some of these time largely solves; others, however, it only intensifies. Among these pragmatic difficulties perhaps the most tangible is the matter of parochial cares. These dash themselves against the priest's waking hours and leave him only broken shards of time in which to seek that "quiet and repose of the humors" during which, St. Albert the Great tells us, "the mind becomes prudent and wise." Closely related to this ever-present problem is the constantly widening distance between the priest and his studies, a gap that the requirements of pastoral work bring about. Add to this the fact that all too often the priest is bitterly aware of how little real training in speaking technique entered into his seminary course, and the sum total is a consciousness of defects that further affects his preaching and his attitude towards it.

Now, while admitting that these are real and everyday problems, they should not be allowed, to obscure what is the most fundamental problem for the conscientious preacher. For without at all detracting from their reality, nor in any sense desiring to appear condescendingly facile, still we note that these practical problems are external to the question of preaching itself and in the long run their solution lies in control and discipline. In saying this, though, it would be folly not to recognize that the acquisition of such control and discipline is an arduous and exacting task and requires long-range patience with oneself. Yet even granting this good will and this control of the situation, they at best only serve to remove the obstacles to good preaching; they do not, of themselves, suffice to produce it. And behind this conclusion is the fact that these things do not directly touch upon the fundamental problem that is inherent in the object of the Catholic sermon—the conveyance of Catholic truth to the mind of the hearer.

It must be borne in mind, however, that this last statement is not without its necessary limitations. First, Catholic truth contains, in the words of the Vatican council, "mysteries which so exceed the created intellect that even when they are revealed to us they are covered by the veil of faith and remain so while we walk in this life."[1] And no sermon is expected to convey what revelation itself has not conveyed. At the same time it is quite clear that a full understanding of Catholic theological teaching requires a technical background that not too many Catholics possess. After all, as has been rather pointedly remarked, all men are called to salvation, but not all men are called to be metaphysicians. It is therefore in the field that lies between these two limits that the fundamental sermon problem abides. It concerns itself with the relation between Catholic truth as it has been given to the priest and as the years have enriched it in his mind, and his ability to place it in the mind of his hearer as a real and moving thing. It is by way of presenting one possible solution that this article on Cardinal Newman's sermons is written.

The first thing that Cardinal Newman's sermon work has to offer, at least for the present writer, is that he is primarily a preacher, rather than a pulpit orator in the classical tradition of oratory. For while no one denies the importance and the eminent place of a Bossuet or a Massillon, still the classical pulpit oratory is limited both by the occasions which call for it and by the talent that it requires, if it is to be at all effective. Preaching, on the other hand, is a tool that admits of constant and almost universal employment, nor does it necessarily demand the wide range of talent that is essential to good pulpit oratory. The pulpit orator, at least in the classical tradition, works on a large canvas; Catholic truth is presented in stately cadence and martial array; the orator himself thinks in terms

---

[1] Denzinger-Bannwart-Umberg; *Enchiridion Symbolorum* (Freiburg im Breisgau: Herder & Co., 1937), 1796.

of vistas and perspectives and calls on the massed display of Catholic thought and history. In contradistinction to this, the preacher is content to etch out a single point or aspect of Catholic truth, and so develop it that he may set it firmly and efficaciously in the mind of his hearer. Finally, though both the orator and the preacher seek to move their hearers, the former would move the group to a fuller appreciation of the magnificence or order or beauty of Catholicism; or, perhaps, the immensity of the burden of sin, or its untold horrors. The preacher is concerned with moving the individuals present to take this one step towards the total perfection demanded of the Christian. The difference might be summed up thus: the immediate concern of the preacher is the individual, whereas the immediate aim of the orator is the group and the occasion. Yet, in all this, it is to be noted that in the actual sermon the preacher will often achieve genuine oratorical levels, and the orator will not be without power to move the individual. The abstract distinctions made here rest solely on immediate aims and basic methods.

How, then, do the sermons of Cardinal Newman exemplify the primary end of the preacher? The answer is implicit in the preceding paragraph. His whole thought is colored and dominated by his concern for the individual. This is apparent in both the selection of subject and in the manner in which it is presented and developed. By way of illustration one might take almost any sermon of his, analyze it, and see how manifest is his abiding concern with the individual. Indicative of such an approach are the sermon titles themselves. Thus: "The Difficulty of Realizing Sacred Privileges,"[2] "Secret Faults,"[3] "Promising Without Doing,"[4] "Contracted Views in Religion,"[5] all evidence the direct approach and the restriction of subject matter. The same concern might be illustrated from the structure of the sermons but that will be treated more fully in another connection. Here, however, the point is rather to show how important a place this concern for the individual held in Cardinal Newman's own mind, a point upon which the sermons offer considerable self-revelation.

---

[2] *Parochial and Plain Sermons* (London: Longmans, Green and Co., 1902), VI, 94.

[3] *Ibid.*, I, 41.   [4] *Ibid.*, I, 165.   [5] *Ibid.*, III, 102.

For the writer, the sermon that offers the most convincing witness to the great Oratorian's understanding and concern for the individual is "The Individuality of the Soul,"[6] because what is said in this sermon could only be the flowering of a great deal of personal thought and meditation. His very statement of the problem evinces this.

> Nothing is more difficult than to realize that every man has a distinct soul, that every one of the millions who live or have lived is as whole and independent a being as if there were no one else in the whole world but he.[7]

Again and again in the course of the sermon he describes how easy it is to forget this fact. Typical of this emphasis is the passage:

> Or again survey some populous town: crowds are pouring through the streets; some on foot, some in carriages; while the shops are full, and the houses too could we see them. Every part of it is full of life. Hence we gain a general idea of splendour, magnificence, opulence and energy. But what is the truth? why that every being in that great concourse is his own centre, and that all things about him are but shades, but a "vain shadow" in which "he walketh and disquieteth himself can really touch him, can touch his soul, his sires, judgments, and aims; he is everything to himself, and no one else is really anything. No one outside himself in vain." He has his own hopes and fears, de-immortality; he must live with himself for ever. He has a depth within him that is unfathomable, an infinite abyss of existence; and the scene in which he bears part for the moment is but like a gleam upon its surface.[8]

This awareness of the uniqueness of the individual is further specified when it is shown how far-reaching this conception is, having its place in even the most casual contacts.

> We may recollect when children, perhaps, once seeing a certain person; and it is almost like a dream to us now that we did. It seems like an accident which goes and is all over, like some creature of the moment, which has no existence beyond it. . . . But if we have

---

[6] Ibid., IV, 80.   [7] Ibid., pp. 80 f.   [8] Ibid., pp. 82 f.

once seen any child of Adam, we have seen an immortal soul. It has not passed away as a breeze or sunshine, but it lives at this moment in one of those places whether of bliss or of misery, in which all souls are reserved to the end.[9]

Any number of passages similar to those just quoted might be adduced. One might instance his moving description of Christ's concern for the individual in "A Particular Providence Revealed in the Gospel";[10] or in the same sermon the scripturally rich section that paints God's care for each of us.[11] Since, however, the quotations are only by way of indicating the color of Cardinal Newman's mind in the matter of preaching, the purpose will be better served and complemented by setting down his own analysis of the reasons for such concern on the part of the preacher.

If we are sure that the most Holy Redeemer has shed his blood for all men, is it not a very plain and simple consequence that we, His servants, His brethren, His priests should be unwilling to see that blood shed in vain—wasted I might say as regards you, and should wish to make you partakers of the benefits which have been vouchsafed to ourselves? . . . What is so powerful an incentive to preaching, as the sure belief that it is the preaching of the truth? What so constrains to the conversion of souls, as the consciousness that they are at present in guilt and peril? What so great a persuasive to bring men into the Church as the conviction that it is the special means by which God effects the salvation of those whom the world trains in sin and unbelief? . . . We come among you, because we believe there is but one way of salvation marked out from the beginning and that you are not walking along it; we come among you as the ministers of the extraordinary grace of God which you need; we come among you. . . . because we dare not hide in a napkin those mercies and that grace of God which have been given us, not for our own sake only, but for the benefit of others.[12]

[9] *Ibid.*, pp. 85 f. [10] *Ibid.*, III, 120 ff.

[11] *Ibid.*, p. 125. Another sermon along this same line is "The Immortality of the Soul," *Parochial and Plain Sermons*, I, 15.

[12] "The Salvation of the Hearer the Motive of the Preacher," *Discourses Addressed to Mixed Congregations* (London: Longmans, Green and Co., 1902), pp. 17 f.

If the passage just quoted be taken in conjunction with the preceding ones, there is given to us not only an insight into the mind of Newman the preacher, but there is also offered a basic description of any true preacher's mind. In fact, a preacher who imbibes of such thoughts and whose work is called into being by such convictions cannot help but be aware that he is directing his efforts to distinct, unique, and infinitely important individuals and not to some faceless group. Likewise, as the preacher becomes increasingly aware of the importance to God of each of his hearers and, at the same time, is growingly conscious of the supreme necessity of his saving message, then he will also be mindful that his sermons are not casual affairs but matters of weighty obligation. Nor does it seem too far-fetched to think that the personal realization of these basic facts lays the foundation for a vital contact between the preacher and his hearers. Certainly, a living concern for those whom he addresses and an abiding awareness of the necessity of the truth that he carries will release the well-springs of his own convictions. This, in turn, will cause them to flow towards his hearers, and it is this vital reaching out that will be the bridge over which Catholic truth will best pass.

But while these things are fundamental and of the essence of good preaching they do not, of themselves, dispense with good technique. It is true, of course, that such convictions are the informing soul of technique, and that without them even the best technique degenerates into conscious or unconscious charlatanry. None the less, good technique can give to these convictions a fullness and an effectiveness that the preacher cannot otherwise supply save perhaps through a *gratia gratis data*—a gratuitious gift which, to say the least, it would be presumptuous of the preacher to depend on every time he delivers a sermon. Consequently, it will be of real value to view some elements of Cardinal Newman's own sermon technique. For, if his fundamental cast of mind and his technique be recognized as forming a living whole, then, perhaps, the careful reading of his sermons may be of assistance in formulating effective sermons of one's own.

The first element of technique presented here is one that would seem to be the Cardinal's most characteristic and effective method. It is one that not only abounds in his sermons, but is employed extensively in his controversial writings and gives to them much of their power. This element of his technique may be described as: *the analysis and formulation for his hearers of their own personal reactions and behavior when they come into contact with religious realities.* Sometimes this particular technique is the very structure of the sermon.[13] In any case, it occurs in all of his sermons either explicitly or implicitly. Its effectiveness arises from the fact that it crystallizes the question, or problem, or truth in such a personal way that the answer itself has an immediate and personal significance.

Since it is an almost impossible task to make universally satisfying selections from the countless examples at hand, the illustrations given are chosen because of their personal appeal. So on the question of duty:

> To find fault with the circumstances in which we find ourselves is our ready and familiar excuse when our conduct is arraigned in any particular. . . . In truth, nothing is more easy to the imagination than duty in the abstract, that is, duty in name and not reality. It is when it assumes a definite and actual shape, when it comes upon us under circumstances (and it is obvious it can come no other way), then it is difficult and troublesome. Circumstances are the very trial of obedience. Yet, plain as this is, it is very common to fancy our peculiar condition particularly hard, and that we should be better and happier men in any other.[14]

This approach lays its finger upon a common form of self-deception, but it does it so impersonally that even the reader feels as though he were examining his own conscience, and finds himself furnishing his own illustrations.

An even more powerful use of this technique is seen in the analysis of the growth of an irreligious cast of mind in a young man.

> He has aspirations and ambitions which home does not satisfy. He wants more than home can give. . . .

---

[13] Cf. "Human Responsibility, As Independent of Circumstances," *Sermons Preached Before the University of Oxford* (London: Longmans, Green and Co., 1902), p. 136.

[14] *Ibid.,* pp. 140 f.

he listens to views and discussions which are incon-
sistent with sanctity and religious faith. At first he has
no temptation to adopt them; he only wishes to know
what is "said." As time goes on, however, living with
companions who have no fixed principle, and who, if
they do not oppose at least do not take for granted,
any of the most elementary truths; or worse, hearing
or reading what is directly against religion, at length
without being conscious of it, he admits a sceptical
influence on his mind. He does not know it, he does
not recognize it but there it is; and *before* he recognizes
it, it leads him to a fretful, impatient way of speaking
of the persons, conduct, words and measures of
religious men. . . . And so he goes on, approximating
more and more closely to sceptics and infidels and feeling more and more congeniality with their modes of
thinking, till some day suddenly, from some accident,
the fact breaks upon him, and he sees clearly that he is
an unbeliever himself.[15]

Here each step in the road to unbelief has been laid bare. At any
step the individual who has begun this journey can see how far
he has travelled and where he now tarries. To all appearances
neither praise nor blame has been laid, but the blindness and
folly of the individual is patent in every descriptive touch.

An example of the same approach used positively may be seen
in his sermon, "Waiting for Christ."

. . . .do you not know what it is to so love and live
upon a person who is present to you, that your eyes follow his, that you read his soul, that you see its changes
in his countenance, that you anticipate his wants, that
you are sad in his sadness, troubled when he is vexed,
restless when you cannot understand him, relieved,
comforted when you have cleared up the mystery?

This is the state of mind, when our Lord and Saviour
is its Object, not intelligible at first sight to the world,
not easy to nature, yet of so ordinary fulfillment in the
Church in all ages, as to become the sign of the Presence

---

[15] "Intellect, the Instrument of Religious Training," *Sermons Preached
on Various Occasions* (London: Longmans, Green and Co., 1902), pp. 10 f.

of Him who is unseen, and to be a sort of note of the divinity of our religion.[16]

These three illustrations of this technique (to which any reader of Cardinal Newman will be able to add a hundred) exemplify a number of points that can help in the building of effective sermons. First and foremost, through its skillful use one can actually bring truth into living contact with the individual. Almost unknown to himself the hearer's mind can be made to face itself in the light of such an analysis. More than this, it is not the preacher but the hearer who sits in judgment upon himself, measuring his acts in the light of Catholic truth and principle. By such a method, too, there is made possible some release from a complete dependence on stories and badly crippled similes. Instead of dragging in stories by the most tenuous of connections, the hearer himself furnishes the best of all illustrations, his own actions and reactions. He can be led to apply this truth or this norm to himself and see his own needs and shortcomings. Clothed with apparent impersonality this technique can be developed to the point where it becomes the articulate voice of conscience calling to the will to act upon what it now sees.

Yet, while admiring Cardinal Newman's skillful and flexible use of this technique, it should not be thought that it is outside the competence of the ordinary priest. No one, of course, will deny Newman's mastery, or say that he can use it in exactly the same way. A priest, however, does deal with a variety and number of individuals in their most intimate and revealing moments. After a few years of pastoral work, he can have in his grasp a working knowledge of human nature in act. He has certainly come to some realization of the complexities of motivation and rationalization that enter in human acts and living. And the reactions of types and ages and varying cultural levels to Catholic truth and principles are for him a fairly familiar land, since so much of his work is done there. He has therefore a rich mine out of which he may draw the material for this technique.

---

[16] "Waiting for Christ," *ibid.*, p. 36. Here might be added his description and analysis of the sinner turning from sin in "Saintliness Not Forfeited by the Penitent," *Sermons Bearing on Subjects of the Day* (London: Longmans, Green and Co., 1902), p. 18.

Nor is this source of the raw material confined to his observation of others. He himself is just as rich with this ore. Almost from the time he has been capable of grasping abstract ideas, he has been in constant contact with Catholic realities and truths. Through the weighing of individual acts in the light of clear-cut and objective moral principles, he has achieved a greater degree of objectivity than he is liable to be aware of. At the same time, retreats, spiritual reading, meditations, and examinations of conscience extended over the years have put into his hands a real capacity for objective introspection, more perhaps than he realizes. All these are at his service here, because as a human being his fundamental responses to high aspirations are not alien to human life. Bound, as he is, to all men by the cords of Adam, his own life mirrors the basic elements of reaction and behavior in the face of religious truth; it reflects the difficulties of depending on faith and not sight; and it images the corrosion that daily duty and routine spiritual activity can produce. With such self-knowledge at his call, plus his own experience as a priest, the preacher carries within him not only the material out of which this form of sermon technique is molded, but at the very least a basic power so to mold it.

The full power of this technique, though, calls for another element which goes hand in hand with it: the use of words. And in such usage Cardinal Newman has much to offer his reader. Almost without exception the words used in his sermons are simple and easily apprehended. Their force lies in the color which they give to his thought. Variety and fluency are introduced by a series of adjectives, adverbs or phrases. Each one of these adds a note to the idea or reveals another of its facets. When they are taken together they give to the idea a color and a vividness that catch the mental eye of the listener because they convey that idea pictorially. In instance of this, take his picture of the young Augustine:

> With his young ambition and his intellectual energy, and his turbulent appetites; educated yet untaught; with powers strengthened, sharpened, refined by exercise, unenlightened and untrained,—[he] goes forth into the world ardent, self-willed, reckless, headstrong,

inexperienced. . . , to become the victim of heresy and
sin.[17]

With an economy of stroke a complete picture of the young
Augustine is set before our eyes. Using only adjectives and ad-
jectival phrases the whole history is limned out: *"With his young
ambition and his intellectual energy, and his turbulent appetites."*
The combination lends to the idea a rich pictorial color. Similarly
in the striking etching of Augustine's early career: *"[he] goes
forth. . . .into the world ardent, self-willed, reckless, headstrong,
inexperienced."* Each word gives voice to a whole history and
combined they form a vivid cross-section of that history.

The use of this method to bring out contrasting realities is
equally effective, as in his delineation of Christ's gift of peace.

> It was a peace but a new peace, "not as the world
> giveth;" not the exultation of the young, light-hearted
> and simple, easily created, easily lost: but a serious,
> sober, lasting comfort, full of reverence, deep in con-
> templation.[18]

Here the purpose is to show what Christian peace really is,
and its difference from the peace of the world. It might be
done by a story. It could be served by presenting the abstract
notions that are implied. Instead, by a rich flow of words, each
of which conveys these abstractions in a vivid and concrete
way, the full idea is driven into the mind. The contrast emphasizes the whole thing: "serious" is opposed to "exultation,"
"sober" to "light-hearted," "lasting comfort" to "easily created,
easily lost," and then "full of reverence, deep in contemplation."

One somewhat more lengthy passage will conclude these examples. This passage is a particularly felicitous combination of the
two elements that have been noted in this article: the analysis of
human behavior and the use of words.

> . . .when a man feels himself possessed of good abili-
> ties; of quickness in entering into a subject, or of powers
> of argument to discourse readily upon it, or of acute-
> ness to detect fallacies in dispute with little effort, or of

---

[17] "Intellect the Instrument of Religious Training," *Sermons Preached on
Various Occasions,* pp. 4 f.

[18] "Christian Nobleness," *Sermons Bearing on Subjects of the Day,* p. 141.

a delicate and cultivated taste, so as to separate with precision the correct and beautiful in thought and feeling from the faulty and irregular, how shall such a one be tempted to self-complacency and self-approbation! How apt will he be to rely upon himself, to rest contented with himself; to be harsh and impetuous; or supercilious; or to be fastidious, indolent, unpractical; and to despise the pure, self-denying temper of religion, as something irrational, dull, enthusiastic, or needlessly rigorous![19]

A careful perusal of the ideas contained here and a consideration of the number and variety of terms chosen to make those ideas live will indicate the depths that go into this proper use of words. There is presented a careful analysis of the type of man described and a clearly and sharply drawn set of pictures. The whole process is the result of a judicious selection and accumulation of words that complement and enrich one another. By way of tasting the full flavor of this method, one might read aloud the words "fastidious, indolent, unpractical" and "irrational, dull, enthusiastic or needlessly rigorous." If they are read with an effort to express what they contain, it will be found that their idea content depicts the reality intended and the very sound co-operates in conveying the same thing.

Many other elements of the great convert's sermon work might be treated. Mention might be made of his use of Scripture and scriptural language; his use of the Fathers and of patristic ideas; his sense of the history of Catholicism and his personal awareness of the place and beauty of the Church of Christ. Limitations of space prevent taking these up here. What has been seen, though, might be termed the fundamental elements of his sermon technique and work. The purpose in treating them at all was to lay down general lines for the formulation of effective sermons. Hence, if thought is evoked in this field the article has accomplished its aim.

Lest, however, all this seem too remote a presentation, attention should be called to the presupposition that underlies the effective use of the methods described and analyzed. For the development which such technique assumes presupposes work.

---

[19] "Temporal Advantages," *Parochial and Plain Sermons*, VII, 65.

Sermon technique is an art, and as an art it demands consistent and careful practice. A dozen tries will not enable the tyro to translate the music sheets into the music of Chopin. Neither does the ability to recognize the notes of the scale make a singer, nor does a good sense of color make a painter. Consistent practice in correct methods, experiment, and new attempts after failure are the tools which develop the art. The mere use of Newman's words will not transform the preacher into another Newman. He is a master of English prose and much of his mastery lies in this very selection of words. But a wide and flexible command of words is not an impossible task for the priest, any more than the ability to analyze human behavior is outside his scope. Reading, speaking, and writing can each contribute to this. It is not impossible to read one sermon of his a week with these ideas in mind and then to try to translate some of it into one's own efforts. This very habit could be a beginning if it were now and again accompanied by the careful writing of a sermon. Still, all this is the dull and unrewarding work of practice, and ultimately the willingness to submit oneself to the task of practice stems from the personal conviction that it is a matter of personal obligation. And a real and personal sense of obligation has its source in the full understanding of what it means to be a priest, the minister of Christ the Divine Teacher, the coadjutor of God the Revealer.

VIII

FOR THE MODERN READER

For The Modern Reader

Daniel M. O'Connell

What better tribute could we pay to John Henry Cardinal Newman than to enlarge the circle of his readers? He is easy reading, even for those who lack a collegiate or indeed a high school education. They can enjoy and study many of his works. Master of English prose, as he is universally proclaimed, he is at the same time an artist of the ordinary, common word. He strove for such a command. A comparative study of the 1864 and 1865 editions of the *Apologia Pro Vita Sua* illustrates this. This book was written under great pressure of time, as its chapters appeared weekly. In his 1865 changes of words he substituted generally an Anglo-Saxon for a Latin vocable. And his thought is always crystal clear.

In urging even the formally uneducated layman to read certain works of the illustrious Oratorian, I am thinking, I hope not too exclusively, of Catholic men and women like the late Honorable Alfred E. Smith. He was never accorded any privileges mentioned in the Latin sheepskin of a bachelor of arts. His mind was trained, nevertheless, much as was Abraham Lincoln's. I am sure that "Al's" intellect, clear and incisive as it was undoubtedly, would have enjoyed certain works of Cardinal Newman. Did he? I confess I never heard that he did. I am confident, though, that he could, and so my plea is, give the laity—educated and uneducated—a chance to enjoy Cardinal Newman by placing some of his works in their hands.

I have enlarged the "entrance requirements" to take in the formally educated laity, as, unfortunately, I am afraid many of them have read Cardinal Newman only in anthologies. And what is the good of an anthology if it does not induce one to read the original works of the author? How many educated Catholic laymen have read one volume of John Henry Cardinal Newman's? But that is the past. There are today's arguments for building up a Newman reading clientele, not excluding the clergy! Newman belongs to the ages and it is never too late to make his acquaintance.

As a matter of encouragement to all of us, one of his most brilliantly written books was addressed to the ordinary lay people of Birmingham, the "Brethren of the Oratory." I refer to *The Present Position of Catholics in England,* a series of nine lectures, which are approaching the time-approved popularity of a hundred years, having been delivered in 1851. Moreover, the subject matter is as timely today, unfortunately, as it was nearly a century ago in England, viz., the anti-Catholic point of view taken by many non-Catholics.

Father Newman, a convert of six years, was fully cognizant of the inside aspect of prejudice as few other priests could have been. He recognized further the obligation of this advantage and that his ability to portray the malady was rather unique in the Catholic Church of his day. Further, he must have felt a zeal for God's house that stimulated his native energy to slay the dragon of "No-Popery." There was aroused in him, too, almost for the first and last time, a delicate wit and humor and delicious irony that have placed *The Present Position of Catholics in England* and *Difficulties of Anglicans* in an exclusive category among his books and even among English prose writings.

Practically every large anthology on English literature contains passages from the first series of lectures. Newman immediately caught the attention of his audience by the now famous descriptions of "The Man and the Lion" and of the Russian anti-English mob. In the former, the sedate lecturer retells how the Lion was entertained most courteously and treated as a human guest by the Man. Set out most prominently in a rich collection of sculpture and painting in the Man's house were images of a Lion. But the latter was always the victim when there was a conflict between man and himself. Furthermore, the Lion was done into "extravagant forms, as if he were not only the slave and creature but the very creation of man. . . .in short, there was no misconception of excess or indignity which was thought too great for the lord of the forest and the king of brutes." All the time the Man was unconscious of the humiliation he was heaping upon the Lion. When his guest was ready to depart, the Man asked the Lion what the latter thought of such splendors of art. The guest answered: "Lions would have fared better had lions been the artists." And Newman added: "You see the application before I make it."[1] Catholics were the Lion to the England of 1851.

This fable was a "softening-up" barrage for the "beachhead" the lecturer was about to make in his famous caricature of the anti-Catholic Englishman of his day in the person of an anti-English agitator haranguing a Russian mob and arousing it to fanaticism against the British constitution.

> "I hold in my hand," continued the speaker, "a book which I have obtained under very remarkable circumstances. . . . It is called 'Blackstone's Commentaries on the Laws of England,' and I am happy to make known to the universe its odious and shocking mysteries. . . . I open the book, gentlemen, and what are the first words which meet my eyes '*The King can do no wrong*.' . . . 'In the law,' says Blackstone, 'the Sovereign is said *never to die!*' Again, with still more hideous expressiveness, 'The law ascribes to the Sovereign an ABSOLUTE IMMORTALITY. THE KING NEVER DIES!'"[2]

In concluding his first lecture, Newman protests that he has not caricatured at all this parallel to anti-Catholicism; that no absurdities contained in his sketch "can surpass those which are firmly believed of Catholics by sensible, kind-hearted, well-intentioned Protestants." Then comes a manifestation of that sympathetic Newman, whom Englishmen eventually came to appreciate: "Such is the consequence of having looked at things all on one side, and shutting the eyes to the other."[3]

Is this not an enticing preview of *The Present Position of Catholics in England* for the mental screen of my ordinary layman? I will gamble my literary fortune on this: bachelor of arts or non-bachelor, after reading this first lecture, will finish one book written by Cardinal Newman. What a triumph! For today how many people, I wonder, read through one serious book a

---

[1] Cf. *The Present Position of Catholics in England* (London: Longmans, Green and Co., 1896), pp. 2 ff.

[2] *Ibid.*, pp. 29-39.   [3] *Ibid.*, p. 41.

year! With the description of this imaginary Russian mob taking
on a current note of interest, let my collegiate or non-collegiate
layman read on.   He has tasted but the *antipasto*.   A banquet
awaits him in the succeeding eight lectures. Here is a glance at
the menu.

Great passages in all literatures arise naturally.   They belong
to the occasion, as the wild flower to the woods. And so in enum-
erating the spreading of prosaic anti-Catholic rumors, Newman,
the artist of word and phrase and of repetition without sameness,
in a later chapter breaks into a brilliant onomatopoeic narration
of how, at the faintest whisper of Catholicism, "spontaneously
the bells of the steeple begin to sound. . . .swinging and booming,
tolling and chiming, with nervous intenseness, and thickening
emotion, and deepening volume, the old ding-dong which has
scared town and country this weary time; tolling and chiming
away, jingling and clamoring and ringing the changes on their
poor half-dozen notes. . . ."[4] This description in its entirety has
been considered a prose rival of Poe's famous "The Bells."   Its
appropriate music is readily recognized and appreciated by any
one as a help to the full sense of the theme.

A diary of the time, kept by Miss Giberne, mentions the peals
of laughter which were audible from outside the hall where Newman was giving these lectures.[5] He felt sure of himself in exposing
"No-Popery" according to the rule that ridicule is a test of truth.
Tradition and fable were the supports of bigotry; prejudice, its
life; assumed principles the intellectual ground, and ignorance
was the protection of the Protestant view. Thus ran Newman's
arguments through the eight lectures.   In the fifth, however,
Father Newman dropped all his bombs of keen irony and biting
sarcasm in a devastating attack on the ex-priest and degenerate,
Achilli, who had been embraced and exploited by an anti-Catholic group in England.   He was attaining the notoriety of another
Maria Monk. Newman pictured him as saying: "I have been a
Catholic and an infidel; I have been a Roman priest and a hypo-
crite; I have been a profligate under a cowl." He continued with

---

[4] *Ibid.*, pp. 76 f.

[5] Cf. Wilfrid Ward, *The Life of John Henry Cardinal Newman* (New
York: Longmans, Green and Co., 1912), I, 264.

an enumeration of Achilli's various immoralities and then: "Look on me, ye mothers of England, a confessor against Popery, for ye 'ne'er may look upon my like again'. . . . And now attend to me, such as I am, and you shall see what you shall see about the barbarity and profligacy of the Inquisitors of Rome."[6] Achilli in his bold libel suit against the lecturer was supported by the anti-Catholic group. The verdict, as the London *Times* declared, was a deep stain on the administration of justice in England. Father Newman was found guilty and fined one hundred pounds. This was promptly paid by friends, but the cost of the suit, which reached the enormous sum of twelve thousand pounds, also fell on the penniless Newman. Fortunately, public subscriptions in Europe and America paid the entire amount. Newman appreciated this brotherly affection of Catholics. He dedicated *The Idea of a University* to them in a beautiful gem of English prose.

To skip to the ninth and last discourse, Newman, as another St. Paul, pointed out to Catholics, especially to the laity, their duties towards this Protestant view. He ended with no general apostrophe, but a very plain, intelligible appeal to their individual lives. "Oblige men to know you; persuade them: importune them, shame them into knowing you."[7] These forcible words might be called the climax of what had gone before. Every Catholic layman will feel proud as he reads this chapter: "In all times the laity have been the measure of the Catholic spirit; they saved the Irish Church three centuries ago, and they betrayed the Church in England."[8] He pleads for a laity, "not arrogant, not rash in speech, not disputatious, but men who know their religion."[9] He recognizes that his audience is such, but he would have them enlarge their knowledge, cultivate their reason, get an insight into the relation of truth to truth, understand how faith and reason stand to each other.[10] Newman advised his audience "not to fret at insults, to bear imputations, and to interpret the actions of all in the best sense you possibly can."[11] Did this seem almost a worldly way of speaking, with

---

[6] *Ibid.*, I, 279 n.
[7] *The Present Position of Catholics in England,* p. 372.
[8] *Ibid.*, pp. 390 f.   [9] *Ibid.*, p. 390.   [10] *Cf. ibid.*
[11] *Ibid.*, p. 392.

no reference to Christian charity? He would not "adopt a tone too high for the occasion," yet every age has its martyrs.[12] Will this? "I only say that if it were to be a time for calling out the martyr's spirit, you and I, through God's grace, have it in us."[13] Holding forth such heroism as a possible reality, Newman could with greater force urge home a practical lesson to be had by his lay audience. And in 1945 it is the same for the American layman of his day as for the English one of 1851. "Look at home, there lies your work; what you have to do, and what you can do, are one and the same. Prove to the people of Birmingham, as you can prove to them, that your priests and yourselves are not without conscience, or honour, or morality. . . . If, then, a battle is coming on, stand on your own ground. . . .be found where you are known; make yourselves and your religion known more and more, for in that knowledge is your victory."[14]

To the laity, with or without that bachelor's degree, I would close my brief for their reading *The Present Position of Catholics in England* with the following attractive sentences from the concluding paragraphs of the last lecture. "Good is never done except at the expense of those who do it. . . .nothing would be done at all, if a man waited till he could do it so well that no one could find fault with it."[15]

The Idea of a University, in contrast, is probably the most academic in matter of Newman's writings, as the titles of the book and of its chapters indicate. It is, moreover, the best example of Newman's literary style. For these two especial reasons it is studied in English and American seats of learning. Such varied high praises have been bestowed on it that it would be impossible to pick out the most striking rose in the bouquet. One such would be that of Sir Arthur Quiller-Couch. As his last book, *Memories and Opinions*, has refreshed our recollections of him, let that be the deciding factor for quoting from him: "And here let me say that of all the books written in these hundred years there is perhaps none you can more profitably thumb and ponder than. . . . *The Idea of a University*. . . . the book is so wise—so eminently wise—as to deserve being

---

12 Cf. *ibid.*
14 *Ibid.*, p. 385.

13 *Ibid.*, p. 400.
15 *Ibid.*, pp. 402 f.

bound by the young student of literature for a frontlet on his brow and a talisman on his writing wrist."[16] Any serious-minded lay person, no matter whether he or she has attended college, could be urged to read this volume. Assure him or her of delightful hours in doing so.

If, however, *The Idea of a University* seems impregnable for the ordinary lay person, let him by-pass that salient and consider instead the contents of Newman's autobiography, the "explanation of his life," his *Apologia Pro Vita Sua*. Many consider it to be Newman's masterpiece, and one of the three great auto-biographies of all time! It, too, was addressed, though in writing, to the laity, the man in the streets of England in 1864. It had a large distribution, being issued weekly in pamphlet form during the time of its writing.

All men naturally resent being called a liar, and so did Father Newman. He was shocked to read such an accusation against him and his fellow priests by the well-known writer, Charles Kingsley, in the following passage of a book review contributed to a popular magazine. "Truth, for its own sake, had never been a virtue with the Roman clergy. Father Newman informs us that it need not, and on the whole ought not to be;—that cunning is the weapon which heaven has given to the Saints wherewith to stand the brute male force of the wicked world which marries and is given in marriage. Whether his notion be doctrinally correct or not, it is at least historically so."[17]

Here was the clear incentive that Father Newman had long awaited. Now it was not merely his private reputation and character which were at stake but the good name of every priest and so of himself as a member of the *regale sacerdotium*, the royal priesthood of the Roman, Holy, Catholic, and Apostolic Church for which he had sacrificed his previous welfare. He wrote to the publishers, Macmillan and Company, expressing his surprise that "There is no reference at the foot of the page to any words of mine, much less any quotation from my writings in justification of this statement. . . . I do but wish to draw the at-

---

[16] *On the Art of Writing* (New York: G. P. Putnam's Sons, 1916), p. 37.

[17] Quoted in *Newman's Apologia Pro Vita Sua* (Oxford University Press, 1931), p. 6.

tention of yourselves, as gentlemen, to a grave and gratuitous slander, with which I feel confident you will be sorry to find associated a name so eminent as yours."[18]

And so, nineteen years after his conversion to the Church, Newman began one of the most famous of all epistolary controversies, that between the "Rev. Charles Kingsley and Dr. John Henry Newman." While not a part of the *Apologia Pro Vita Sua*, the correspondence is given usually as an appendix to the book. Newman showed himself a master in smoking out his opponent. He acknowledged Kingsley's letter "referring generally to a Protestant sermon of mine. . . .published by me, as Vicar of St. Mary's, in 1844. . . .and also referring to my works *passim;* in justification of your statement, categorical and definite that Father Newman informs us,' etc."[19]   Kingsley retorted: "What then does Dr. Newman mean?"

"What then does Dr. Newman mean?" This question kept recurring to Newman's mind. At last, he realized that it was not Kingsley but England that asked the question. To England the answer would be given in the history of his life. Away with Kingsley, the appeal is to the English people. And how opportune was to be Newman's appeal can be judged by the following extract which a nonfriendly critic addressed to Father Newman: "All England has been laughing with you and those who knew you of old have rejoiced to see you once more come forth like a lion from his lair, with undiminished strength of muscle, and they have smiled as they watched you carry off the remains of Mr. Charles Kingsley (no mean prey) lashing your sides with your tail, and growling and muttering as you retreat into your den."[20] To a third party, who had interposed, in a written communication suggesting a truce, Newman's answer was brilliant: "Most wonderful phenomenon! An educated man, breathing English air, and walking in the light of the nineteenth century, thinks that neither I nor any members of my communion feel any difficulty in allowing that 'Truth for its own sake need not, and on the whole ought not to be, a virtue with the Roman clergy;' nay, that they are not at all surprised to be told that 'Father Newman

---

[18] *Ibid.*, p. 7.   [19] *Ibid.*, p. 9.
[20] Wilfrid Ward., *op cit.*, II, 34.

had informed' the world, that such is the standard of morality acknowledged, acquiesced in, by his co-religionists!"[21]

Newman realized that rapid and continuous firing was of the essence in his present attack on the hitherto complacent English anti-Catholics. He wrote for as many as twenty hours a day during those weeks. Despite the strain, he was always the gentleman he pictured so forcibly in *The Idea of a University*. Urbanity is conceded even to this polemical writing, done under a white heat of strong personal feeling. This period was a great crisis in Newman's life, but he triumphed, as was evidenced, for example, by the changed and enthusiastic reviews in the London *Times* of Newman's following works. Kingsley, to his own credit, declared that he had joined swords with one who was too strong for him.

The *Apologia Pro Vita Sua* illustrates its author's general style, "common English made perfect." You may challenge, then, an intelligent layman to read the *Apologia* with the attention he gives to the editorial page of his daily newspaper. He will have joined the ranks of those who know Cardinal Newman not from a disconnected, syncopated anthology but from having read one of his complete volumes. How numerous will such valiant laymen be? The answer to that question must be left to the future. For myself, I am willing to put off the answer with the great hope that time will multiply those numbers in geometric proportions.

---

[21] Quoted in *Newman's Apologia Pro Vita Sua* (Oxford University Press, 1931), p. 10.

IX

NEWMAN AND MODERN EDUCATIONAL THOUGHT

Newman And Modern Educational Thought

J. F. Leddy

When we consider the wide range of Newman's interests, and the high distinction of his achievement in so many fields it seems ungracious, as well as inaccurate, to view his work under one aspect alone, and to stress that aspect to the neglect of others. In most instances it requires considerable skill to compose such a special study without false emphasis or misleading suggestions about Newman's work as a whole. However, an exception may be made in the case of his opinions on educational problems.

He spent many years immersed in educational matters, living by turns the life of a student, a professor, and finally an administrator. He was at home in a school, and completely at ease in a university. He passed his youth and early middle age at Oxford, the prime of life deep in plans for the new university in Ireland, and after these had failed, although he was elderly, he nursed hopes of a return to Oxford. During this time many letters, essays, and books came from his pen, all devoted to the educational questions of his day and of our day as well.

His thought was commonly cast in an academic mold, and his expression attuned to the prevailing fashion and tendency of intellectual discussion. His approach to nearly every question was academic—in the best sense of the word. Even in fiction or in verse Newman is didactic. He may range beyond this aim, and his motive in a given work may be more complex but he never altogether ceases to be the teacher. It is significant that his celebrated poem, *The Dream of Gerontius*, which grows steadily in reputation, is fundamentally a theological treatise.

There is no need to labor the point. Newman was always the educator—he might be more, but never less. There are several methods of finding our way through the rich maze of his thought, but one at least is the silver thread of his educational writings. It is instructive to read them in their entirety and to supplement them with the letters and minor papers which Ward[1] has reprinted in the standard biography. The industrious student will soon perceive an order, a consistency, which binds together these scattered works into a logical system, and he will naturally ask what was the reception accorded to Newman's ideas when they first appeared in print, and what has been their subsequent reputation.

It is a natural question, for Newman was a great man, widely appreciated in his own lifetime, and in the half-century since his death. He is a figure set in another age, and it should be possible to assess his influence today. If, as we have insisted, his educational interests were of such importance, we should expect to find, even if many of these writings now have no contemporary interest, that he has influenced in some degree the course of educational thinking since, certainly among his fellow Catholics, and possibly among others. This expectation would appear to be justified when we observe the existence of many "Newman Clubs" serving the interests of Catholic university students, and note the continuing fame of his great work, *The Idea of a University*. We are here concerned with both practical and theoretical problems in higher education, and it will be useful to deal with them in greater detail.

Although the Newman Club is now a well-known institution in Canada and the United States, it should not be taken for granted or casually accepted as a familiar and elementary matter. It is based upon far-reaching principles, and throws a flood of light on the practical implications of Newman's thought. An examination of them will serve to correct the popular notion that he was exclusively intellectual in his treatment of educational problems. (For the purpose of this paper the term "Newman Club" is applied only to an organization of Catholic students, guided by a chaplain, fully sanctioned by ecclesiastical authority, in connection with a state or non-denominational university, and is meant to signify the whole arrangement under which Catholic students are permitted to attend such institutions.)

---

[1] Cf. Wilfrid Ward, *The Life of John Henry Cardinal Newman*, 2 vols. (London: Longmans, Green and Co., 1912).

These clubs are not named after Newman merely to honor a great churchman and scholar. He was in fact the inventor, and the chief advocate of the Newman Club as we know it. The story should be better known than it is.

In Newman's day the Oxford and Cambridge graduate dominated every phase of life in England. The men whom he had known when he was a student and then a tutor at Oxford were later the bishops, the cabinet ministers, the bankers, and the eminent writers who directed public opinion to so large an extent. They were, of course, Anglican, and they constituted the great bulwark of that church. With his conversion Newman dropped out of this powerful group and learned at first hand how different were the circumstances and the influence of Catholics. He perceived that Catholic doctrine suffered in popular prestige from the weakness and insignificance of the Catholic community itself. Catholics without a university education lacked opportunities in their careers, and Catholic champions were sometimes at a disadvantage in dispute with opponents of wider learning and education. Further, the university was in the nature of the case the usual origin of new intellectual movements. Free from Catholic influence, these would probably be infidel and heretic in character, and the eventual cause of much harm to true doctrine. It was too much to hope that the Oxford movement would be repeated.

Newman's first solution was the traditional and approved one—the Catholic university, and he struggled for some years to establish one in Ireland, expecting that English Catholics would also attend it.[2] When this plan failed he reduced his hopes and began to consider some arrangement which would permit Catholics to attend Oxford with safeguards for their

[2] Monsignor Guilday considers that Newman's efforts at this time to secure funds and to establish the need of a Catholic university were indirectly a stimulus to Americans in their preliminary attempts to found the Catholic University of America. Cf. Peter Guilday, "The Founding of the Catholic Unversity of America." *The American Ecclesiastical Review,* CIX, 1 (Jan., 1944), 4.

faith.[3] By this time, the religious test had been discarded at Oxford and so far as the authorities there were concerned Catholics were free to attend.

The suggestion horrified many Catholics and roused violent opposton. No effort on Newman's part could reassure them, and each of his proposals was turned aside. Oxford was then completely Anglican in atmosphere, with the great majority of the tutors still in Anglican orders. That situation was soon to pass away, and Newman knew it, but others were not convinced. On March 23, 1865, the bishops "discountenanced, to the practical effect of a prohibition" the attendance of Catholics at Oxford, and this ruling closed the issue for nearly thirty years. But this period served only to emphasize Newman's contention that the resources of the Catholics of England were inadequate to provide an institution of higher learning, and that the alternative for them was attendance at one of the established universities, or no university education at all.

In these circumstances the question was eventually reopened in 1893, after Newman's death, and his plan[4] was at long last accepted in England and then approved by Rome. Catholic students were permitted to attend the universities, but a special chaplain was established at each one, with precise rules to govern him in the care of his flock. The chaplain, chosen for his own academic distinction and for his familiarity with university life, was directed to give a series of sermons and to invite other eminent clergymen to preach. Needless to say, these instructions are carefully followed, and Catholic graduates of Oxford, of whom I may speak with some knowledge, recall these special sermons with particular gratitude and admiration.

This pattern was copied by Catholic authorities in the British dominions and in the United States in settling their relations with state universities, and it has proved a success wherever similar care in the choice of a chaplain has been exercised. At the

---

[3] The story is told in detail by Ward, op. cit., II, Chapters XXI, XXIV-XXVI; and from a different point of view by Cuthbert Butler, The Life and Times of Bishop Ullathorne, 2 vols. (London: Burns, Oates, and Washbourne, 1926), II, 1-39.

[4] It is set forth with special clarity in a private letter written on June 8, 1872, and reprinted by Ward, op cit., II, 555.

present time the arrangement represents a compromise between, on the one hand, the pressing claims of the current generation of Catholic youth who in a given locality may have no hope of the early establishment of a Catholic university, and on the other, the proper misgiving and anxiety with which Catholic authorities regard "mixed" education at a state university.

The wide adoption of Newman's famous scheme has not silenced all criticisms. The arguments advanced against it in his lifetime are sometimes repeated today. It is held that he underestimated the dangers to the faith of a Catholic in the modern university. He was himself so strong a character, dominating his environment, that he could not quite realize the plight of weaker men. It is also suggested that in his day Oxford and Cambridge were still Christian in their sentiment, but today these and other public universities are at best indifferent, and are commonly hostile, to religion.

I do not believe that these objections are valid, at least in the sense that they imply a lack of full appreciation on Newman's part. He had clearly foreseen that the skepticism of the German universities would appear in England, and run its course there as well. In spite of the plausible tribute to the unique strength of his character, in contrast to the common frailty, it is absurd to declare that Newman—a great writer on the psychology of faith, a shrewd observer of his fellow man, and the author of many searching descriptions of human weakness and imperfection—was insensitive to the reaction of the average man. The question, if argued, must be pursued on other lines. Newman weighed all the factors, was fully aware of the possible dangers, estimated as always the loss and the gain, and then decided in favor of the compromise. One may question his judgment and condemn his decision, if one is so disposed, but it is not possible to deny that he possessed a full knowledge of the issues before he made his final choice.

It should always be remembered that Newman regarded the completely Catholic institution, Louvain, for example, as ideal[5] and preferred to consider anything less as provisional and tentative. He would probably have been disappointed if he could

---

[5] Cf. Ward, *op. cit.*, II, 50.

have foreseen the existence of so many Newman Clubs today, implying as they do the continuing incompleteness of the Catholic education system. Yet the whole trend of modern education indicates that this situation will not change for some time. If no more than an arts college is required, many Catholic communities are now in a position to provide it, and fifty years ago such an institution would have been willingly accepted as a university. But today few students desire this training and large numbers demand professional courses instead. As a rule it is beyond the means of any Catholic groups, except those concentrated in the metropolitan areas of the United States, to provide such professional colleges, which are very expensive and difficult to staff adequately. The state university therefore continues to improve its favored position and will attract Catholic students who, unless they are free to travel considerable distances, can find no other entry to such professions as law, medicine, and engineering, and this situation ensures the continuance of what we have been calling the Newman Club arrangement. Since it is a matter of policy, changing circumstances may lead to its eventual abandonment, but for the present this seems a remote possibility.

For our purposes in this paper it is sufficient to note that Newman is the first author and the acknowledged champion of an educational device which has won general adoption and has proven acceptable in a wide variety of circumstances. This is surely ecclesiastical statesmanship of a high order.

The Idea of a University is a classic, often reprinted[6] and much admired. Like any classic it is a blend of the temporary and the timeless. Some passages take us back to the Dublin of ninety years ago, and to the Europe of the nineteenth century. In this setting Newman speaks for a moment as a child of his own time, and the reader, although charmed, murmurs to him-

---

[6] All quotations are from the standard edition, published by Longmans and frequently reissued. My copy is London, 1919. A very helpful college text has been edited by Daniel M. O'Connell, S.J. (New York: The America Press, 1941), omitting certain brief passages and adding some useful material. The discourses and one of the lectures on university subjects have been printed in the Everyman series, under the title: "On the Scope and Nature of University Education," with an introduction by Ward (London, 1939).

self, "This was indeed long ago." But such interludes are short and are followed by magnificent pages in which all barriers of distance fall away and we cease to be conscious that almost a century has passed since Newman wrote. The nine great discourses contain much that almost startles us with deep clarity of reasoning and clear force of logic. Men do not think and write so today, and when we recall that they were read in Newman's magic voice we recognize that the Dublin lectures must have remained the memory of a lifetime for those who were privileged to hear them.

In print, however, it seems that the series was slow to win fame. There are not many references to it by the critics of the day, some of whom do not trouble to list it among Newman's chief works, and for some time afterwards citations are very casual. Newman himself was not well pleased with the discourses and declared that "They belong to a time, when he was tried both by sorrow and by anxiety, and by indisposition also, and required greater effort to write, and gave him less satisfaction when written, than any of his Volumes."[7] Walter Pater, however, took the view that it was "the perfect handling of a theory,"[8] and early indifference began to pass until today *The Idea of a University* is generally esteemed as the second of Newman's works, scarcely less famous than the *Apologia*. This gradual increase in reputation is largely based on evident merit, but a certain share of credit must be assigned to the English critic, Sir Arthur Quiller-Couch. He was the author of many literary studies and enjoyed a wide popularity as a lecturer. He was fashionable but he deserved to be. *On the Art of Writing* and *On the Art of Reading* are favorites with many readers who relish the wit and smooth urbanity which do not quite conceal the vigor of his mind. In both books, which ran into many editions, he quotes Newman warmly and generously, and in the first he gives almost extravagant praise to the university lectures: "And here let me say that of all the books written in these hundred years there is perhaps none you can more profitably thumb

---

[7] Everyman edition, p. xxx. (Note also the dedication, a superb example of Newman's style.)

[8] See O'Connell, *op. cit.*, pp. ix f., for several other estimates.

and ponder than. . . . *The Idea of a University*. . . . It has missed
to be appraised at its true worth, partly no doubt by reason of
the colour it derives from a religion still unpopular in England."[9]
This enthusiasm aroused the curiosity of readers who might
otherwise have had no interest in Newman. Sir Arthur himself has recently revealed that his own attention was first engaged
when as a freshman at Oxford he was assigned to Newman's old
rooms.[10] This routine act of the college bursar deserves at least
a footnote in the history of literary appreciation in England.

Why did it require such vehement praise to bring the book
into proper notice? Why was Newman himself not satisfied
with it? The reasons tell us much about the subject and the
times.

The first reason is one commonly overlooked even by admirers
of Newman. He was a pioneer, much in advance of his time,
and with the gift of accurate anticipation. He sensed the direction of events, and from the first beginnings, not yet perceived
by others, he predicted the future development. From his youth
he constantly foretold the wide spread of indifference to religion.
Today we see the full realization of this prophecy and think that
there was nothing remarkable in Newman's view. His contemporaries, however, did not accept it and were in fact somewhat irritated by it. They disliked heartily his gloomy predic-
tion of an age of infidelity and free thought. Something of the
sort happened in the case of *The Idea of a University*. Many
motives, interacting, impelled Newman to compose the work.
He wished to clarify his own thoughts, to instruct others, but
also to oppose certain opinions on the subject which he judged
to be wrong and harmful, and to be gaining strength. Until
his contemporaries were brought to share his belief that these
were significant tendencies deserving of immediate attention his
book could not exercise its full influence. Newman delivered
the university lectures between 1852 and 1858, about thirty years
before English and American universities began to enter into
the period of change and ferment from which they emerged in

---

[9] *On the Art of Writing* (Cambridge University Press, 1923), pp. 26 f.,
with some omissions.

[10] *Memories and Opinions* (Cambridge University Press, 1945), pp. 71 f.

their present form.   When these lectures were given only a few
acute observers realized that long-established traditions were
about to be roughly handled and in some cases rejected.   As
the universities have increasingly lost their original character to
become professional schools with a narrow and immediate utilitarian purpose, those who still believe in a general education, and
that knowledge is an end in itself, have come to appreciate that
Newman's presentation of this case is still the best available to
them.   Where others would fumble for words, his argument
crystalizes again and again into clear gems which cannot be
denied quotation:

> Knowledge is capable of being its own end.   Such is
> the constitution of the human mind, that any kind of
> knowledge, if it be really such, is its own reward
> (p. 103).
>
> I am prepared to maintain that there is a knowledge
> worth possessing for what it is, and not merely for
> what it does. . . . (p. 114).
>
> Truth of whatever kind is the proper object of the
> intellect; its cultivation then lies in fitting it to appre-
> hend and contemplate truth (p. 151).
>
> We feel our minds to be growing and expanding
> *then*, when we not only learn, but refer what we learn
> to what we know already (p. 134).
>
> And therefore a truly great intellect. . . .is one which
> takes a connected view of old and new, past and pres-
> ent, far and near, and which has an insight into the in-
> fluence of all these one on another; without which there
> is no whole, and no centre.   It possesses the knowledge,
> not only of things, but also of their mutual and true
> relations; knowledge, not merely considered as acquire-
> ment, but as philosophy (p. 134).
>
> That perfection of the Intellect. . . .is the clear, calm
> accurate vision and comprehension of all things, as far
> as the finite mind can embrace them, each in its place,
> and with its own characteristics upon it (p. 139).

And then, should you think that his views are restricted to the intellectual aspect of man, there are many other quotations, of
which the following are typical:

> But a University training is the great ordinary means
> to a great but ordinary end; it aims at raising the intel-

lectual tone of society, at cultivating the public mind, at purifying the national taste, at supplying true principles to popular enthusiasm and fixed aims to popular aspiration, at giving enlargement and sobriety to the ideas of the age, at facilitating the exercise of political power, and refining the intercourse of private life (pp. 177 f).

He [a university graduate] has the repose of a mind which lives in itself, while it lives in the world, and which has resources for its happiness at home when it cannot go abroad. He has a gift which serves him in public, and supports him in retirement, without which good fortune is but vulgar, and with which failure and disappointment have a charm (p. 178).

. . . . [cultivation of the intellect] is but a temporal subject, and a transitory possession; but so are other things in themselves which we make much of and pursue. The moralist will tell us that man, in all his functions, is but a flower which blossoms and fades except so far as a higher principle breathes upon him, and makes him and what he is immortal. . . . We attain to heaven by using this world well, though it is to pass away; we perfect our nature, not by undoing it, but by adding to it what is more than nature, and directing it towards aims higher than its own (p. 123).

The lectures are adorned by phrases and passages which are the delight of the anthologist, and the despair of any man who has for a moment flattered himself that he can write:

Alas! what are we doing all through life, both as a necessity and as a duty, but unlearning the world's poetry, and attaining to its prose! (pp. 331 f.)

The stimulating system [of encouraging students by rivalry] may easily be overdone, and does not answer on the long run. A blaze among the stubble, and then all is dark (p. 493).

We cannot do without a view, and we put up with an illusion, when we cannot get a truth (p. 76).

It is tempting to continue these quotations, for they redeem even the most inadequate article on Newman, but space compels us to be content with a mere reference to certain lengthy passages, in which Newman leaves behind patient logic and sweeps forward with mounting eloquence until he has achieved one of those memorable, all-embracing definitions which illuminate the nature of man, definitions which somehow enlarge rather than restrict their subject. The most familiar is the famous description of the true gentleman (pp. 208-211), but no less worthy is his picture of the ideal university graduate, quoted in part above (pp. 177 f.), and his bold paragraphs on sinful and imperfect man (pp. 229-31).

By such qualities *The Idea of a University* has won an assured position in any list of English classics. To read it for the first time is a delight even for students who have given no previous thought to the problems of education; for those who have, it is a revelation. Why then was Newman himself dissatisfied with it?

This is not an idle question, nor can it be settled with the suggestion that Newman was influenced unduly by the ultimate failure of the Dublin scheme. In his introduction to the Everyman edition, Ward, who remains a standard authority, found an answer in the argument that the discourses, given in 1852, are incomplete without the further lectures on university subjects delivered between 1854 and 1858. This is true enough as far as it goes, but much more is involved.

Newman had ventured into a field of inquiry where he could expect little help. He was ranging over a new and vast area, forced to make bold decisions, and he was fully aware of the fact.[11] The part of the pioneer may be exhilarating, but it also has its anxieties. Furthermore, he sought to address himself persuasively to two opposing groups, to those believers who were inclined to underestimate the value of secular and scientific learning, and to unbelievers who were scornful of theology. The necessity of keeping this double audience always in mind imposed an additional strain which doubtless affected Newman in his estimate of the work. However, I believe that there was a specific reason for his dissatisfaction—he felt a certain disappointment with the second, third, and fourth discourses, those entitled: "Theology a Branch of Knowledge," "Bearing of Theology on Other Knowledge," and "Bearing of Other Knowledge on Theology."

I cannot prove this assertion and I therefore mention it with hesitation, but most readers will agree that the fifth, and part

---

[11] *The Idea of a University*, p. 213.

of the sixth discourse, namely, "Knowledge its Own End," and "Knowledge Viewed in Relation to Learning," contain some of the most profound and finished pages in all Newman's writing. They constitute the peak of his effort in the book, and they carry the remaining chapters to a triumphant conclusion. It is my impression on the other hand that the three earlier sections on theology, fine as they are, do not quite reach the same magnificent level. And yet they are more basic, and Newman there attempted his most important and difficult demonstrations. The distinction may be invidious, and for that matter quite invalid, but if there were even a slight difference in the level of success between the early and later parts of the books, we can be sure that Newman would sense it, and would be disturbed.[12]   Of course it is impertinent and dangerous to impute one's own literary judgments to Newman himself, and he may have been quite well satisfied with these earlier discourses, but if an unsupported opinion may be allowed, I do not think so. In this connection it is not altogether irrelevant to mention that these are the very chapters which sometimes fail to carry conviction to a modern reader.

We live in an age of very vigorous speculation concerning the philosophy of education.[13] For more than forty years, ever since the early writings of John Dewey appeared, the American educator in particular has been most active in developing and presenting his views on the philosophy of education. Many books have been written, programs have been promulgated and supported with evangelical zeal, cliques and claques have been

---

[12] Note the important place in the plan of the book which Ward assigns to the discourses on theology, op. cit., I, 391 f., 390.

[13] A good general presentation is given by J. S. Brubacher, Modern Philosophies of Education (New York: McGraw-Hill Book Co., 1939). The Catholic point of view, which was for many years inadequately represented, is now available in many excellent publications, of which two recent studies may be particularly recommended—W. F. Cunningham, The Pivotal Problems of Education (New York: Macmillan, 1940); J. D. Redden and F. A. Ryan, A Catholic Philosophy of Education (Milwaukee: The Bruce Publishing Co., 1943). Both books have ample bibliographies. The reader who prefers a shorter statement cannot do better than consult the pamphlet of Father W. J. McGucken, S.J., The Philosophy of Catholic Education (New York: The America Press, 1944).

formed, but the results of this ferment are not impressive, and it is difficult not to be indignant and impatient with much that has been offered as the new dispensation. Tag ends of utilitarianism, confident scientism, nineteenth-century "liberalism," free thought, and pragmatism have been tossed into the pot, and the resulting stew has been tricked out with catchwords such as "democracy" and "freedom," and then served up as something new and significant. Maritain has surveyed this prevailing school of thought with devastating criticism, but with his usual industry and charity has found some things of which he can speak kindly.[14] Perhaps we should do likewise, for it would be unjust to deny that in practice the modern "progressive" educator has done many good things and has sought sincerely to serve the interests of education as he understands them, but it would also be unjust not to charge him with a naive and muddled philosophy which has brought confusion and triviality to the American educational scene.

Against this background the reader will hardly expect Newman's ideas to have played a very significant role, and he will be right. On visits to several university libraries I have examined the standard books on the history and on the philosophy of education, and in very few of them is Newman ever mentioned, either in the index of incidental references, or in the text where one might look for his name.[15] I am further informed by several educators whose views seem to be typical that Newman has nothing for us today, and that he represents an extreme and outmoded intellectualist position.

Some of this same spirit has even appeared among Catholic writers who in consequence ignore Newman or display a surprisingly critical attitude and maintain that he was not suf-

---

[14] *Education at the Crossroads* (New Haven: Yale University Press, 1943).

[15] Where there is a reference, it is almost always the same one, to the very first lines of the preface of *The Idea of a University*, in which Newman states that in his view a university is a place of *teaching* universal *knowledge*, and not of research. The usual comment on this leaves one with the painful feeling that these eminent authors have read no further and have taken no trouble to understand Newman's full and subtle opinion.

ficiently practical.[16] I suppose that we are all contaminated to some extent by the pragmatism which is native to the air of the modern world, but there is no excuse for this attitude. We must have sound theory before we can hope for good practice, and if an author, with great effort and originality, has given us such a theory, let us be thankful, and make no criticism if he leaves the details of administration to others.

But it would not be right to end the matter on this discouraging note. Newman may have had little influence with the modern policy makers in education, but, as we have indicated above, the prestige of *The Idea of a University* is still great. Scholars, especially in the field of English, continue to savor it, and men of culture find therein the charter of their way of life. This gentle, reasonable tradition goes on, outshouted for the moment by the bluster of noisy technicians, but exhibiting a steady strength and a tenacity which give a fair prospect of a new day in education.

There are many signs of that change. President Hutchins of Chicago, to summarize his views too simply, feels that there is not enough hope of agreement in theology to make it the unifying force in a university, and offers a metaphysic in its stead, but in much else he is in the closest agreement with Newman, and so are many others who have lately begun to fight so effectively for a revival of liberal education, in the old tradition, but in a modern setting. Since we are not attempting a sketch of current educational thought, we must not linger over these new and, on the whole, encouraging trends which hold great promise of a real challenge to the "progressive" educator, but it would be very surprising if most of these spirited rebels did not know and thoroughly appreciate Newman's work, and were not conscious of a great debt to him. Perhaps in certain cases this is not so, and the coincidence of views has come about without their knowledge, but this would only serve to emphasize what is Newman's chief claim on our attention. We should not read him and follow him simply because he is Newman, but because he is right. If we study the nature of man, and the facts of

---

[16] Cf. E. Leen, *What is Education?* (London: Sheed and Ward, 1943), p. 18.

this world long enough and hard enough, we will reach very much the same views as Newman did, even if we do not realize it. What he once said of Aristotle in philosophy we may well say of Newman himself in education: "He has told us the meaning of our own words and ideas, before we were born. In many subject-matters, to think correctly, is to think like [him], and we are his disciples whether we will or no, though we may not know it."[17] Shall we then "go back" to Newman? No, we shall use his work as he would have wished—we shall *begin* with Newman.

---

[17] *The Idea of a University,* p. 109-110.

X

NEWMAN AND THE LIBERAL ARTS

Newman And The Liberal Arts

JOHN E. WISE

Cardinal Newman's *Idea of a University* is the most complete *ad hoc* exposition of the meaning of liberal education ever written. Is it equally the soundest? The liberal arts mean historically the formal training of man's highest powers, an intermediate stage in the educational process, and the transmission with organic growth of great truths in the Graeco-Roman-Hebrew-Christian culture. On this last point Cardinal Newman is clear.

> In the nineteenth century, in a country which looks out upon a new world, and anticipates a coming age, we have been engaged in opening the Schools dedicated to the studies of polite literature and liberal science, or what are called the Arts, as a first step towards the establishment on Catholic ground of a Catholic University. And while we thus recur to Greece and Athens with pleasure and affection, and recognize in that famous land the source and the school of intellectual culture, it would be strange indeed if we forgot to look further south also, and there to bow before a more glorious luminary, and a more sacred oracle of truth, and the source of another sort of knowledge, high and supernatural, which is seated in Palestine. Jerusalem is the fountain-head of religious knowledge, as Athens is of secular. . . . Each leaves an heir and successor in the West, and that heir and successor is one and the same. The grace stored in Jerusalem, and the gifts which radiate from Athens, are made over and concentrated in Rome. This is true as a matter of history.[1]

Cardinal Newman is deep in the culture of the West, and knows that the liberal arts are part of it. Is he equally as clear concerning the formation of man's highest powers, and concerning the preparatory, intermediate function of liberal edu-

---

[1] John Henry Cardinal Newman, *The Idea of a University Defined and Illustrated* (New York: Longmans, Green and Co., 1931), pp. 264-65.

cation? He calls knowledge "its own end." Does this mean
that he neglects the training of the will? Again, he calls knowledge "its own end." Does he neglect the preparatory function?
Does he forget what benefits a liberal education confers on
future professional men and on suitable pursuits of leisure?
Does he forget the uses of knowledge for the business of life?

The question concerning the training of the will is most
important. If Cardinal Newman thinks that true knowledge is
to be gained without virtue, he stands against the tide of
history. The Greeks, the Romans, the Fathers of the Church,
the medieval scholastics, and the renaissance revival of classic
ideals echoed the Socratic aphorism that "knowledge is virtue,"
with the proper Aristotelian qualification that, although virtue
depends on right ideas, these must be acted upon by the
will. Then came the Roman *vir bonus, dicendi peritus,* and
the Augustinian *Noverim me, noverim te,* which implies the
knowledge of God and self, the intimate knowledge of one's
own nature, as a prerequisite for high virtue. St. Thomas is
pellucid in his exposition of the moral and intellectual virtues.
The guiding hand is prudence, the *recta ratio agibilium,* the
power of correctly applying one's knowledge. The early Protestants stressed knowledge of the Bible, but placed faith more
in feeling, *confidentia fiducialis,* against the Catholic concept of
an intellectual consent in faith, "the substance of things to be
hoped for, the evidence of things that appear not."[2] But in
both cases there is an association of knowledge and virtue,
knowledge helping virtue, and virtue helping knowledge, since
the pure of heart see God.

Does Cardinal Newman make knowledge and virtue independent? Does he neglect the training of the will? Even an
earnest opponent of the great man gives an indication of where
the answer lies. "Many exponents of Newman's mind and
thought can advance the view that he is essentially anti-intel-
lectual; while others can appeal to his emphatic declaration
that intellectual excellence, the cultivation of *the intellect as
such,* constitutes the work of a University, and is coterminous

---

[2] St. Paul, *Epistle to the Hebrews,* 11:1.

with Liberal Education."[3] The reason why some interpreters think that Newman is an intellectualist is because he repeats with emphasis and abundant illustration that knowledge is its own end, as if it lacked important relationship with virtue. The reason why some interpreters think that Newman is anti-intellectualist is because such a concept of knowledge, and of its ability to exist in atheistic genius or saintly wisdom, is to lower the value of learning to a thing quite indifferent to the true purpose of life. What is the answer to this dilemma? Where does Newman's idea of knowledge stand in relation to virtue?

One would hope to find the answer in the concept of Christian wisdom, namely, that Newman means by his "knowledge," wisdom, which includes virtue. Then knowledge could be an end in itself. This wisdom includes the knowledge of God, not without His love.[4] This wisdom is prudence, ordering human actions to their right end.[5] This wisdom is concerned with first principles,[6] with things eternal[7] and with the last

---

[3] T. Corcoran, Newman: Selected Discourses on Liberal Knowledge (Dublin: University College, 1929), p. lxviii. This author's view of Newman's "philosophy of severance," the alleged disassociation of knowledge and virtue, is also given in "Liberal Studies and Moral Aims: a Critical Study of Newman's Position," THOUGHT, I (June, 1926), pp. 54-71.

[4] St. Augustine, Enarratio in Psalmum 135. 8 (Migne, Vol. 37, col. 1760), "intelligimus sapientiam in cognitione et dilectione ejus quod semper est. . . .quod Deus est."

[5] St. Thomas Aquinas, Summa Theologica, I. q. I. a. 6, resp., "prudens sapiens dicitur, inquantum ordinat humanos actus ad debitum finem. Unde dicitur Prover. 10, 'Sapientia est viro prudentia.'" Newman, op cit., p. 124, "wisdom. . . .has a direct relation to conduct, and to human life."

[6] Aristotle, Metaphysics, I. 1, trans. W. D. Ross, "all men suppose what is called Wisdom to deal with the first causes and the principles of things." Cf. Richard McKeon, editor, The Basic Works of Aristotle (New York: Random House, 1941) p. 601.

[7] St. Augustine, De Trinitate, XII. 15. 25, (Migne, Vol. 42, col. 1012), "Si ergo haec est sapientiae et scientiae recta distinctio, ut ad sapientiam pertineat aeternarum rerum cognitio intellectualis; ad scientiam vero, temporalium rerum cognitio rationalis. . . ."

cause.[8] It is almost Newman's realized knowledge, "the ideas, which are the secret life of a Christian,"[9] of the heart as well as the head, of reason as well as faith. This would be an easy answer to the problem of knowledge as an end in itself. But Cardinal Newman, despite his empiricist philosophy, despite his emphasis on the unity of man in sensible, historical, experiential, living knowledge, as contrasted to the dangers of the notional and abstract,[10] does not mean by his "knowledge" in *The Idea of a University*, Christian wisdom. He means intellectual culture.

> Knowledge is one thing, virtue is another; good sense is not conscience, refinement is not humility, nor is largeness and justness of view faith. Philosophy, however enlightened, however profound, gives no command over the passions, no influential motives, no vivifying principles. Liberal Education makes not the Christian, not the Catholic, but the gentlemen. It is well to be a gentleman, it is well to have a cultivated intellect, a delicate taste, a candid, equitable, dispassionate mind, a noble and courteous bearing in the conduct of life;—these are the connatural qualities of a large knowledge; they are the objects of a University.[11]

Or, still more clearly, "When I speak of Knowledge, I mean something intellectual. . . .something which takes a view of

---

[8] St. Thomas, *loc. cit.*, "Ille igitur, qui considerat simpliciter altissimam causam totius universi, quae Deus est, maxime sapiens dicitur. Unde et sapientia dicitur esse divinorum cognitio, ut pateat per Augustinum, *de Trinit.* XII. 14."

[9] Newman, "The Theory of Developments in Religious Doctrine," *Fifteen Sermons Preached before the University of Oxford* (New York: Longmans, Green, and Co., 1896), p. 327.

[10] Newman, *An Essay in Aid of a Grammar of Assent* (New York: Longmans, Green, and Co., 1930), pp. 90-1, "Real assent or belief, . . .being concerned with things concrete, not abstract, which variously excite the mind from their moral and imaginative properties, has for its objects, not only directly what is true, but inclusively what is beautiful, useful, admirable, heroic; objects which kindle devotion, rouse the passions, and attach the affections; and thus it leads the way to actions of every kind, to the establishment of principles, and the formation of character, and is thus again intimately connected with what is individual and personal."

[11] Newman, *Idea of a University*, pp. 120-21.

things. . . .which reasons upon what it sees, and while it sees; which invests it with an idea."[12]

How can such a knowledge be an end in itself? The answer would seem to be in the formal concept of a University, its specific, characterizing object. It does not exclude virtue, but was created for knowledge, just as the Church may be said to exist for the salvation of souls, rather than for knowledge as such. The formal object of the Church is certainly not the intellectual culture described by Cardinal Newman, though the Church can use these gifts in its members to great advantage.

The proof that Cardinal Newman is talking about the formal object of a university—and he uses the term as quite synonymous, at least in purpose, with a liberal education and with the liberal art[13]—appears especially in his luminous comparisons of mental knowledge with bodily health and with moral virtue.

> It were well if the English, like the Greek language, possessed some definite word to express, simply and generally, intellectual proficiency or perfection, such as "health" is used with reference to the animal frame, and "virtue," with reference to our moral nature.[14]

The perfection of the body is physical health, of the will, moral virtue, and of the intellect, knowledge, the active power of judging, of "discriminating between truth and falsehood,"[15] of seeing things whole, in all their relationships.[16] This is good health of mind, a perfection in itself, just as virtue is perfection for the will and health for the body. Now a good healthy body can be used to serve God in pursuits intellectual

---

[12] *Ibid.*, p. 113.

[13] "It is needless to trace out further the formation of the courses of liberal education; it is sufficient to have given some specimens in illustration of it. The studies which it was found to involve, were four principal ones, Grammar, Rhetoric, Logic, and Mathematics; and the science of Mathematics, again, was divided into four, Geometry, Arithmetic, Astronomy, and Music; making in all seven, which are known by the name of the Seven Liberal Arts," *ibid.*, p. 259. This liberal knowledge, defined not merely as content, but as largeness of view and the ability to reason well, is the scope of a university. *Cf. ibid.*, pp. 125-6.

[14] *Ibid.*, p. 124.   [15] *Ibid.*, p. 152.   [16] Cf. *ibid.*, p. 134.

or manual, in the apostolic ministry or in legitimate recrea-
tion, or it can be used to fight an unjust war, or to lead recal-
citrant racketeers in robbery. So of a strong mind. What
geniuses some of the gangsters of history have been, what
profligates some litterateurs, what egotists, some composers!
Shrewd judgment serves the unjust as well as the just, and a
strong body can also serve both. But with virtue it is different.
A strong will, which may exist in St. Bernard as well as in
Julian the Apostate, is not necessarily a perfect will, for the
object of the will is good, and a will which adheres to evil
is not perfect, but perverted. But a healthy body is a healthy
body, regardless of who owns it, and a bright mind is a bright
mind, even in Satan, the Angel of Light.

Now health is a good in itself, and so is knowledge. There is
nothing that is evil in bodily health as such, nor is there anything evil in knowledge as such. Knowledge, therefore, just
as health, can be an end in itself. In its own order it is the
ultimate well-being. It is only in relation to a further use that
evil appears, not in the health, not in the knowledge, but in
the will. Health can be abused, just as knowledge can. But
bodily health, in itself, is a good, just as intellectual discernment
or quickness is a good in itself, and, in its own order, its
own end. The trouble does not come from bodily health, but
from its misuse, and thus the Christian practice of mortification, not against health as its own end, but against health as
man's end. Health is an end in itself, but it is not man's end.
Knowledge is an end in itself, but it is not man's end. In relation
to the whole man, health is a means of perfection, just as
knowledge, in relation to the whole man, is a means of perfection; and therefore follows the subjection of knowledge, in the
matter of faith and morals, to the good of the whole man. Just
as Christian mortification usually works even to the better health
of the body in itself, so it is that the norm of faith, which is
really a higher knowledge, usually makes for better natural
health of mind.

Cardinal Newman, therefore, as proper to his subject, enters
into the various relationships of knowledge. This is a proof
that he is considering knowledge in itself; otherwise the whole
man could scarcely be said to have relationships to himself.

But he wishes to know the place of this mental power, this strong reason, this refined taste, in man's makeup.

> . . . .the work of a Hospital lies in healing the sick or wounded, of a Riding or Fencing School, or of a Gymnasium, in exercising the limbs, of an Almshouse, in aiding and solacing the old, of an Orphanage, in protecting innocence, of a Penitentiary, in restoring the guilty. . . .a University, taken *in its bare idea, and before we view it as an instrument of the Church,* has this object and this mission; it contemplates neither moral impression nor mechanical production; it professes to exercise the mind neither in art nor in duty; its function is intellectual culture; here it may leave its scholars, and it has done its work when it has done as much as this. It educates the intellect to reason well in all matters, to reach out towards truth, and to grasp it.[17]

Cardinal Newman is dealing with the formal idea of a university, its specifying function. This is seen in the very title of his book, *The Idea of a University.* Education can go on in an orphanage, even in a penitentiary, but education is not the primary purpose of these institutions. Similarly, a university may shelter the unwanted scion of neglectful parents, may even have penal statutes, but such concomitant works do not characterize the place. Even in pagan times, universities were possible, however much the institutions of Athens and Alexandria depart from the corporate concept of the Middle Ages. The idea of a university does not consist even in its organization, but in its specific purpose, strength of mind, and breadth of vision.

Having clarified the function of a university,—and it may be repeated that this function and purpose is understood in Newman's essay as synonymous with the function and purpose of a liberal education and of the liberal arts, prescinding from professional education,[18]—the author delineates, as he should,

---

[17] Newman, *op. cit.,* p. 125, *italics mine.*

[18] "A liberal education is a real benefit to the subjects of it, as members of society, in the various duties and circumstances and accidents of life. . . . over and above those direct services which might fairly be expected of it, it actually subserves the discharge of those particular functions, and the pursuit of those particular advantages, which are connected with professional exertion, and to which Professional Education is directed," *ibid.,* p. 172.

the relation of this specific function to the needs of the whole
man. And here he reigns supreme. No one at all has ever
described better than he the relation of mental culture, of intellectual ability, to human perfection, to the perfection of the
whole man. Far from minimizing the place of virtue, the
place of faith, the function of the Church, in a university, no
one has ever made more of it than Newman. He tells of the
dangers of mental culture, which is all good in itself, far more
vividly than one could describe the simpler phenomenon of
brute health, a good in itself, running wild.

> Lord Bacon has set down the abuse, of which I am
> speaking, among the impediments to the Advance-
> ment of the Sciences, when he observes that "men have
> used to infect their meditations, opinions, and doctrines,
> with some conceits which they have most admired, or
> *some Sciences which they have most applied;* and give
> all thing else a *tincture* according to them *utterly untrue
> and improper.* . . . So have the alchemists made a phi-
> losophy out of a few experiments of the furnace; and
> Gilbertus, our countryman, hath made a philosophy out
> of the observations of a lodestone. So Cicero, when,
> reciting the several opinions of the nature of the soul,
> he found a musician that held the soul was but a har-
> mony, saith pleasantly, 'hic ab arte sua non recessit,'
> 'he was true to his art.' "[19]

The illustrations are not always so curious, nor are they
always so remote from life today. They can be in history, of
course, as Julian the Apostate, whose simplicity of manners,
frugality, austerity of life, singular disdain of sensual pleasure,
military heroism, application to business, literary diligence,
modesty, and clemency were accomplishments that "go to make
him one of the most eminent specimens of pagan virtue which
the world has ever seen."[20] Was his reason rightly used?
"Reason rightly exercised," says Cardinal Newman, "leads the
mind to the Catholic Faith."[21] That is how much the convert
thinks of the apostate. That is how much he esteems the place
of faith and of Christian virtue. He sees human accomplishments, even of genius and power, capable of perversion, perhaps even more frequently associated with religious indiffer-

---

[19] *Ibid.*, p. 77.   [20] *Ibid.*, p. 194.   [21] *Ibid.*, p. 181.

ence.[22] The place of faith and virtue and of the Church in a university is, therefore, the more necessary as the intellectual excellence is greater. Those critics are wrong who call Newman an intellectualist, and who quote the encyclicals about the purposes of a Catholic university, saying that its purpose is virtue and wisdom. They have not penetrated as deeply as Newman into the real work of a university, one of the greatest in the line of human endeavor, intellectual excellence; they have not isolated the specific function; they have not outlined as clearly the place of intellectual excellence in life and in a university. The insistence of papal documents on knowledge and virtue is precisely because the Church understands, as no one individual, the uses and the pitfalls of secular learning. The Church does not necessarily explain philosophically what is a university. Her work is the glory of God and the salvation of souls. All human gifts, including that of philosophy, she would save from abuse and turn to fruitful talents. The Church is in the orphanage, in the prison, in the gymnasium, in the state, in the university. The more noble the work and the higher the attainment, the closer must be the Church; for the more valuable is the talent, the more likely may be its waste in time, without interest in eternity. "Such, I say, is the danger which awaits a

---

[22] Cf. Newman, *Discussions and Arguments on Various Subjects* (New York: Longmans, Green and Co., 1891), pp. 274-75. Secular knowledge is not a direct means of moral improvement, but even a temptation to unbelief. Poetry can lead to sentimentalism, and experimental science, to skepticism. "Christianity, and nothing short of it, must be made the element and principle of all education. Where it has been laid as the first stone, and acknowledged as the governing spirit, it will take up into itself, assimilate, and give a character to literature and science." *Cf. Idea of a University*, p. 227, "If the interposition of the Church is necessary in the Schools of Science, still more imperatively is it demanded in the other main constituent portion of the subject-matter of Liberal Education,—Literature." This juxtaposition of sciences and literature is interesting, because later (*ibid.*, p. 263), Newman disesteems the training value of the sciences, though here he says, "Literature stands related to Man, as Science stands to Nature," an excellent expression, with his clear inclusion of Theology and God, of the liberal arts content. The training value of the experimental sciences is brought out well in a modern work, F. Charmot, *"La Teste Bien Faicte"* (Paris: Editions Spes, 1932), pp. 113-22.

civilized age; such is its besetting sin (not inevitable, God forbid! or we must abandon the use of God's own gifts), but still the ordinary sin of the Intellect."[23]

No critic of Newman as an "intellectualist" has ever painted with such master strokes the soul of a fallen Angel of Light. Newman cries more than his critics for virtue and faith and the Church in the university. Newman sees more clearly than they why it was the Church which started universities, why the ages of faith were also the ages of the schools. Newman sees more clearly than they the rights of the Church. This is the cardinal point of his discussion: "the radical difference indeed of this mental refinement from genuine religion."[24] He has illustrated it from history; he will show its subtle truth in his own times; and who would say the picture does not fit today?

Newman's example is a political economist. His high character is unknowing of motives of sordid money making. His religious views make him dear to an institution in which religion is revered. He places, however, political economy high in the realm of *moral* sciences, and his colleagues hear him without excitement. For he raises his own objection to his own thesis, that the pursuit of wealth is an humble occupation, and that it cannot claim to be necessarily joined to happiness. But he answers this objection with fine flourish.

> "My answer," he says, "is, first, that the pursuit of wealth, that is, the endeavour to accumulate the means of future subsistence and enjoyment, is, to the mass of mankind, the great source of *moral* improvement. . . .
> "No institution," he continues, "could be more beneficial to the morals of the lower orders, that is to at least nine-tenths of the whole body of any people, than one which should increase their power and their wish to accumulate; none more mischievous than one which should diminish their motives and means to save."[25]

---

[23] Newman, *Idea of a University*, p. 191.

[24] *Ibid.*, p. 190. *Cf.* also p. 216, "Liberal knowledge has a special tendency, not necessary or rightful, but a tendency in fact, when cultivated by beings such as we are, to impress us with a mere philosophical theory of life and conduct in the place of Revelation."

[25] *Ibid.*, pp. 91-92.

There is a great deal of truth in these statements. The earning of daily bread, and the business aiding thereunto, is a protection for one's moral life, if only in the avoidance of idleness. Moreover, the highest perfection can be associated with performing well the duties of one's state in life, with providing generously for one's own, and with the faithful assumption of domestic or civil responsibility. There are truths related to the political economy of our savant. But these truths in isolation, political economy, not only as a self-contained field, granted its hypotheses, but as an adequate and proper human end for moral perfection, contradict reason and revelation. The pursuit of wealth is not "the great source of moral improvement," but at least one great source of spiritual ruin. The wish to accumulate, however good it be in itself, needs to be reconciled with the counsel, "Lay not up to yourselves treasures on earth." Thus, the self-contained scientist makes of his science a philosophy and a theology. His hypotheses he makes into conclusions never proved; the proof is the further development of his own science. His architectonic is monotectonic; his *weltanschauung* is a deeper hiding of his head in the sand.

This is far from the predication of knowledge as the end of man. Newman's work is, in fact, an exposition of the interrelationships of knowledge, of the bearing of mental culture to religious duty, of the duties of the Church to knowledge, of "Christianity and Letters," of "Christianity and Physical Science," of the relation of knowledge to professional skill. We see clearly, then, what he means by "knowledge."

> Since then sciences are the results of mental processes about one and the same subject-matter, viewed under its various aspects, and are true results, as far as they go, yet at the same time separate and partial, it follows that on the one hand they need external assistance, one by one, by reason of their incompleteness, and on the other that they are able to afford it to each other, by reason, first, of their independence in themselves, and then of their connexion in their subject-matter.[26]

26 *Ibid.*, p. 47.

Any particular science is an aspect of the whole. The medical practitioner should no more prescribe for the needs of the soul than should the theologian prescribe for pneumonia. If there is an apparent conflict, if the danger of death, from the physician's viewpoint, should not be told to the patient, because "the thought of religion will disturb his mind and imperil his recovery," the decision is the priest's from a higher science, to minister to the soul lest the patient "should die without due preparation."[27]

This subject is extensive, and Cardinal Newman has done well, whatever be incidental points of controversy in a pioneer thinker. He was not the first to treat the function of mental power; perhaps his treatise is not the least in error. Alone the claim is made for it that the province proper to every science is well defined, and that simultaneously with the proper sovereignty of each science, not only the danger of irrational isolation, and the inevitable trespassing of apparently coexisting essential rights is truly exposed, but the place of virtue and wisdom and prudence is emphasized in clear reason. Cardinal Newman has analyzed the idea of a university with consummate skill. He spent his whole life on it. The lectures were not merely gotten up for the occasion,[28] the founding of the Catholic University of Ireland, though there is nothing wrong in getting up one's talks for an occasion, providing the preparation is suitable, and the reasonings well founded. But it was different with *The Idea of a University*.

> The views to which I have referred have grown into my whole system of thought, and are, as it were, part of myself. Many changes has my mind gone through: here it has known no variation or vacillation of opinion, and though this by itself is no proof of the truth of my principles, it puts a seal upon conviction and is a justification of earnestness and zeal. Those principles, which I am now to set forth under the sanction of the Catholic Church, were my profession at that early period of my life, when religion was to me more a matter of feeling and experience than of faith. They did but

<hr>

[27] *Ibid.*, pp. 511-12.   [28] *Cf. ibid.*, p. 3.

take greater hold upon me, as I was introduced to the records of Christian Antiquity, and approached in sentiment and desire to Catholicism; and my sense of their correctness has been increased with the events of my every year since I have been brought within its pale.[29]

Father Corcoran is in error, therefore, when he attributes Newman's conception of a university and of liberal studies to a relatively ephemeral reformation of academic Oxford.[30] Newman's thought was colored by the surroundings of his life, and this coloring was favorable as well as not; but to say that his thought was entirely limited by his life and times is to impugn the basic power of objective judgment in any age.

The objections, however, to the present interpretation of *The Idea of a University* may be stated. "Cardinal Newman does include character development in his idea of knowledge; this 'knowledge' may be interpreted as wisdom." This position is supported by such statements as: "Education is a higher word; it implies an action upon our mental nature, and the formation of a character; it is something individual and permanent, and is commonly spoken of in connexion with religion and virtue."[31]

> In a word, Religious Truth is not only a portion, but a condition of general knowledge. To blot it out is nothing short, if I may so speak, of unravelling the web of University Teaching. It is, according to the Greek proverb, to take the Spring from out of the year; it is to imitate the preposterous proceeding of those tragedians who represented a drama with the omission of its principal part.[32]

This second quotation is a confirmation of the interpretation of knowledge as an end in itself. It merely tells the purpose of religious knowledge in itself, a science, which, with philos-

---

29 *Ibid.*, p. 4.
30 *Cf.* Corcoran, *Newman: Selected Discourses*, pp. xv-xvi.
31 Newman, *Idea of a University*, p. 114.
32 *Ibid.*, p. 70.

ophy, is an ordering norm for other sciences.[33] Theology itself
can be a means of virtue or, unfortunately, separated from
virtue. This is to keep the concept clear. This is what Newman does.

The other quotation, which includes character formation in
education, regardless of the turn of thought Cardinal Newman
may wish to give, cannot stand against the thesis that refinement of mind is not virtue and that this mental culture is the
end of a liberal education.[34] The "cardinal point" of the discussion is to show "the radical difference indeed of this mental
refinement from genuine religion."[35]   Now genuine religion includes virtue.   Intellectual culture and the amenities of social
usage, as Newman goes on to say, are not synonymous with
conscience and God's law.

"If Cardinal Newman does not bring virtue into his concept
of knowledge, he should." But this would harm the clarity
of his thinking. He is talking about mental health as "a bare
idea," just as bodily health can be considered in itself, previous
to the settlement of its use as a means of virtue. It must be
repeated that Newman's analysis of the culture of the mind
is his point of excellence. His synthesis suffers from the vis-
ibility of the component parts, much as one should see the
steel girders in a completed skyscraper or view the heart in
an x-ray. It is asking much that architect and engineer be
combined, not only in the same individual, but even in the
same work, that the same human be at once a master of diagno-
sis and an accomplished artist of the portrait of man. New-

---

[33] "The comprehension of the bearings of one science on another, and
the use of each to each, and the location and limitation and adjustment
and due appreciation of them all, one with another, this belongs, I con-
ceive, to a sort of science distinct from all of them, and in some sense
a science of sciences, which is my own conception of what is meant by
Philosophy, in the true sense of the word, and of a philosophical habit
of mind," Ibid., p. 51. "Granting Theology is a real science, we cannot
exclude it, and still call ourselves philosophers. . . .if there be Religious
Truth at all, we cannot shut our eyes to it without prejudice to truth of
every kind, physical, metaphysical, historical, and moral; for it bears upon
all truth," Ibid., p. 52.

[34] Cf. ibid., p. 115.   [35] Ibid., p. 190.

man can paint man too, as in his essay on literature, or in his sermons. That he is also capable of philosophical abstraction is only a point in his favor.

Finally, expressions will be brought forth, with great emphasis, to show that Newman's bent of mind, that his adequate concept and feeling, belittled the place of virtue, of faith and of the Church in profane knowledge. In the revision of 1859 he even "replaces the word 'implicate' by the word ·'burden,' "[36] in the passage: "I consider Knowledge to have its end in itself. For all its friends, or its enemies, may say, I insist upon it, that it is as real a mistake to burden it with virtue or religion as with the mechanical arts."[37] Newman is insistent, and the reason is not far to seek. Knowledge has been so often confused with virtue, mental culture has been so often substituted for Christianity and for Christ, that he will have none of such a capital human crime. Knowledge is not only an end in itself, but it is also a means. It is a means, moreover, so powerful for good or for evil that it must be penetrated with Christianity, or it will be penetrated with error.

> "Good" indeed means one thing, and "useful" means another; but I lay it down as a principle, which will save us a great deal of anxiety, that, though the useful is not always good, the good is always useful. . . . If then the intellect is so excellent a portion of us, and its cultivation so excellent, it is not only beautiful, perfect, admirable, and noble in itself, but in a true and high sense it must be useful to the possessor and to all around him; not useful in any low, mechanical, mercantile sense, but as diffusing good, or as a blessing, or a gift, or power, or a treasure, first to the owner, then through him to the world. I say then, if a liberal education be good, it must necessarily be useful too.[38]

The liberal culture of the mind, the "freedom" of its powers,[39] is an end in itself, but it is simultaneously a means for good, as illustrated, or evil.[40]

---

[36] Corcoran, *op. cit.*, p. lxvii.   [37] Newman, *Idea of a University*, p. 120.
[38] *Ibid.*, p. 164.   [39] *Ibid.*, p. 101.
[40] "Basil and Julian were fellow-students at the schools of Athens; and one became the Saint and Doctor of the Church, the other her scoffing and relentless foe." *Ibid.*, p. 211.

Newman's concept, therefore, of knowledge as an end in itself does not militate against the propaedeutic function of the liberal arts, that they are a preparatory and intermediate stage in education.

> When the intellect has once been properly trained and formed to have a connected view or grasp of things, it will display its powers with more or less effect according to its particular quality and capacity in the individual. In the case of most men it makes itself felt in the good sense, sobriety of thought, reasonableness, candour, self-command, and steadiness of view, which characterize it. In some it will have developed habits of business, power of influencing others, and sagacity. In others it will elicit the talent of philosophical speculation, and lead the mind forward to eminence in this or that intellectual department. In all it will be a faculty of entering with comparative ease into any subject of thought, and of taking up with aptitude any science or profession.[41]

This is the historic claim of the liberal arts, rarely expressed better than here, that they are the best preparation for life if one is fitted for them. It is well to mention, too, the place Newman assigns to religion in the liberal arts, considered as preparatory studies. Even in the formal concept of mental culture, the proper largeness of view, the proper inter-relationship of the sciences, is not possible without study of the final questions of religion. Theology, in the liberal arts, is not studied professionally, but for fullness of knowledge and viewpoint, for proper mental orientation of any man. And yet theology and religion are subjects almost unknown in many secular universities. This is hard to understand, for taking theology even from a natural viewpoint, sketching even the questions of its content matter, without affirming truth or falsity, it cannot fail, considered as knowledge, "to exert a powerful influence on philosophy, literature, and every intellectual creation or discovery whatever."[42] Even in intermediate studies, for the mere intellectual purpose of schooling, theology is necessary.

---

[41] *Ibid.*, pp. xvii-xviii.   [42] *Ibid.*, p. 66.

Cardinal Newman has given us the content matter of the liberal arts, theology and letters and the sciences. He gives us the clear aim, mental power and breadth of vision, and the clear dangers, when this mental health, as bodily health is wont to do, in a lesser disorder, refuses to recognize a law and purpose superior to its own laws and purposes. This is the greater sin in the intellect, since the intellect is made to see the truth and to see it whole, so that man can live the truth[43] and act on it. Cardinal Newman has given us also, the intermediate function of such mental vigor, in the classic passage just quoted, "when the intellect has once been properly trained. . . ." The third function of the liberal arts, besides their content, and preparatory aim, is the exercise of man's highest powers. The training of the intellect, Newman describes well and assigns the proper function of the liberal arts as the cultivation of the understanding and the improving of the talent for speculation and original inquiry, and (agreeing with Locke at least in this), "the habit of pushing things up to their first principles." This is "a principal portion of a *good* or *liberal* education,"[44] the "exercise and growth in certain habits, moral or intellectual."[45] The will is not left out. It comes in somehow. Even the formal concept of mental culture has a relation to virtue. True knowledge tends to good, can be the instrument of good.[46] True principles are the moving forces of the will. The teachers of mankind have ever attempted to make men virtuous, and this by liberal knowledge.[47] Abstraction can gain formal concepts of things, but reality finds them in union. Newman is an empiricist, and we rarely find him tempted to dialectical divisions so mutually exclusive that they bear the taint of falsity. He treats man as a living subject, never reducing him to a *caput mortuum* of abstractions.[48] Even his formal idea

---

[43] *Cf.* St. Paul, *Epistle to the Ephesians,* IV. 15, "doing the truth in charity."

[44] Newman, *Idea of a University,* p. 163.   [45] *Ibid.,* p. xi.

[46] *Cf. ibid.,* p. 164.   [47] *Cf. ibid.,* p. 115.

[48] *Cf.* Jean Guitton, *La Philosophie de Newman* (Paris: Boivin et Cie., Editeurs, 1933), p. 81. Newman's divisions are not always mutually exclusive, "se fondent la plupart du temps sur la prédominance de tel ou tel élément, parce qu'il vise à traiter un sujet vivant sans le réduire à un *caput mortuum* d'abstractions."

of mental culture insinuates the uses of virtue. Much more clearly, when this formal idea steps to its place in the hierarchy of being, does it bow to virtue and faith. No one more than Newman fears the misuse of knowledge; no one honors more its service of the good. The liberal arts, the universities, cannot assure, cannot assume the responsibility of virtue and faith; rather it is virtue and faith, Christianity and the Church, which have the duty to assure the integrity of the universities and the arts.[49]

Cardinal Newman deepens, as did many of his predecessors, the concept of the liberal arts. This concept, like religious doctrine, is capable of organic growth and development. Remaining itself, like man, this great human education gains ever more experience; its essentials remaining the same, it is adaptable to all ages, ever old, ever new.

---

[49] Not all who reject character training as the specific purpose of a university accept the present conclusions concerning the authority of the Church. *Cf.* Robert Maynard Hutchins, *The Higher Learning in America* (New Haven: Yale University Press, 1936), pp. 28-32.

XI

UNIVERSITY—ACTUALITY OR IDEA?

University---Actuality Or Idea?

CHARLES F. DONOVAN

It does not take a bold prophet to predict that when the current emergency years have passed there either will be a swing away from utilitarianism in collegiate education or there will not. The disjunction is complete, for so long as curricula are chosen by the rule of expediency, mere dabbling in "cultural" subjects will not liberalize our colleges. The philosophy of utility is antithetic to the philosophy of liberal education. For the Catholic educator the postwar prospect is not only a disjunction; it is a dilemma. Either alternative is a horn. If utilitarianism remains in possession, we must not only hold our ground against it; we must regain the ground we were forced to yield when wartime urgency made specialization a necessity. Whereas, if there should be a reaction against vocationalism and a reversion to the liberal curriculum, we will be faced with perhaps a more dangerous evil: a natural, irreligious humanism, alluringly charming and intoxicating to a world which has too long been starved of true intellectual adventure.

For the next few years, say during the seven years that lie between this centenary of Newman's conversion and the centenary of his renowned Dublin lectures, we would do well to reread and ponder and draw argument and deepened conviction from Newman's educational pronouncements. In his Tamworth Reading Room articles, his Dublin lectures, and his university addresses, he attacks two major issues, and they are precisely the issues that constitute our dilemma—vocational as opposed to humanistic education and secularist as opposed to religious education.

In page upon page and chapter upon chapter of lucid exposition Newman constructs his thesis—that a full, a humane, a universal education must be a combination, respecting due order, of religious and liberal knowledge. His plea for each of the complementary parts of this total university program stands as

153

the most cogent refutation of materialism and utility in education that our language, perhaps any language, knows. The idea of a university propounded by Newman was old when he stated it. Had he never spoken, it would have been, and would be still, the only true idea of a university. But though his concepts were not original, they were expressed with a classic clarity and finality that make almost canonical books for Catholic educators, especially in this day when the tide of scepticism, infidelity, and expediency has risen far higher than it stood when Newman struck out against secularism and professionalism.

It is heartening, amid today's encircling gloom, to read definitive maxims like these, written before Newman's conversion, under the pen name "Catholicus":

> Christianity, and nothing short of it, must be made the element and principle of all education. Where it has been laid as the first stone, and acknowledged as the governing spirit, it will take up into itself, assimilate, and give a character to literature and science.

> If we attempt to effect a moral improvement by means of poetry, we shall but mature into a mawkish, frivolous, and fastidious sentimentalism;—if by means of argument, into a dry, unamiable long-headedness;—if by good society, into a polished outside, with hollowness within, in which vice has lost its grossness and perhaps increased its malignity;—if by experimental science, into an uppish, supercilious temper, much inclined to scepticism. But reverse the order of things: put Faith first and Knowledge second; let the University minister to the Church, and then classical poetry becomes the type of Gospel truth, and political science a comment on Genesis of Job, and Aristotle changes into Butler, and Arcesilas into Berkeley.

> . . . . greater insight into Nature will lead a man to say: "How great and wise is the Creator, who has done this!" True: but it is possible that his thoughts may take the form of "How clever is the creature who has discovered it!" and self-conceit may stand proxy for adoration. This is no idle apprehension.[1]

---

[1] *The Tamworth Reading Room* in *Discussions and Arguments on Various Subjects* (London: Longmans, Green and Co., 1888), pp. 274, 275, 301.

Heartening, too, are dicta like the following, written when Newman was "Catholicus" in the fullest sense:

> I cannot so construct my definition of the subject-matter of University Knowledge, and so draw my boundary lines around it, as to include therein the other sciences commonly studied at Universities and to exclude the science of Religion. . . . Admit a God, and you introduce among the subjects of your knowledge, a fact encompassing, closing in upon, absorbing, every other fact conceivable. How can we investigate any part of any order of Knowledge, and stop short of that which enters into every order? All true principles run over with it, all phenomena converge to it; it is truly the First and the Last. . . . You will soon break up into fragments the whole circle of secular knowledge if you begin the mutilation with divine.

> In a word, Religious Truth is not only a portion, but a condition of general knowledge. To blot it out is nothing short, if I may so speak, of unravelling the web of University Teaching.

> Knowledge is one thing, virtue is another; good sense is not conscience, refinement is not humility, nor is largeness and justness of view faith. Philosophy, however enlightened, however profound, gives no command over the passions, no influential motives, no vivifying principles. Liberal Education makes not the Christian, not the Catholic, but the gentleman.

> Surely it is very intelligible to say, and that is what I say here, that Liberal Education, viewed in itself, is simply the cultivation of the intellect, as such, and its object is nothing more or less than intellectual excellence.

> . . . .a great memory, as I have already said, does not make a philosopher, any more than a dictionary can be called a grammar. There are men who embrace in their minds a vast multitude of ideas, but with little sensibility about their real relations towards each other. These may be antiquarians, annalists, naturalists; they may be learned in the law; they may be versed in statistics; they are most useful in their own place; I should shrink from speaking disrepectfully of them; still, there is nothing in such attainments to guarantee the absence of narrowness of mind.

> A University is, according to the usual designation,
> an Alma Mater, knowing her children one by one, not
> a foundry or a mint, or a treadmill.
>
> Shut your College gates against the votary of knowl-
> edge, throw him back upon the searchings and the
> efforts of his own mind; he will gain by being spared
> an entrance into your Babel.[2]

By such a concatenation of texts, taken almost at random
from the luminous pages of *The Idea of a University,* the simple,
the vast, the true concept of a university is outlined. It is *our*
idea. Catholic education alone can fulfill its specifications.
Catholic education alone professes and attempts to do so. We
have the field to ourselves. Others fail in one department or
the other, either in the secular or in the religious, by not afford-
ing the enlargement of mind that can come only from a liberal
curriculum, or by offering a humanism which, without the basis
and complement of religious knowledge, is sapless, false, and
barren.

But let complacency be far from us. We, and we alone, have
the idea of a university. But where is the actuality? As we
review the catechetical principles of collegiate education laid
down by Newman, let us examine our consciences. Are we fulfilling our profession and our promise in either province, religious or cultural?

After bleak decades of specialization, useful facts, and labora-
tory bondage, if in collegiate circles there arose an institution
which literally fulfilled the prescriptions of liberal education as
enunciated by Newman, which gave enlargement of mind, "a
clear, calm, accurate vision and comprehension of all things, as
far as the finite mind can embrace them, each in its place, and
with its own characteristics upon it;" if there were a college
which made men philosophers in the literal sense; which gave
them a familiarity and fellowship with the great minds of history; which made intellectual pursuits—reading, thinking and
writing—not a four-year drudgery but a lifetime's adventure;
which turned out graduates who were artists at least to the

---

[2] *The Idea of a University* (London: Longmans, Green, and Co., 1898),
pp. 25, 26, 70, 120, 121, 135, 144 f., 148.

extent of intelligently fraternizing with the world's great artists—
if such a school arose, would not students flock to it from all
parts of America, as Europeans flocked to medieval Paris or
Salamanca?

We have been true to the humanistic ideal. But it is no
small thing to give the amplitude, the elevation, the enrich-
ment of mind that that ideal implies. And the ideal will not
be realized by mechanical imitation of the humanistic method
or by catalogue- and syllabus-service to the great humanistic
tradition. It will not be realized through the labored translation
of scraps of classical authors, through arid contact with scattered verse and fragments of prose, through the memorizing
of authors, titles, and dates, through rote learning of proofs and
definitions. Only under the influence of inspired and inspiring
teachers who demand and evoke mature effort can the student's
mind expand and grow to meet great artists and thinkers on
their own, not on a schoolboy's, ground. The student has a
right to experience the exhilaration, the lift, the expansiveness
that come from high intellectual companionship, from *personal
mastery* of some part of the great and beautiful things of the
world.

If there should be a resurgence of liberal education, if professors and young men became alive to the zest and emancipat-
ing joy of intellectual life, could Catholic colleges, on the
strength of present performance, meet the challenge and draw
the "votary of knowledge" to themselves? Whatever and however valid our excuses may be, we can hardly boast that we
have generally fulfilled our aim. Perhaps we have lost the spirit
ourselves. Perhaps we have been stressing the wrong things.
We have extolled the disciplinary value of a classical education
with almost Teutonic enthusiasm. Mental discipline is essential,
it is necessary in all true education, it is a by-product of the
humanistic tradition. But it will not keep that tradition alive.
Only enjoyment will do so. Stuffy people may be permanently
motivated by the desire for intellectual discipline; others will
not. Normal human beings do hard non-utilitarian work—and
mature thinking and reading are hard work—only because they
enjoy it, because they love it, because they find it soul-filling,

satisfying, enriching. The real humanist, the philosopher, he who possesses the intellectual health, excellence, and cultivation of which Newman speaks, is not a mere student, trainee, acquaintance or analyst of wisdom. He is, according to the parent language, wisdom's *lover*.

In the field of religion, Catholic education naturally stands on securer ground. Without doubt or cavil, we possess the truth, natural and supernatural; and our commission is from Christ. We are relatively unique, in this day, in centering our education on the *Summa Veritas*, the supreme object of the intellect. We are absolutely unique in teaching by God's authorization. But our norm for self-evaluation should not be those institutions which have neither the truth nor the authority to speak it. Rather it should be the very exactions and responsibilities of our high office.

It is encouraging to find among Catholic educators a lack of complacency about their work in teaching religion. They go over and over the ground in articles, surveys, regional and national meetings, trying to find an improved curriculum and improved techniques. Some feel that our approach is too moralistic, others that we give little more than advanced catechism; some contend that religion courses should present unwatered theology, others that we have had too much theology and not enough spiritual guidance. Whatever be the answer, so long as we remain restless, dissatisfied with routine or slipshod handling of religion courses, anxious for improvement in so vital a department of education, the prospect is good that we may one day achieve our total aim—schools and campuses alive with Christian humanism, offering the best for mind and soul, the best in the natural and supernatural orders, ministering to students who are, in dead earnest and in very practice, lovers of wisdom and lovers of Christ.

Finally, it may not be impertinent in a paper somewhat commemorative of Newman's philosophy of education to observe that Newman would hardly approve of the compromise by which Catholic students attend secular colleges and gather for religious exercises and instruction in clubs bearing his name. This is entirely apart from any question of the necessity or value or the ecclesiastical support of such clubs. There is question here only of what Newman's opinion of them would be. For him religion is not an appendage to the curriculum, an afterthought, an enterprise organized and conducted privately and tolerated by collegiate authorities. It must be integral to the college program—"the element and principle of all education, laid as the first stone, acknowledged as the governing spirit."

Let it not be said in retort that Newman himself once contemplated a Catholic establishment at Oxford. Remember that, even after his conversion, Oxford was to him an essentially ecclesiastical institution, paying homage to religion and acknowledging its primacy in the hierarchy of learning. The type of school Newman combatted was the irreligious, wholly secularist college which denied any place to theological studies, such as the then newly established London University. And surely the great majority of American colleges today bear a far stronger resemblance to the London than to the Oxford of Newman's day. Such being the case, a modern secular school plus a Newman Club adds up to a sadly inadequate fulfilment of Newman's idea of a university.

XII

NEWMAN AND PAPAL INFALLIBILITY

Newman And Papal Infallibility

JOSEPH CLIFFORD FENTON

John Henry Newman's teaching on the Vatican council definition of papal infallibility stands apart from all his other contributions to Catholic thought. The great English churchman made
valuable additions to the Catholic literature on the history of
dogma, on the spiritual life (particularly in the field of priestly
perfection), and on the philosophy of education. His works on
the genesis of faith and on the process of conversion to Catholic
truth have placed the Church forever in his debt. The volumes
which treat of these subjects, and which deal with the work of
practical apologetic, represent the best and the characteristic
thought of the most distinguished convert of the nineteenth
century. They are far superior to his writings on the subject
of papal infallibility.

Yet, on this happy occasion of the Newman centenary, I
believe that it will be not only helpful but actually almost
necessary to consider this weakest section of Newman's teachings. Newman has suffered what is for him the supreme indignity of becoming fashionable. Far more indiscriminate praise
than really critical study has been given to his writings. Modern
Catholic literature has tended to make a hero of Newman,
and has endeavored to justify rather than explain his con-
tentions.[1] As a result, his attitude towards the Vatican council's
definition of papal infallibility has been put on a level with the
rest of his teachings.

The effect has been most unfortunate. Some Catholics, and
not a few of those outside the true Church, have been led to
accept on the authority of Newman what, in the last analysis, is
an imperfect and inexact statement of the conciliar doctrine.
Furthermore the rest of Newman's teachings have, in a certain
measure, been eclipsed. They have been made to look like

---

[1] For every critical and discriminating study like Dr. Benard's *A Preface
to Newman's Theology*, there are half a dozen works which becloud the
ideas of Newman through their very anxiety to eulogize him.

what was, objectively, the least acceptable portion of his doctrine.

So, on the occasion of this twofold jubilee, the hundredth anniversary of Newman's entrance into the true Church of Jesus Christ and the seventy-fifth anniversary of the Vatican council, it will be interesting to review the teachings of Newman on the subject of papal infallibility and to examine the process in which these views were formulated and expressed. If the student is enabled to see something of the emotional strain under which Newman labored during the course of the Vatican council discussion and to understand what he thought of the issues involved in the definition, he will be in a position to appreciate the injustice that is done to Newman by those indiscriminate admirers who place his infallibility teachings on a level with his other doctrines, and to realize the impossibility of accepting Newman's teachings on this one point as representative of Catholic truth.

Prior to the Vatican council Newman frequently acknowledged his acceptance of a doctrine of papal infallibility. What Newman regarded as an absolute enunciation of the doctrine was found in the original text of his *Discourses on University Education.*

> Deeply do I feel, ever will I protest, *for I can appeal to the ample testimony of history to bear me out,* that in questions of right and wrong, there is nothing really strong in the whole world, nothing decisive and operative, but the voice of Him, to whom have been committed the Keys of the Kingdom, and the oversight of Christ's flock. That voice is now, as ever it has been, a real authority, *infallible* when it teaches, prosperous when it commands, ever taking the lead wisely and distinctly in its own province, adding certainty to what is probable and persuasion to what is certain. Before it speaks, the most saintly may mistake; and after it has spoken, the most gifted must obey.[2]

---

[2] Newman cites this passage in a letter to the *Guardian,* written in September, 1872. It had been included in the 1852 edition of the *Discourses on University Education,* but was left out the definitive edition of 1859. The letter to the *Guardian* is printed in *The Life of John Henry Cardinal Newman,* by Wilfrid Ward (London: Longmans, Green and Co., 1912), II, 558 f.

The *Apologia pro Vita Sua,* written in 1864, contains yet another expression of Newman's belief in papal infallibility. "It is," he tells us, "to the Pope in Ecumenical Council that we look, as to the normal seat of Infallibility."[3]

Yet by all means the most important feature of Newman's view of papal infallibility was his absolute insistence that this doctrine should be treated as a matter of mere theological opinion. A detailed statement of Newman's thought on the quality of the assent due this thesis is found in a letter to Dr. Edward Bouverie Pusey.

> Applying this principle [that a man may be obliged to believe a doctrine on grounds either of faith or of "religiousness"] to the Pope's Infallibility, (N.B. this of course is mine own opinion only, *meo periculo*) a man will find it a religious duty to *believe* it *or* may safely *disbelieve* it, in *proportion* as he thinks it probable or improbable that Church might or will define it, or does hold it, and that it is the doctrine of the Apostles. For myself, (still to illustrate what I mean, not as arguing) I think that the Church *may* define it (i.e. it possibly may turn out to belong to the original *depositum*), but that she will not ever define it; and again I do not see that she can be said to hold it. She never *can* simply act upon it, (being undefined, as it is) and I believe never has;—moreover, on the other hand, I think there is a good deal of evidence, on the very surface of history and the Fathers in its favour. On the whole then I hold it; but I should account it no sin if, on the grounds of reason, I doubted it.[4]

Writing to Peter le Page Renouf in 1868 Newman repeated his basic contention. "I hold the Pope's Infallibility," he stated, "not as a dogma, but as theological opinion; that is, not as a certainty, but as a probability."[5] In a letter written on June 27, 1870, nine days after the Vatican council had issued its definition, he offers the same assertion. "For myself, ever since

---

[3] *Newman's Apologia pro Vita Sua. The two versions of 1864 and 1865 preceded by Newman's and Kingsley's pamphlets,* with an introduction by Wilfrid Ward (London: Oxford University Press, 1931), p. 347.

[4] Ward, *op. cit.,* II, 221. The letter was written March 23, 1867.

[5] *Ibid.,* p. 236.

I was a Catholic, I have held the Pope's infallibility as a matter of theological opinion."[6]

It must be remembered that the chief cause of Newman's fierce opposition to William George Ward, and to Archbishop Manning and the others who advocated a definition of papal infallibility, was his quite emphatic insistence that the doctrine be left on the level of a mere theological opinion. It is perfectly true that he differed from the archbishop of Westminster and from the other proponents of the Holy Father's prerogative on questions concerning the limits and the exercise of the Church's inerrancy. Still, he did not resent their statement of the doctrine of infallibility in a way that differed from his own. What moved him to bitter and continued anger was his opponents' contention that the thesis on papal infallibility was not a matter of mere theological opinion at all. His polemic was directed primarily, not against an exaggerated or an extremist notion of papal infallibility, but against its presentation or definition as Catholic dogma.

A strange letter from Newman to Ward, written on May 9, 1867, brings out this most important element in Newman's attitude towards the thesis. He accepts with serenity the fact that Ward's teachings on infallibility differ sharply from his own. Newman's basic contention is that these differences are unimportant and inevitable. He is infuriated because Ward persists in viewing these differences as important. He could look with equanimity on statements contradicting his own tenets on the subject of the Holy Father's infallibility as long as these statements were presented as opinions which could be accepted or rejected freely. He is intolerant and indignant when such teachings are offered as dogmatic truth.

> Let me observe then that in former years, *and now,*
> I have considered the theological differences between
> us as unimportant in themselves; that is, such as to be
> simply compatible with a reception both by you and by
> me of the whole theological teaching of the Church in
> the widest sense of the word teaching; and again now,

---

[6] *Certain Difficulties Felt by Anglicans in Catholic Teaching,* by John Henry Cardinal Newman (London: Longmans, Green and Co., 1896), II, 304.

and in former years too, I have considered one phenomenon in you to be "momentous," nay, portentous,
that you will persist in calling the said unimportant,
allowable, inevitable differences, which must occur between mind and mind, not unimportant, but of great
moment. In this utterly uncatholic, not so much opinion
as feeling and sentiment, you have grown in the course
of years, whereas I consider that I remain myself in the
same temper of forbearance and sobriety which I have
ever wished to cultivate.

His charge against Ward is that "you are doing your best to
make a party in the Catholic Church, and in St. Paul's words are
dividing Christ by exalting your opinions into dogmas." The
letter ends on that note to harshness which Newman seemed to
reserve for those who differed from him on the question of papal
infallibility.

I protest then again, not against your tenets, but
against what I must call your schismatical spirit. I dis-
own your intended praise of me, viz. that I hold your
theological opinions in "the greatest aversion," and I
pray God that I may never denounce, as you do, what
the Church has not denounced.[7]

Newman's own attitude towards the theological details of the
doctrine of papal infallibility is quite clearly expressed in a letter to Henry Wilberforce, written on July 21, 1867. In this letter
he reveals himself as not greatly concerned about the extent and
the subject of ecclesiastical inerrancy.   The only matter of
moment to him is the fact that the Church itself is infallible.
He holds himself bound to accept on divine faith only what is
universally taught and universally believed.   He acknowledges
that the arguments set forth in favor of papal infallibility are
not such as to convince him that this doctrine falls into the class
of those truths which have been expounded and accepted always and everywhere within the Church.   It is Newman's contention that, should the doctrine of papal infallibility really
belong to the divine message, the purity of his own faith is
saved by the fact that he believes it implicitly in accepting as
the revealed word of God everything thus presented by the
Catholic Church.   Thus Newman's stand did not involve any

---

[7] Ward, *op. cit.*, II, 232 f.

denial on his part that the doctrine of papal infallibility is actually a part of divine public revelation. He was perfectly willing to admit that this teaching was probably included in God's message to mankind. His whole polemic was directed towards withholding from the doctrine of papal infallibility anything more than an implicit assent of divine faith. Explicitly he would concede to it only the status of an opinion.

The pertinent passage, although somewhat long, is far too important to be neglected by one who seeks to understand Newman's attitude towards the Vatican definition.

> For myself I have never taken any great interest in the question of the limits and seat of infallibility. I was converted simply because the Church was to last to the end, and that no communion answered to the Church of the first ages but the Roman Communion, both in substantial likeness and in actual descent. And as to faith, my great principle was: "*Securus judicat orbis terrarum.*" So I say now—and in all these questions of detail I say to myself, I believe whatever the Church teaches as the voice of God—and this or that particular inclusively, *if* she teaches this—it is this *fides implicita* which is our comfort in these irritating times. And I cannot go beyond this—I see arguments here, arguments there—I incline one way today another tomorrow—on the whole I more than incline in one direction—but I do not dogmatise—and I detest any dogmatism where the Church has not clearly spoken. And if I am told: "The Church has spoken," then I ask when? and if, instead of having anything plain shown me, I am put off with a string of arguments, or some strong words of the Pope himself, I consider this a sophistical evasion, I have only an opinion at best (not faith) that the Pope *is* infallible, and a string of arguments can only end in an opinion—and I comfort myself with the principle: "Lex dubia non obligat"—what is not taught universally, what is not believed universally, has no claim on me—and, if it be true after all and divine, my faith in it is included in the *implicita fides* which I have in the Church.[8]

Objecting to the practice of proposing the doctrine of papal infallibility as a dogma, although he was ingenuously ready to

___
[8] *Ibid.,* pp. 234 f.

admit that it might be numbered among those truths included
in the deposit of divine public revelation, the full force of Newman's wrath was turned, long before the actual convening of
the Vatican council, upon those who were urging that the council define papal infallibility as a dogma. As early as November
10, 1867, we find Newman complaining of the "intrigue, trickery,
and imperiousness" of those who favored a definition of the
Holy Father's infallibility. This strong language was occasioned
by Archbishop Manning's pastoral.

> Here is the Archbishop in a Pastoral or Pamphlet
> putting out extreme views—getting it read to the Pope,
> and circulating that the Pope approved of it—all with a
> view of anticipating and practising upon the judgments
> of the Bishops, when they meet for a General Council.
> Of course what the General Council speaks is the word
> of God—but still we may well feel indignant at the in-
> trigue, trickery, and imperiousness which is the human
> side of its history—and it seems a dereliction of duty
> not to do one's part to meet them.[9]

Newman's personal contribution to the campaign against the
definition against infallibility in the days before the opening of
the council included his encouragement and support of pamphlets by Father Ignatius Ryder and by Peter le Page Renouf.
Father Ryder's brochure was entitled *Idealism in Theology* and
it was meant to take the form of a personal attack on William
George Ward, whose writings on papal infallibility were understood to have the support of Archbishop Manning. In a letter
to Ward, sent on April 30, 1845, Newman asserted that Ryder
had written without, as far as Newman knew, receiving even a
suggestion from any other person. He claimed that "it was written simply and entirely on his [Ryder's] own idea, without any
suggestion (as far as I know) from anyone here or elsewhere."[10]
Somewhat different is Newman's account of the matter to Canon
Walker, in a letter written on May 11, 1867.

> My own share in it is this—that I thought it was good
> generalship for various reasons directly to attack Ward,
> not in the first place his opinions. I wanted him to

[9] *Ibid.*, p. 240.   [10] *Ibid.*, p. 224.

show from Ward's character of mind how untrustworthy
he was. . . .[11]

Ryder had foolishly characterized himself as a Gallican. Newman will not condemn even this absurdity. For a review in
which such writers as Acton sought to turn Catholics away
from the Vicar of Christ Newman can find no harsh words. The
only vehemently bitter expressions he is able to form during all
this period of conflict are directed against the proponents of the
Holy Father's infallibility.

> As to his [Ryder's] professing himself, not in any
> *true* sense, but in the sense people sometimes injuriously
> use the word, a Gallican, he *wished* to say what he has
> said—and I confess *I* have a great impatience at being
> obliged to trim my language by conventional rule, to
> purse up my mouth, and mince my words, because it's
> the fashion. And as to the *Home and Foreign,* I detest
> the persecuting spirit which has pursued it.[12]

The situation becomes openly ridiculous when we find Newman inveighing against the proponents of infallibility because
one of their number, a Jesuit, had presumed to answer Renouf
in the very tone which Newman admitted Renouf himself had
used.[13] A sharp attack on the doctrine of papal infallibility
received Newman's support. A sharp and decisive rejoinder to
that attack drew only his lofty disapproval. Acerbity was acceptable, but only in anti-infallibilist writings.

An outstanding characteristic of Newman's attitude to the
question of papal infallibility prior to the Vatican council is
his unrelenting and violent aversion for the proponents of the
definition. One can search in vain through his writings of this
period for one scant word of approval, for one admission that
they might have had some not too-outrageous reason for believing that the doctrine should be defined. For some reason
or other Newman seemed to regard it as a sacred duty to oppose
the projects of his metropolitan. Writing about Ryder's pamphlet to Father St. John, who was then in Rome, Newman
speaks thus about the archbishop.

> As to clamour and slander, whoever opposes the three
> Tailors of Tooley Street [Manning, Ward, and Vaughn]

---

[11] *Ibid.,* p. 229.   [12] *Ibid.*   [13] Cf. *ibid.,* pp. 297 f.

must incur a great deal, must suffer—but it is worth the
suffering if we effectually oppose them. . . .[14]

Newman considered that, in opposing Archbishop Manning
and his followers, he was fighting a "formidable conspiracy,
which is in action against the theological liberty of Catholics,"[15]
and men "making a Church within a Church, as the Novatians
of old did within the Catholic pale."[16]   The doctrines against
which Ryder was encouraged to write were characterized as
"the ὕβρις ὀρθίων κνωδάλων, " (the wantonness of rearing beasts),
and as "the arrogant *ipse dixits* of various persons who would
crush every opinion in theology which is not theirs."[17]

The first session of the Vatican council was held on December
8, 1869. Two weeks later the rector, the dean, and ten of the
professors of Louvain's great theological faculty addressed to the
council a petition that the Fathers should define as a dogma of
faith the doctrine that "when he prescribes to the universal
Church of Christ in solemn definition that some dogma is di-
vinely revealed and to be received with divine faith, or when
he condemns some assertion as contrary to divine revelation,
the Roman Pontiff, the successor of St. Peter, cannot err."
The Louvain petition proudly listed the names of the glorious
lights of the ancient faculty who had held this doctrine, naming
James Latomus, John Driedo, Ruard Tapper, Jodocus Ravestyn,
John Hessels, William Lindanus, Martin Rythovius, Cornelius
Jansen, the bishop of Ghent, Thomas Stapleton, William Estius,
John Malderus, and Christian Lupus.[18]   On January 7, 1870,
all the bishops of Belgium, led by Archbishop Dechamps of
Malines, presented the Louvain petition to the council.[19]   The
Louvain action rendered impossible, once and for all, any seri-
ous contention that the world of scholarship was opposed to the
definition.

During the month of January, 1870, petitions for and against
the definition of papal infallibility were circulated among the
members of the council.[20]   It soon became apparent that the

---

[14] *Ibid.*, pp. 154 f.   [15] *Ibid.*, p. 230.   [16] *Ibid.*, p. 233.   [17] *Ibid.*, p. 241
[18] Cf. *Acta et Decreta Sacrorum Conciliorum Recentiorum, Collectio Lacensis* (Freiburg im Breisgau: Herder, 1890), VII, cols. 942 f.
[19] Cf. *ibid.*, col. 942.   [20] Cf. *ibid.*, cols. 923 ff.

great majority was in favor of some definition. Newman was reacting to these events when he sent to Bishop Ullathorne the letter around which centered all of his public statements on the Vatican definition during the time the council was in session.

On January 20, 1870, Bishop Ullathorne despatched to Newman a letter which included some penetrating observations on the council, the statement of his conviction that it "will ultimately do a good work for the Church," and a declaration of his decision to "put hand to no petitions or propositions on this side or that." Newman answered on January 28 with what he considered "one of the most passionate and confidential letters I ever wrote in my life."[21] Evidently his ordinary did not consider it completely confidential, because he promptly showed it to four English bishops, all of them friends of Newman. One of these, William Joseph Clifford, bishop of Clifton, the man who had served Newman's first mass and who remained his most devoted friend in the English hierarchy, asked and obtained from Bishop Ullathorne permission to take the letter home with him. When he returned the letter in the morning, he surprised and annoyed Bishop Ullathorne by announcing that he had made a copy of the document for himself. When copies of the letter were shown around Rome some time later, Bishop Ullathorne accused Bishop Clifford of having given it abroad. Bishop Clifford solemnly denied the charge, and claimed that no one could have seen or obtained a text of his copy. There the matter rests to this day.[22]

Newman's letter contained a bitter and powerful protest against the actions of the leaders of the majority at the council. The council itself is accused of "infusing into us by the accredited organs of Rome and its partisans (such as the *Civiltà*, the *Armonia*, the *Univers*, and the *Tablet*) little else than fear and dismay." Through the action of the council, "No impending danger is to be averted, but a great difficulty is to be created." Newman contended that all Catholics believed in the pope's infallibility, but that the proposed definition was a test of faith.

---

[21] Cf. *The Life and Times of Bishop Ullathorne*, by Dom Cuthbert Butler (New York, Cincinnati, Chicago: Benziger Brothers, 1926), II, 56 f.; 59.

[22] Cf. *ibid.*, pp. 61 f.

Disclaiming any possibility of difficulty for himself, he declares that "I cannot help suffering with the various souls which are suffering, and I look with anxiety at the prospect of having to defend decisions which may not be difficult to my private judgment, but which may be most difficult to maintain logically in the face of historical facts." He complains that "an aggressive insolent faction" should be allowed "to make the heart of the just to mourn, whom the Lord hath not made sorrowful," and informs his ordinary that "some of the best minds" are reacting, among other ways, by becoming "angry with the Holy See for listening to the flattery of a clique of Jesuits, Redemptorists, and converts." He adverts to "the store of pontifical scandals in the history of eighteen centuries" and indicates the "blight" which is falling upon certain Anglican ritualists at even the prospect of the definition. He so far forgets himself as to declare that what the infamous and scurrilous anti-Catholic lecturer Murphy had inflicted upon the Church, the distinguished journalist, Louis Veuillot, was indirectly bringing upon it now, presumably through his advocacy of the definition.

The depth and bitterness of his feelings on the subject may be gathered from the final paragraph of the letter.

> With these thoughts before me, I am continually asking myself whether I ought not to make my feelings public; but all I do is to pray those great early Doctors of the Church, whose intercession would decide the matter—Augustine and the rest—to avert so great a calamity. If it is God's Will that the Pope's infallibility should be defined, then it is His blessed Will to throw back 'the times and the moments' of that triumph which He has destined for His kingdom; and I shall feel I have but to bow my head to His adorable, inscrutable Providence.[23]

Naturally enough, Newman's letter to Bishop Ullathorne was considered sensational. On March 14, *The Standard*, an English newspaper, published a report that Newman had written to his bishop "stigmatising the Promoters of Papal Infallibility as an insolent, aggressive faction."[24] Newman had apparently kept only a very imperfect copy of his letter, and he was under the impres-

---

[23] *Ibid.*, pp. 58 f.   [24] *Collectio Lacensis*, VII, col. 1514 n.

sion that the words attributed to him had not entered into its composition. Acting on that assumption, he wrote to *The Standard* on the following day disavowing the use of the terms attributed to him. He took the opportunity, however, to make the following pronouncement.

> That I deeply deplore the policy, the spirit, the measures of various persons, lay and ecclesiastical, who are urging the definition of that theological opinion, I have neither the intention nor wish to deny; just the contrary. But, on the other hand, I have a firm belief, and have had all along, that a Greater Power than that of any man or set of men will overrule the deliberations of the Council to the determination of Catholic and Apostolic truth, and that what its Fathers eventually will proclaim with one voice will be the Word of God.[25]

Two days later the reporter who had made the statement attributing the expression "insolent, aggressive faction" to Newman returned to the case and reaffirmed his belief that the words had actually been employed. On March 22, Newman wrote again to *The Standard*, acknowledging that its reporter had been correct in his statement. This time he insisted that when he had spoken of the faction, he had "neither meant that great body of Bishops who are said to be in favour of the definition of the doctrine, nor any ecclesiastical order or society external to the Council." Apparently still relying on the bad copy, and forgetting that they had been classed, along with Redemptorists and converts, as components of a clique engaged in flattering the Holy Father, Newman solemnly announced: "As to the Jesuits, I wish distinctly to state that I have all along separated them in my mind, as a body, from the movement which I so much deplore." The "faction" turns out to be "a collection of persons drawn together from various ranks and conditions in the Church."[26] Later Newman released the text of the greater part of his letter to *The Standard*. It was published in that journal on April 6.

On the whole Newman seemed strangely pleased about the whole affair. Writing on March 27 to Sir John Simeon, he rejoiced that he had made the mistake about the content of

---

25 *Ibid.*, col. 1514   26 *Ibid.*, col. 1515.

his own letter. The mistake had given him the opportunity to publicize his views twice, once in correcting what he took to be another's error, and once in the process of acknowledging his own.[27] His only fear seemed to be that some one would make his communication the occasion for a counterdemonstration in favor of the definition. "If it leads to some counter demonstration, it will be very sad," wrote Newman to his friend De Lisle.[28] On more than one occasion, he asserted that he believed the definition impossible. He rejoiced to hear from Simeon that a protest against the definition would be largely signed, and expressed his desire for such a lay movement to De Lisle.

His condemnation of the leaders in the fight for the definition became more virulent than ever. "Nothing can be worse," he writes, "than the conduct of many in and out of the Council who are taking the side which is likely to prevail."[29] These leaders "have been taking matters with a very high hand and with much of silent intrigue for a considerable time."[30] Even the despicable writings of such a man as Acton can be explained by Newman as "the retributive consequence of tyranny."[31] Writing on the subject of the definition to David Moriarty, bishop of Kerry, like Bishop Clifford both an intimate friend of Newman and a vigorous opponent of the majority policy, he declares that he "cannot bear to think of the tyrannousness and cruelty of its advocates—for tyrannousness and cruelty it will be, though it is successful."[32]

One of the most amazing factors in Newman's opposition to the definition during the time of the council was his repeated conviction that he and his followers ought to act in this debate as though they were themselves gifted with infallibility. He expresses this sentiment once in the letter to De Lisle, and again in a letter to Father Whitty. He thus expresses himself in the latter communication.

> One can but go by one's best light. Whoever is infallible, I am not; but I am bound to argue out the matter and to act as if I were, till the Council decides; and then, if God's Infallibility is against me, to submit at once, still not repenting of having taken the part which I felt to be right, any more than a lawyer in Court may

[27] Cf. Ward, *op. cit.*, II, 291 f.   [28] *Ibid.*, p. 293.   [29] *Ibid.*, p. 283.
[30] *Ibid.*, p. 284.   [31] *Ibid.*, p. 285.   [32] *Ibid.*, p. 289.

repent of believing in a cause and advocating a point
of law, which the Bench of Judges ultimately give
against him.[33]

In this case we have either an inept analogy or a real index
of a mistaken attitude on the part of Newman. A lawyer may
argue a case before the highest tribunal. In the event that the
decision is given against him, he is of course bound to accept
that decision.   But in no case is he bound to think that the
court has decided correctly. He can still be convinced that his
own side was the right one, and he can legitimately hope that
at some future date the tribunal will incline towards the views
which he has defended.   There is no legitimate parallel between this case and that of a man who has taken a side against
which an infallible dogmatic decision of the Catholic Church is
issued.   It is unfortunate that Newman imagined that such an
analogy was valid.

In the letter to Father Whitty, Newman set forth what seem
to have been his strongest reasons against the procedure of
the majority in the council.   Basically, he argued against what
he considered undue haste in the formation of the decision.   It
was his contention that "It is enough for one Pope to have passed
one doctrine (on the Immac. Concept.) into the list of dogmata."

Passing to what he regards as specific reasons against the definition of papal infallibility by the council, Newman adduces four
points. The first of these is merely one of the cardinal principles
of the old Gallicanism.   The advocates of the definition are
warned that they "must not flout and insult the existing tradition of countries." He denies that the traditions of Ireland and
England are on the side of papal infallibility, and insists that
what he terms ultramontane views are comparatively recent
both in those countries and in France and Germany.   In voicing
this opinion Newman manifested, as perhaps nowhere else, the
spectacular intellectual weakness of his own cause.   He appeals
to what is at best a highly suspect theological principle, and, in
branding the "ultramontane" views as "recent," he showed little knowledge of the history of scholastic theology.

---

[33] *Ibid.*, p. 295.

The second point alleged in this letter consists in a rehash of the old attack against the promotors of the definition. This time the particular charge is that they had kept the other members of the council from knowing about their purpose to work towards the definition. "I declare," wrote Newman, "unless I were too old to be angry, I should be very angry." He recollects a statement attributed to poor Msgr. Talbot to the effect that what made the definition of the Immaculate Conception such an acceptable thing was the fact that it opened the way towards a definition of the Holy Father's infallibility. Newman professed himself shocked at the thought and, meditating "on such crooked ways," he turned to the consideration of our Lord's warning about scandal. Never once did it seem to enter his mind that there was even a faint chance that his own conduct in the affair might possibly have given scandal.

The third point is interesting. It was Newman's contention that the intense theological study which had preceded the *Ineffabilis Deus* "had brought Catholic Schools into union about it, while it secured the accuracy of each." He believed that each of the two schools of thought which had previously existed on the subject of our Lady's Immaculate Conception "had its own extreme points eliminated, and they became one, because the truth to which they converged was one." Newman seemed to assert that the only means of doctrinal progress was along the Hegelian lines of thesis, antithesis, and synthesis. He apparently imagined that when two groups are opposed on some issue, the ultimate resolution can come only through a sort of compromise, in which the "extreme" points of both opposing theories are abandoned while all the contestants unite in their adherence to a middle position. He seems not to have considered the possibility of a situation in which two parties might debate, and one turn out to have defended a truth which the other had attacked.

The final argument adduced in the letter to Father Whitty takes the form of a protest against the definition on the grounds that it will be "dated," as meant merely to give support to the syllabus. Furthermore, he finds that it is inexpedient for England since its very prospect has proved disquieting to the ultra-pontifical Mr. Gladstone, and to a certain unsavory, convent-baiting politician named Newdegate.[34]

On July 18, 1870, the Vatican council adopted and promulgated the constitution *Pastor aeternus* containing the Catholic definition of papal infallibility. To Newman, who had hoped against hope that the definition would never be made, the act of the council came as a stunning blow. It was not long however before he manifested the attitude which he was to adopt towards the new definition.

At first he refused adamantly to accept the definition as a *de fide* pronouncement. It remained for him in the status of an opinion. The acts of a council, he contended, do not seem certainly binding until they are promulgated at the termination of that gathering. Before the end of the council, things could be expected to right themselves.

Again, he thought that nothing more had been defined than what he had always believed. His position stands out clearly in a letter he wrote on August 8, 1870.

> It is too soon to give an opinion about the definition. I want to know what the Bishops of the minority say on the subject, and what they mean to do. As I have ever believed as much as the definition says, I have a dfficulty in putting myself into the position of mind of those who have not. As far as I can see, no one is bound to believe it at this moment, certainly not till the end of the Council. This I hold in spite of Dr. Manning. At the same time, since the Pope has pronounced the definition, I think it safer to accept it at once. I very much doubt if at this moment—before the end of the Council, I could get myself publicly to say it was *de fide*, whatever came of it—though I believe the doctrine itself.[35]

Less than a week after the definition had been made by the council, Newman had confided his attitude to one of his friends. "I saw the new definition yesterday," he wrote, "and am pleased

---

[34] *Ibid.*, pp. 295 ff. The remarks about the letter to Father Whitty do not, of course, describe Newman's considered teaching on doctrinal development, as set forth in the *Essay*.

[35] *Ibid.*, pp. 308 f.

at its moderation—that is, if the doctrine in question is to be defined at all. The terms are vague and comprehensive; and, personally, I have no difficulty in admitting it."[36] The old passion for admitting the doctrine exclusively as an opinion appears even in this letter. Newman sets himself to inquire whether or not the definition comes to him "with the authority of an Ecumenical Council." He answers this question in the negative. The authority of an ecumenical council is certainly accorded only to those doctrines which councils proclaim with moral unanimity, according to Newman. At the moment when the Vatican council proclaimed the doctrine of papal infallibility it did not possess, as far as he was able to judge, the moral unanimity which would have made it necessary for all Catholics to accept its definition with the assent of divine faith. All of the definition's claim to be a *de fide* pronouncement was said to hinge on the future conduct of the minority bishops, on later sessions of the council, and finally on the reception accorded the conciliar definition by "the whole body of the faithful."

Newman was careful to state that, even as the proposition stood, and by reason of the authority of the assembly which had proclaimed it, the definition had a high claim upon the belief of Catholics. "Even as it is," he wrote, "if I were called upon to profess it, I should be unable, considering it came from the Holy Father and the competent local authorities, at once to refuse to do so. On the other hand, it cannot be denied that there are reasons for a Catholic, till better informed, to suspend his judgment on its validity."[37] As far as he was concerned, even after July 18, 1870, the doctrine of papal infallibility remained in the last analysis an opinion, even though he was quite cheerfully ready to acknowledge that it was a highly probable opinion.

Later he was willing to accord it the status of a dogma, but only under conditions which could be made to justify his previous stand. Had he not expressed himself as not too greatly concerned with questions about the seat and the limits of infallibility? Was not his own favorite and ultimate organ of infallibility the consent of the universal Church, the factor described in the words *Securus judicat orbis terrarum,* so intimately

---

[36] *Difficulties of Anglicans,* II, 301.   [37] *Ibid.,* p. 301 f.

connected with his own entrance into the true Church? Well, this could be the effective agent for constituting the doctrine of papal infallibility as a Catholic dogma.[38]

After all, there was no other way of accepting the definition as a dogma consistent with his principles. It would be absurd to take the pope's word as a *de fide* profession of his own infallibility. According to Newman the Roman Pontiff's infallibility had hitherto been merely a matter of opinion, and one who is only probably infallible can certainly not issue a definitive doctrinal judgment on his own authority. The council was a broken reed, since, apart from any other consideration, it had never been formally closed. Only the *Securus judicat orbis terrarum* is left, and "This indeed is a broad principle by which all acts of the rulers of the Church are ratified." "In this passage of my private letter," Newman later explained, "I meant by 'ratified' brought home to us as authentic. At this moment it is certainly the handy, obvious, and serviceable argument for our accepting the Vatican definition of the Pope's Infallibility."[39]

Newman's original position in the infallibility controversy had been in favor of treating this doctrine as an opinion. It was basically on this point that he lashed out against his opponents before the council, and it was with this in view that he deplored the attempts a definition within the council and for a time refused to acknowledge the *de fide* status of the teaching even after the council had spoken. Finally, after there could be no doubt concerning the judgment of the great body of the faithful, he found a means for reestablishing the domain of opinion in this field. The instrument that he employed was his beloved doctrine of "minimizing." Newman asserted that the Church "has ever shown the utmost care to contract, as far as possible, the range of truths and the sense of propositions, of which she demands this absolute reception [of divine faith]."[40] As for the Church's own pronouncements, according to Newman's theory, "She speaks only when it is necessary to speak; but hardly has she spoken out magisterially some great general principle, when she sets her theologians to work to explain her meaning in the concrete, by strict interpretation of its wording, by the illustra-

---

[38] Cf. *ibid.*, p. 372   [39] *Loc. cit.*   [40] *Ibid.*, p. 320.

tion of its circumstances, and by the recognition of exceptions, in order to make it as tolerable as possible, and the least of a temptation, to self-willed, independent, or wrongly educated minds."[41]

The dogmatic pronouncements with which minimizing is concerned fall into two classes. Some are positive statements of doctrine. Others are negative in form, presented as condemnations of teaching judged inacceptable by the Church. For all practical purposes, the meaning of any proposition in either class must be determined by theologians, which decisions may be accurate, but are certainly never binding.

The negative judgments of the Church, qualifying some proposition as heretical, erroneous, or the like, are primarily commands issued to Catholics to avoid these propositions in teaching. The judgment about the meaning of the condemned doctrine belongs to the theologian, and hence, according to Newman's minimism, to the domain of opinion. The affirmative propositions, on the other hand, with the exception of those dealing directly with the Godhead or with our Lady and the saints "are but general, and so far, in consequence, admit of exceptions in their actual application—these exceptions being determined either by other authoritative utterances, or by the scrutinizing vigilance, acuteness, and subtlety of the *Schola Theologorum*."[42]

Such was the doctrine set forth by Newman in the famed *Letter to the Duke of Norfolk*. Unfortunately, the rancor which he had always felt towards the leaders in the movement for the definition manifests itself in the *Letter* in such a way as to make it very tiresome reading. Newman never loses an opportunity for an expression of bitterness towards a group which included, after all, the leading prelates of Christendom. He has only expressions of courtesy for the bumbling politician who had ventured to attack the Church of God. He has only expressions of sympathy for those opponents of the definition who had left the Church. His harsh words are reserved for a group that included men like Archbishop Spalding and Archbishop Manning. In 1872 he had not a word to retract from the violent letter he had sent to Bishop Ullathorne.[43] In the

---

[41] *Ibid.*, p. 321. [42] *Ibid.*, p. 334. [43] Cf. Ward, *op. cit.*, II, 559.

Letter to the Duke of Norfolk he withdraws this lamentable document only to the extent of asserting that it had not been meant for the public eye.[44]   Indeed, the *Letter to the Duke of Norfolk* seems to have been considered by Newman himself as an attack on Archbishop Manning as much as a defence of the Catholic body against the libels of Gladstone.[45]   It is characteristic of the relations of the two great English churchmen that, when the then Prefect of Propaganda, Cardinal Franchi, wrote to Archbishop Manning on the subject of censurable propositions in the *Letter to the Duke of Norfolk*, Manning hastened to reply, begging that no public action be taken against Father Newman, and giving as his first and principal reason the assertion that "The heart of the revered Father Newman is as right and as Catholic as it is possible to be."[46]

As a whole, Newman's stand on the doctrine of papal infallibiltiy was doctrinally inexact and unfortunate in its influence. In his controversial efforts against the definition, he seems never to have adverted to the factor which rendered this conciliar act not only beneficial, but morally necessary to the Church of God. The great ecclesiologists of the golden age, almost without exception, had insisted upon the infallibility of the Holy Father's definitive dogmatic pronouncements They had pointed to the fact that his decisions were irreformable of themselves, whether he spoke in concert with the rest of the apostolic college, or alone in his capacity as the supreme teacher of the true Church of Jesus Christ. The long list of theologians cited by the Louvain faculty in its petition to the Vatican council covers only a portion of the body of classical ecclesiologists who taught this doctrine.   Men like St. Robert Bellarmine, Francis Suarez, Francis Sylvius, and John Wiggers considered this teaching as a part of the deposit of Catholic faith.

The infamous Gallican articles darkened the theology of the eighteenth and the early nineteenth centuries.   The Gallicans did not simply deny papal infallibility, but they would recognize as infallible only those pronouncements which the Holy Father makes in concert with the Catholic bishops throughout

---

[44] *Difficulties of Anglicans*, II, 301.
[45] Cf. Ward, *op. cit.*, II, 402.   [46] Butler, *op. cit.*, II, 101.

the world.   The confusion caused by this politico-theological doctrine manifested itself in a relatively poor quality of teaching *De Romano Pontifice* in mid-nineteenth-century theology. Only an occasional ecclesiologist, like Patrick Murray of Maynooth, managed to achieve the clarity and adequacy which had been characteristic of this tract in former years.[47]   As a result of the Gallican teachings, there had been a regress rather than a progress in an important portion of theology.   The definition of papal infallibility was meant to remove this harm from the Church.   Unfortunately, Newman seemed unaware of the immediate issue and of its chief implications.

Acton, who was in constant touch with Newman during the time of the infallibility debates and who was sympathetic to Newman's attitude, seems to have considered the great Oratorian's explanation of the Vatican decrees as being, for all intents and purposes, an emptying of their content.   Writing to "dear Mr. Gladstone" in December 1874, Acton made no secret of the fact that it was his wish "to make the evils of Ultramontanism so manifest that men will shrink from them, and so explain away or stultify the Vatican Council as to make it innocuous."[48]   After the *Letter to the Duke of Norfolk* had appeared, Acton, apparently still unwilling to do other than "explain away" the Vatican definitions, announced to Lady Blennerhassett that "Newman's conditions would make it possible, technically, to accept the whole of the decrees."[49]   Even before the council had made its definition, Newman had written to O'Neill Daunt, contending that "if anything is passed, it will be in so mild a form, as practically to mean little or nothing."[50]

The most unfortunate effect of this attitude on the part of Newman has been the emergence of an opinion that, after all, the Vatican definition of papal infallibility was of little import. This impression has been spread, not so much by Newman's own

---

[47] Murray, the outstanding ecclesiologist of the nineteenth century, is among those accused by Newman of attempting "to bring in a new theory of Papal Infallibility." (Cf. Ward, *op. cit.*, II, 152 f.).

[48] *Selections from the Correspondence of the First Lord Acton* (London: Longmans, Green and Co., 1917), I, 147.

[49] *Ibid.*, p. 155.   [50] Ward, *op. cit.*, I, 299.

writings, which of themselves are not very convincing on this point, as by Wilfrid Ward's official biography of Newman. Ward's *Life,* one of the few really influential modern Catholic works in the English language, sees the issues only through the eyes of Newman himself. Newman's opponents are, for Wilfrid Ward, only the "untheological school,"[51] and the persons who have the temerity to question Newman's position are "good but not far-seeing people,"[52] or "men whose education was not equal to their piety."[53] Without the faintest attempt to appeal to evidence, he leads his readers to believe that the Vatican council saw a conflict between two groups of extremists, his own father and Louis Veuillot on one side against men like Doellinger on the other. The actual definition is supposed to have represented a victory for certain moderates, among whom Newman himself was to be found. Something of the same spirit has gone into the writing of Dom Cuthbert Butler's *The Vatican Council.* It is principally from this last-named book that Trevor Gervase Jalland has taken what he regards as the modern Catholic attitude towards papal infallibility, the impression that this doctrine means very little in the dogma of the Catholic Church. It is regrettable that Dr. Jalland can give to the non-Catholic scholarly world such an ill-advised description of Catholic attitude towards the definition as that which he has taken from Butler: "Rather does it seem to give point to Salmon's gibe—or was it Whateley's?—that the Pope is infallible so long as he defines nothing."[54]

Actually, the opinion of Newman on the definition of papal infallibility is only a kind of unwarranted exception to the theological explanation of the decrees. In the light of the traditional and scientific exposition of papal infallibility, found at its best in works like Billot's *De Ecclesia,* Newman's position is inexact and his uncritical apologists are misleading.

Some popular accounts of Newman's life seem calculated to make us believe that his position on the Vatican council's

---

[51] Cf. *ibid.,* p. 282.   [52] Cf. *ibid.,* p. 279   [53] Cf. *ibid.,* p. 280.

[54] *The Vatican Council* (London: Longmans, Green and Co., 1936), II, 228. The sentence is quoted in Jalland's *The Church and the Papacy* (London: Society for Promoting Christian Knowledge, 1944), p. 534.

definition was basically quite satisfactory. Such a belief would be inaccurate, and harmful both to the Church and to Newman himself. The divine message which we possess within the Catholic Church is too precious a thing to be obscured by the unfortunate theory of even so great a man as Newman. Furthermore, his capacity for good is too powerful to allow us to dally with the notion that his stand on the infallibility controversies is as valuable as his other contributions to Catholic thought.

XIII

THE BEAUTY EVER ANCIENT, EVER NEW

The Beauty Ever Ancient, Ever New

WALTER P. BURKE

The charge of "dogmatism" is the usual accusation that any forceful writer of Catholic convictions must expect. But as Chesterton retorted to Arnold Bennett: "In truth there are only two kinds of people, those who accept dogmas and know it, and those who accept dogmas and don't know it."[1] This two-edged thrust could well be aimed at Carlyle, who found himself so ruffled by Cardinal Newman's apparent dogmatism that he made the unwarranted assertion that Newman possessed "the brain of a moderate sized rabbit."[2] The truth of the matter is that in Newman's writings on Catholic dogmas we find the great mind of the nineteenth century really at its best.

An intense realization of the ancient newness and beauty of Catholic dogmas sparkles all through his writings. He is ever conscious, ever in wonderment, at the dynamic realities, the vital truths, the power and significance of the dogmas of the Church. His appreciation of them makes the colorless black columns of Denzinger-Bannwart really come to life. For after all, words and terms express true ideas—the images by which, through the mysterious power of the mind, we actually come in contact in an intensely intimate way with the realities which these ideas represent.

Newman's glorification of the dogmas of the Church, then, can hardly be considered extravagant. For him, the definitions, the symbols, the dogmatic statements are the trophies "set up in record of the victories of the Faith."[3] The Athanasian creed is "the

---

[1] Maisie Ward, *Gilbert Keith Chesterton* (New York: Sheed and Ward, 1943), p. 217.

[2] *Ibid.*

[3] *Sermons Preached Before the University of Oxford* (London: Long-mans, Green, and Co., 1909), p. 315.

war-song of faith,"[4] "a hymn of praise to the Eternal Trinity."[5]
The definitive pronouncements of the Church are the catalogued
treasures of God's own mind as revealed to man.[6] They are
ever "springing into life with inexhaustible fecundity,"[7] ever
blossoming forth from the perennial Vine of Christ. The ana-
themas and *de fide's* are trumpet blasts of the Church Militant
"to draw the line between truth and heresy."[8] It is by means of
these masterful formulas that the Church has ever been able
"to anticipate or remedy the various aberrations of wrong reason; to combat pride and recklessness with their own arms, and
thus to triumph over the sophist and the innovator." "The
overthrow of the wisdom of the world was one of the earliest
as well as the noblest triumphs of the Church."[9]

There is a master idea behind the writings of Newman which
gives the key to his appreciation of the dogmas of the Church.
It parallels one of the basic principles in the intellectualism of
St. Thomas, who states: "Intelligence is a form of life, and of
living things, it is the most perfect."[10] So, too, for Newman, the
master idea of his intellectualism is that truth is a dynamic, living thing. As long as a truth endures, it must be always manifesting the characteristics of a principle of life. It must be
active and growing. It must constantly be perfecting and developing itself in the minds of men without suffering any substantial change within itself. Thus the dynamic life of a truth
is its cause of development. And the norm for determining
whether or not the doctrinal development of a truth is a genuine development or merely a corruption is that the development
possesses the characteristics proper to a real living thing. Hence

---

[4] *An Essay in Aid of a Grammar of Assent* (London: Longmans, Green,
and Co., 1909), p. 133.

[5] *Parochial and Plain Sermons* (London: Longmans, Green, and Co.,
1908), II, 270.

[6] *The Via Media of the Anglican Church* (London: Longmans, Green,
and Co., 1897), II, 209.

[7] *An Essay in Aid of a Grammar of Assent* (London: Longmans, Green,
and Co., 1909), p. 148.

[8] *Sermons Preached Before the University of Oxford*, p. 313.

[9] *Ibid.*, pp. 313 f.

[10] St. Thomas Aquinas, *In XII libros metaphysicorum*, I, 5.

the master idea of Newman regarding dogmas might be summed up in this statement: The living quality of truth is not only the cause of developments but also the criterion for judging a true development of doctrine.[11]

Newman, an intellectual genius and profound psychologist, has a tremendous insight into the dynamic life of dogmas and their developments because, from his own personal experience, he is so much aware of the intensity of life in the realms of the intellectual. The spirit-world, the sphere of the intellect and the will, is Newman's real world. His writings seem always pregnant with a vision of that spirit-world. Perhaps we might describe that vision as that of a man who views the world of human minds as a mighty sea sparkling with myriads of individual spirit-principles of activity and life, acting and interacting on one another. Added to them and coursing among them with mighty clashes and collisions are the millions of individual ideas acting upon the minds of men, and in turn, being acted upon by them. For each human idea is itself a principle of life and activity. It is in this unseen world of ideas and human minds, vibrant beneath the drab world of sense and space and time, that human life and activity reach their highest peak, their whitest heat. It is such a vision that enriches Newman's analysis of the ebb and tide of thought-trends in history, the birth and death of false philosophies, the crooked course of heresies from corruption to decay, and the perennial life and beauty of ancient Christian dogmas.

Illustrative of this vision is the following passage from the preface to Newman's *Essay on the Development of Christian Doctrine*:

> When an idea, whether real or not, is of a nature to arrest and possess the mind, it may be said to have life, that is, to live in the mind which is its recipient. Thus mathematical ideas, real as they are, can hardly properly be called living, at least ordinarily. But when some great enunciation, whether true or false, about human nature, or present good, or government, or duty, or religion, is carried forward into the public throng of

[11] Wilfrid Ward, *The Life of John Henry Cardinal Newman* (London: Longmans, Green, and Co., 1921), I, 87.

men and draws attention, then it is not merely received passively within them, leading them to an ever-new contemplation of itself, to an application of it in various directions and a propagation of it on every side. . . . Let one such idea get possession of the popular mind, or the mind of any portion of the community, and it is not difficult to understand what will be the result. At first men will not fully realize what it is that moves them, and will express and explain themselves inadequately. There will be a general agitation of thought, and an action of mind upon mind. There will be a time of confusion, when conceptions and misconceptions are in conflict, and it is uncertain whether anything is to come of the idea at all, or which view of it is to get the start of others. New lights will be brought to bear upon the original statements of the doctrine put forward, judgments and aspects will accumulate. After a while, some definite teaching emerges; and as time proceeds, one view will be modified or expanded by another, and then combined with a third; till the idea to which these various aspects belong, will be to each mind separately what at first it was only all together. . . . It will, in proportion to its native vigour and subtlety, introduce itself into the framework and details of social life, changing public opinion, and strengthening or undermining the foundations of established order. Thus in time it will have grown into an ethical code, or into a system of government, or into a theology, or into a ritual, according to its capabilities: and this body of thought, thus laboriously gained, will after all be little more than the proper representative of one idea, being in substance what that idea meant from the first, its complete image as seen in a combination of diversified aspects, with the suggestions and corrections of many minds, and the illustration of many experiences.

This process, whether it be longer or shorter in point of time, by which the aspects of an idea are brought into consistency and form, I call its development, being the germination and maturation of some truth or apparent truth on a large mental field.[12]

He continues farther on: "In time, it enters upon strange territory; points of controversy alter their bearing; parties rise and

---

[12] *An Essay on the Development of Christian Doctrine* (London: Longmans, Green, and Co., 1909), p. 36 ff.

fall around it; dangers and hopes appear in new relations; and old principles reappear under new forms. It changes with them in order to remain the same. In a higher world it is otherwise, but here below to live is to change, and to be perfect is to have changed often."[13]

The real richness of Newman's master idea of the living quality of truth and the intensity of life in the intellectual order is not fully seen by viewing it in itself, as we have done, but rather in seeing its actual application to the nature of a dogma and to the development of a dogma. As conscious as Newman is of the dynamism of ideas and their revolutionary effects, still he does not stray from the path of orthodoxy. There is also permanence in the reality of the spirit-world. There is always the objectivity and changelessness of truth itself.

Newman's notion of a dogma is an orthodox one even though it lacks the precise terminology of the schoolmen or of the Vatican council. He does not state: "A dogma is a truth revealed by God and as such, directly set forth by the Church for us to believe."[14] But he does express its equivalent. Newman insisted that his position agreed substantially with that of his critic, Perrone, the Roman theologian.[15] At the same time, he submitted his *Essay on Development* to the Catholic authorities in case they should consider necessary any theological revision.[16]

In Newman's various statements on the notion of a dogma, the elements of the Vatican definition are clearly present, along with the application of his master idea to the nature of a dogma: "Theological dogmas are propositions expressive of the judgments which the mind forms, or the impressions which it receives of the Revealed Truth."[17] "These articles were all hidden, as it were, in the Church's bosom from the first, and brought out into form according to the occasion."[18] ". . . .a dogma

---

13 *Ibid.*, p. 40.

14 E. Dublanchy, "Dogme," *Dictionnaire de théologie catholique* (Paris: Letouzey et Ané, 1911), IV, 2, col. 1575.

15 Wilfrid Ward, *op. cit.*, I, 185 f.   16 *Ibid.*, I, 99, 615.

17 *Sermons Preached Before the University of Oxford*, p. 320.

18 *Via Media*, II, 40.

professes to be a direct contemplation, and, if so be, a definition
of what is infinite and eternal. . . ."[19]   Newman states rather
decisively the authoritative part of the Church in a dogma.
"Every Catholic holds that the Christian dogmas were in the
Church from the time of the apostles; that they were ever in
substance what they are now; that they existed before the
formulas were publicly adopted, in which, as time went on,
they were defined and recorded, and that such formulas, when
sanctioned by due ecclesiastical acts, are binding on the faith
of Catholics, and have a dogmatic authority."[20]

The above quotations certainly clear Newman of any possible
taint of Modernism as regards the nature of a dogma. The Kant-
ian subjectivism and relativity of truth as found in the writings
of Schleiermacher and Loisy are a far cry from Newman, who
looks upon revealed truths as eternal and changeless. For the
Modernist, dogmas are merely the ephemeral bubbles of sentiment raised upon the surface of the sea of the inner religious
experiences of mankind. But for Newman, a dogma is as
changeless and as objective within itself as the reality it represents. Thus he writes: "Surely, if Almighty God is ever one
and the same, and is revealed to us as one and the same; the
true inward impression of Him, made on the recipient of the
revelation, must be one and the same; and, since human nature
proceeds upon fixed laws, the statement of that impression must
be one and the same, so that we may as well say that there are
two God as two Creeds."[21]

Newman is a staunch supporter of the infallibility of the
Church in matters of dogma.[22] The rebellion against the authority of the Church which characterized the modernists has no
place with Newman. He was aware that even the forerunners
of modernism were being swept along by the revolutionary
thought-trends and social changes which were bubbling up as
early as the times of Lammenais. In his essay on the Abbé

---

[19] *Ibid.*, p. 325.

[20] *Tracts Theological and Ecclesiastical* (London: Longmans, Green, and
Co., 1908), p. 333.

[21] *Sermons Preached Before the University of Oxford*, p. 328.

[22] *Apologia pro vita sua* (London: Longmans, Green, and Co., 1905), pp.
250 f.

de Lammenais' *Affaires de Rome* he quotes some of the more powerful passages on the revolutionary ideas and changes then sweeping the continent. Newman wrote this essay even before de Lammenais' fall and he has this to say of the abbé's writings: ". . . .there is just that ill flavour in his doctrine as to make one tremble, lest, under disappointment, he should be led to deny the authority of religion."[23] It may be remarked further that Newman would have preferred to re-edit his *Essay on Development*. Cardinal Wiseman, however, examined the book and advised Newman to leave it in its original terminology lest any modifications might cause it to lose currency with the Anglicans.[24]

So much for the orthodoxy and proper understanding in Newman as to the nature of a dogma. It is with his application of his master idea to the notion of a dogma that we are chiefly concerned. As is evident from the quotations from Newman regarding the nature of a dogma, he is well aware that a dogma is composed of two elements: a formula and a divine truth. The formula, of course, is the organized group of terms which contain and express the divine truth. Even in his appreciation of the formulas, we see the master idea of Newman in action, beholding the formula as itself a living thing and participating in the vitality of the truth that it expresses.

For Newman, the aesthete and mystic as well as historian, the formulas themselves possess a perennial power and beauty. He refers to these formulas as a "watchword. . . .distinguishing Christians from infidels."[25] They are outlines of sound words[26] and abstracts of saving faith.[27] "It is the temper of reverent faith to feel this; to feel that in coming to the Church, it stands before God's representative, and that, as in her Ordinances, so in her Creed, there is something supernatural and beyond us."[28] In his *Via Media*, Newman tells us that "history bears witness to the fact" that the Apostles' creed is "the treasure and legacy of

---

23 *Essays Critical and Historical* (London: Longmans, Green, and Co., 1910), I, 173.

24 Wilfrid Ward, *op. cit.*, pp. 99, 615.

25 *Via Media*, I, 218. 27 Cf. *ibid.*, p. 240.

26 Cf. *ibid.*, p. 249. 28 *Ibid.*, p. 257.

faith."[29]   "In like manner, it was called the *Regula Fidei* or Rule of Faith, as the formulary, by which all statements of doctrine made in the Church were to be measured and estimated."[30]   Of the Athanasian creed he confesses: "For myself, I have ever felt it is the most simple and sublime, the most devotional formulary to which Christianity has given birth, more so even than the *Veni Creator* and the *Te Deum*."[31]

Newman views the formulas as partaking of some of the active power of the truth which they enclothe and at the same time manifest, just as the human body does of the soul: "To object, then, to the number of propositions, upon which an anathema is placed, is altogether to mistake their use; for their multiplication is not intended to enforce many things, but to express one—to form within us that one impression concerning Almighty God, as the ruling principle of our minds, and that, whether we can fully recognize our own possession of it or no."[32]

Yet it must be admitted that Newman does not put too much stress on the beauty and vitality of the formulas themselves, since he is enthralled rather by the truth that they certain. Perhaps it is because he does not have a thoroughly developed epistemology that would bring out clearly the intimate relationship of the term to the vital concept it expresses.   In the principles of St. Thomas, we see the mental processes of conception and definition as identical, and the term as the perfect expression of the object grasped by the mind.[33] The formula, then, is readily comprehended as very intimately sharing in the life of the truth it contains and manifests.

Newman himself admits that by nature and sentiment he prefers the simple, beautiful scriptural language of the days of the *disciplina arcani*.[34] His pious sensitiveness and mystical otherworldliness are not soothed by the thought of bloodshed and suffering and loss of immortal souls involved in the formulation

---

[29] *Ibid.*, p. 218.   [30] *Ibid.*, p. 219.   [31] *Grammar of Assent*, p. 133.

[32] *Sermons Preached Before the University of Oxford*, pp. 336 f.

[33] Pierre Rousselot, S.J., *The Intellectualism of St. Thomas* (London: Longmans, Green, and Co., 1935), pp. 102 f.

[34] *The Arians of the Fourth Century* (London: Longmans, Green, and Co., 1908), pp. 36 ff.

of such terms as ὁμοούσιος and others. He sees the formulas as
the tools of human reason, the powerful arms which the Church
Militant has had to take up in order to defend herself against
heresies. He admits that without precise formulas the Church
is hampered in her defence against attacks, just as she was
against Arianism before Nicea.[35] But it is always the truth of
God contained within the formula that Newman emphasizes.
At times, he so stresses the beauty, the riches, and the depths
of divine truth expressed by the formulas that he seems to obscure the vitality and beauty that he actually does maintain
to be present in the formulas themselves.

It is in this second element, the truth of a dogma, that the
master idea goes into real action. Newman is always filled with
awe and wonderment at the majesty and the fecundity of God's
revealed truth. This is the "pearl of great price" for Newman,
and he sees it ever prolific in life and beauty and yet as substantially changeless as it is ancient. It is not only because
human minds are limited active principles, which only gradually
deepen their comprehension of a truth, that we have doctrinal
developments. It is chiefly because the words of God are fountains "springing up unto life everlasting."

Thus Newman writes:

> This is a phenomenon proper to the Gospel, and a
> note of divinity. Its half sentences, its overflowings of
> language, admit of development; they have a life in
> them which shows itself in progress; a truth, which has
> the token of consistency; a reality, which is fruitful in
> resources; a depth, which extends into mystery: for
> they are the representations of what is actual, and has
> a definite location and necessary bearings and a mean-
> ing in the great system of things, and a harmony in
> what it is, and a compatibility in what it involves.
> What form of Paganism can furnish a parallel? What
> philosopher has left his words to posterity as a talent
> which could be put to usury, as a mine which could be
> wrought?[36]

---

[35] *Ibid.*, p. 141.
[36] *Sermons Preached Before the University of Oxford*, pp. 317 f.

It is this living quality of the divine truth in the dogma that not only causes but necessitates the development of doctrine. Newman describes its action in a typical development:

> Let us quit this survey of the general system, and descend to the history of the formation of any Catholic dogma. What a remarkable sight it is, as almost all unprejudiced persons will admit, to trace the course of the controversy from its first disorders to its exact and determinate issue. Full of deep interest, to see how the great idea takes hold of a thousand minds by its living force, and will not be ruled or stinted, but is "like a burning fire," as the Prophet speaks, "shut up" within them till they are "weary of forbearing and cannot stay," and grows in them, and at length is born through them, perhaps in a long course of years, and even successive generations; so that the doctrine may rather be said to use the minds of Christians, than to be used by them. Wonderful it is to see with what effort, hesitation, suspense, interruption,—with how many swayings to the right and left—with how many reverses, yet with what certainty of advance, with what precision in its march, and with what ultimate completeness, it has been evolved; till the whole truth "self-balanced on its center hung," part answering to part, one, absolute, integral, indissoluble while the world lasts! Wonderful, to see how heresy has but thrown that idea into fresh forms, and drawn out from it farther developments, with an exuberance which exceeded all questioning, and a harmony which baffled all criticism, like Him, its Divine Author, who, when put on trial by the Evil One, was but fortified by the assault, and is ever justified in His sayings, and overcomes when He is judged.[37]

The above passage is beautifully illustrated by the whole history of the doctrinal development of the Incarnation. One cannot help but surmise that the passage is a rich abstract drawn from the cardinal's tremendous study and writings on the Christological heresies. Here in one paragraph, he has x-rayed the turbulent yet colorful and complex course of the doctrine from the time of its first revelation to its final formulation at Chalcedon. St. John, inspired by the Holy Spirit, writes: "The

---

[37] *Ibid.*, p. 316 f.

Word was God. . . .and the Word was made flesh and dwelt amongst us."[38] In these simple yet richly pregnant words, St. John expressed the tremendous truth that God had really and truly become man, a truth that was clearly taught in the gospels and epistles, preached by all the apostles and held by all the faithful of the ancient Church. Yet this was not enough.

The mighty truth of the Incarnation was like a bomb-shell that burst amidst the pagan fortresses of Platonism, Manicheism, and pessimism. It acted like a piece of phosphorous on the stagnant waters of the pagan philosophies that formed the dead sea of the minds of fallen men. Then followed four turbulent centuries of controversies. The intellectual realms of the ancient world surged with new life and became a raging sea of mind clashing with mind, and heart with heart, in the attempts of men to interpret and penetrate this new truth that had come down from heaven in the person of the Son of God.

The whole Christian world became embroiled in a life and death struggle with the Gnostic "higher wisdom" of the world which attempted to twist and corrupt this mighty truth of God into tiny fables about demiurges and intermediate beings. Against each heretic God raised up a giant of sanctity and intellectual brilliance to preserve the divine facts with the protective armor of steel-cut formulas. On the anvil of heresy and human obstinacy, amidst the heat of controversy and even the shedding of blood, these formulas were hammered out and delicately fashioned. The war-like Athanasius turned the tide against the Arians with the term ὁμοούσιος and at Nicaea preserved the divinity of Christ. Cyril at Ephesus in 431 with the term θεοτόκος defeated the Nestorians, who tried to destroy the intimate union of humanity and divinity by insisting on two persons in Christ. Gregory Nazianzen maintained the νοῦς or rational soul in Christ against the Apollinarists and thereby perserved the integrity of the humanity of the God-Man. Finally, Leo the Great vanquished Eutyches, who proclaimed that after the union of the humanity and divinity in Christ the human nature was completely absorbed and swallowed up, as it were, in Christ's divinity.

---

[38] *John* 1:1, 14.

It was then that St. Leo, guided by the Holy Spirit, wrote infallibly in a manner that crystallized four centuries of intense human activity spent in the protecting and the comprehending of the simple statements of the gospels and epistles which had told men that Jesus Christ was truly God and truly man. In his dogmatic letter to Flavian, Leo expressed the same changeless truth as John and Paul and the others before him; but he expressed it in a formula which manifested a real growth in men's comprehension of what God had wrought with the coming of the Saviour into the world. He phrased it in a delicately balanced formula which clarified the truth and at the same time excluded the errors and corruptions of Arianism, Nestorianism, Apollinarianism, and Eutychianism. Thus, three hundred years after John and Paul, their words of revelation were sheathed in these terms:

> . . . .we all confess and teach with one accord, one and the same Lord Jesus Christ, perfect in His divinity and perfect in His humanity, true God and true man, having a rational soul and body, consubstantial with the Father in His divinity and consubstantial with us in His humanity. . . .one and the same Christ. . . .to be confessed in two natures without confusion, without change, division or separation, for the union does not destroy the distinction of natures but rather each retains its own being and characteristics, and is united to the other in one person and hypostasis. . . .[39]

Of this dogmatic statement enunciated by Leo, of this doctrinal development of the Incarnation, Newman's words are most appropriate: ". . . .with what ultimate completeness, it has been evolved; till the whole truth 'self-balanced on its centre hung,' part answering to part, one, absolute, integral, indissoluble while the world lasts!"[40] This dogma as expressed by Leo is for Newman like the other dogmas of the Church. They are the deathless enunciations of saints and scholars, of men like Athanasius and Cyril and Leo and Gregory who spent their lives that the ancient

---

[39] H. J. Schroeder, O.P., *Disciplinary Decrees of the General Councils* (St. Louis: B. Herder Book Co., 1937), p. 83.

[40] Cf. *supra*, p. 317.

beauty and fecundity of divine truth might never be lessened or obscured.

Yet Newman was not content with merely stating that the dynamic life of truth is the cause of doctrinal developments. With his master idea, he penetrated even more deeply into this historical phenomenon. For he saw that every living thing, whether it be in the physical order or in the intellectual order, follows very definite laws in its growth. A thing which is really alive follows an obvious pattern of development and possesses very definite characteristics in its progress. That is why a true growth is easily distinguished from a mere corruption. Newman, in his *Essay on Development*, sets down seven characteristics that are common to living things and especially proper to a living dogma.

The seven qualities of a true growth or development by which a true growth must be characterized are: "A Chronic Vigour," "A Preservation of Type," "The Power of Assimilation," "Continuity of Principles," "Logical Sequence," "Conservative Action," and "Anticipation of its Future."[41] Since these seven qualities are always essential to any true growth, it follows that they can be used as sound criteria for distinguishing a real doctrinal development from a mere corruption or heresy. An easy way to perceive the truth of this line of reasoning is to apply these seven characteristics to some living thing in the physical order, such as an oak tree, and see the principle illustrated in a concrete manner. Then, by way of parallelism, apply it in the intellectual order to a living dogma such as the Incarnation. It is clearly seen that these seven notes form a reliable norm for judging whether a doctrinal development is a truth growth or merely a heresy.

Take, for example, the first note, "Chronic Vigour,"[42] as applied to an oak tree, and then as applied to the doctrine of the Incarnation. An oak tree is a living thing. Therefore, it has within it a principle of life or self-perfecting activity. Hence as long as an oak tree is alive, it must be always growing and developing and perfecting itself. So, too, a living truth must be always manifesting a perennial growth and development, for the sphere of the intellect is life at its highest intensity. The doctrine of

---

[41] *Essay on Development*, pp. 169-206.   [42] *Ibid.*, p. 203.

the Incarnation is characterized by this note. For the truth that "The Word was God. . . .and the Word was made flesh and dwelt amongst us,"[43] has never ceased to grow in the comprehension of itself by human beings. And the depth of its meaning has had an inexhaustible fecundity not only for the minds of men of the caliber of Paul and Augustine and Thomas but for the minds of men of all ages. It has very definitely a "Chronic Vigour."

The second note, "Preservation of Type,"[44] is but another way of saying that any living thing must maintain its substantial identity of nature even while it grows and changes. Thus an oak tree does not turn into a box hedge or into a cedar tree but always remains an oak. Likewise, the essential truth of a doctrine and its intrinsic identity must persist. In the Christological development, the essential truth of the Incarnation as revealed in Scripture has been maintained. For the fact that Christ is both God and man has not been altered by Nicaea or Ephesus or Constantinople or Chalcedon. That is why Arianism lacks this note. It corrupts what is of the very essence of the truth: the divinity of Christ.

The third note, "Power of Assimilation,"[45] means that a living thing must be able to absorb into its own substantial unity elements that are external to it and that help it in its course of growth. There must be a real affinity between the living thing and these elements, and their absorption must take place without its suffering any loss or alteration of its own substantial identity. So it is that an oak tree nourishes itself with the chemical elements in the soil, and the air, and the rain, and absorbs them without losing its nature as an oak, or turning into earth and air itself. It does not absorb what it does not have a natural affinity to; hence it is not corrupted.

In the intellectual order, a truth has a natural relationship to the activities of human minds and to other true ideas. For truth, whether revealed or unrevealed, is the proper object of the human intellect, whether the intellect be that of a pagan or a Christian. The body of Christian revelation is also related to

---

[43] *John* 1:1, 14.   [44] *Essay on Development*, pp. 171 f.
[45] *Ibid.*, pp. 185 f.

the bits of truth of the primitive revelation already scattered throughout the pagan world beforehand. Thus the living truth of the Incarnation marshalled to itself large theological groups and attracted the activity of many minds upon itself. That which was good and true and related to it was used while that which was evil or heretical or utterly foreign was rejected. Philosophical phraseology and Aristotelian logic were absorbed and used for the perfecting of men's penetration of the one truth. The term ὁμοούσιος was cleansed of any wrong connotations and assimilated by the doctrine while the compromising semi-Arian ὅμοιος was rejected. Despite this assimilation of external elements, there is still no essential difference in the truth as expressed at Chalcedon or as expressed in the prologue of St. John's gospel, though there is a very definite growth in the minds of men as regards their penetration and comprehension of the Incarnation.

The fourth note, "Continuity of Principles,"[46] signifies that every living thing has very definite laws or principles by which it nourishes and perfects itself. This regulating law of growth flows from the very nature of the things and is proper to it. As such, it is as changeless as the nature of the thing itself. The principle of growth for an oak tree is that of osmosis and absorption. It could not suddenly begin to masticate and forage for itself, for then its nature would have been changed into that of an animal. The essential principle of growth for a philosophy is the activity of human reason. In theology, it is faith and reason, with faith being supreme. All through the true developments of the Incarnation, the law of development was that of the supremacy of faith over reason, for this is the principle of growth for any truth of Revelation. It was when reason was placed superior to faith and usurped the function of faith that heresy resulted. This was the dominant characteristic of the whole heretical Gnostic movement.

The fifth note is "Logical Sequence,"[47] which means that developments in any living thing must be proportionate to and flow naturally from the very nature of the thing. They must, as it were, be at least virtually contained within it. A conclusion

---

[46] *Ibid.*, pp. 178 f. [47] *Ibid.*, pp. 189 f.

naturally and logically flows from its premises; so, too, the branches of a tree from its trunk. It would be unnatural and "illogical" for the trunk of an oak tree to suddenly put forth the branches and needles of a hemlock tree. Its "logical sequence" is to put forth branches with the same grain and bark and leaves proper to an oak tree. Thus a true development can never be contrary or contradictory to the essence of the truth from which it is derived. When the second council of Constantinople condemned Monotheletism and insisted on the two wills in Christ, it was merely maintaining the logical sequence of development. For the existence of two wills flows logically and necessarily from the fact that there are two intelligent free natures in Christ. Docetism was significantly illogical, for if Christ is true man, He must necessarily and logically possess a true human body. To postulate a mere material husk that is only the appearance of a body is to contradict the fact that Christ is really and truly a man with a real human nature.

The sixth note is "Conservative Action":[48] any new development of a living thing must also protect and preserve all that has come before it. The new branches of an oak tree do not kill the old branches of the tree but are a new source of nourishment and strength for the rest of the tree. Any true doctrinal development must possess a similar conservative action. For there must not only be a new growth in the understanding of the essential truth but this new development must also fortify and protect what is already known about the truth. Thus Chalcedon preserves and improves what was achieved at Nicaea and Ephesus and Constantinople regarding the Incarnation. Monotheletism obviously corrupts what was achieved in those councils for its destroys what is essential to Christ's human nature—a free will.

The seventh note, "Anticipation of its Future,"[49] means that every living thing manifests very definite tendencies in its early stages of growth. These tendencies are maintained throughout the whole course of its development, if no corruption or essential change takes place; for these tendencies flow from its very nature. Thus in looking on the life history of an oak tree, it

---

[48] *Ibid.*, pp. 199 f.   [49] *Ibid.*, pp. 195 f.

will be observed that in its early stages of growth it manifested the same characteristic tendencies as it did in all of its later stages of development. On close examination, an oak seedling manifests the same grain and bark and branch design and leaf formation as the mighty oak of future years. In viewing the history of the development of a doctrine, we should be able to observe the same orthodox and traditional tendencies persevering and being maintained in its later developments. Ephesus is a good example of this. It certainly anticipated Chalcedon in condemning Nestorianism. In maintaining only one person in Christ, it set the way for Chalcedon to explain how there is only one person in Christ and its relation to the two natures. Both Constantinople and Chalcedon manifest the same tendency by insisting on a complete and integral human nature for Christ, and each council did this in its own way.

The striking element of this whole dynamic theory is that amidst all of Newman's stressing of change and growth, he never fails to emphasize at the same time the essential changelessness of the doctrine itself. This is especially evident in his seven criteria. Though he insists that a true doctrine must always be characterized by a chronic vigor, still, it must also be characterized by a very definite immutability within itself. For over the whole course of its development, the doctrine must maintain an identity of nature, an identity of essential tendencies, and an identity of laws of growth. Even the least development must conserve that identity of nature and flow logically from it. Anything which violates this rigorous law of identity is a mere corruption.

Newman is always aware that the growth of a doctrine takes place in the minds of the recipients and not in the revealed truth itself. There is no change in the original revelation nor in the inner consciousness of the Church as regards the revelation which she knew she possessed even from the beginning. For the Church, the growth is the *transitus* from implicit awareness to explicit formulation. By analogy, the facts of a case history are presented to a doctor. He studies them and thereby draws out very explicit conclusions actually contained in the facts already stated. He does all this without any necessary change taking place either in the facts or in the condition of his patient. So, too, for Newman, as for any Catholic, the revealed truth remains ever the same but the comprehension of all that is contained therein increases with the passing of time and the activity of human minds upon the object. Amidst this expansion of understanding on the part of her members, the Church is always accompanied and guided by the authority and enlightenment of the Spirit of Truth working among the members of Christ's Living Body.

As original as is Newman's theory of the development of doctrine, it is far from being completely new. He admits that both De Maistre and Moehler on the continent have preceded him in handling the problem.[50] Yet Moehler's approach and Newman's are quite different. Moehler's is that of a dogmatic theologian, while Newman's is that of a philosopher of ecclesiastical history. Moehler treats of the subject from the point of view of the Church as a living organism of which the Holy Spirit is the vivifying principle.[51] Doctrinal developments are thus seen as but the unfolding of the life of the Church.[52] They are the formal acts of the Mystical Body of Christ. Newman deals with the subject apologetically. He starts with the life of truth and with the intensity of life in the intellectual order which characterizes any field of human activity. In this way, Newman is on common ground even with those outside the Church. Yet the approaches of both men are quite compatible with one another. Both writers are well anchored in the traditions of the past. The writings of Tertullian, Irenaeus, Petavius, and Vincent of Lerins do not allow either of them to be ranked as radical innovators.[53] Not infrequently, Newman refers to · Vincent of Lerins and also quotes a very striking passage from Tertullian regarding the development of doctrine.[54]

---

[50] *Ibid.*, p. 29.

[51] G. Voss, S.J., "Johann Adam Moehler and the Development of Dogma," *Theological Studies*, IV, 1 (March, 1943), 420-44.

[52] *Ibid.*, p. 444.

[53] *Ibid.*, pp. 443 f.

[54] *Essay on Development*, pp. 10-27, f.; cf. also *Via Media*, I, 73.

It is a significant fact that the last writing of Newman as an Anglican was his *Essay*. It was begun just as he was finishing his long journey from Oxford to Rome. In it he glorifies "the beauty ever ancient, ever new"[55] that he found in the dogma of Catholicism.

The *Essay on Development* is almost a *Te Deum* which he composed while standing outside the very threshold of the Church.

---

[55] Cf. Augustine's *Confessions*, Book X, Chapter 27.

NEWMAN CENTENNIAL LITERATURE:

A BIBLIOGRAPHY

Newman Centennial Literature: A Bibliography

That Cardinal Newman's personality and writings are still a vital force in the Catholic world was amply demonstrated by the abundant literature produced on the centenary of his conversion to Catholicism. This work of Catholic—and a few non-Catholic—writers, while inspired by the specific occasion, has more than an occasional value. Much of it is a real and permanent contribution to our knowledge of the great Oxford convert.

Any volume such as this can contain, of course, only a tiny fraction of the material that might well be included. The purpose of the following bibliography is to indicate to students and admirers of Newman the scope and richness of the literature of the Newman centennial, and to assist them in finding what has appeared on particular phases of Newman's life and work in which they might have special interest.

An attempt has been made to list systematically the principal articles in the Catholic publications of the United States, and in those foreign publications readily available here. Most of the material was published during the centennial year, 1945. But numerous items have been included which, although they appeared in 1944 or 1946, may still rightly be called Newman centennial literature.

Collections of essays are noted early in the bibliography, but the various essays they contain are listed among the "Essays and Articles" in what seemed to be their proper places in the general scheme; the essays are referred to their collections by abbreviations or adaptations of the collection titles.

It was frequently difficult to catalogue an essay or article under a specific heading. Many of them contain material which gives them a claim to two or more places in the system. However, in order to prevent the bibliography from becoming unwieldy, each item has been mentioned only once, in the place which appeared, all things considered, most suitable. Thus, for instance, if an essay entitled "Writer and Preacher" is found under the heading "Newman the Poet," it is because the material in the essay seemed to deal with Newman under that aspect more than under the ones the title would suggest.

It was interesting to note, in compiling this bibliography, how an article which dealt specifically with a particular work of Newman really was most concerned with Newman himself as the writer of that work, so that a study of the *Essay on Development,* for example, seemed most at home under the heading "Newman the Theologian." The personality of the Cardinal is so pervasive that it colors and gives form to the most abstract treatise; it can never be forgotten, for the shadow of the man himself lies across the work of his pen. And even the dessicated divisions of this bibliography reflect, in a little, the multi-faceted and various character of the man with whom it deals.

EDMOND DARVIL BENARD

BOOKS ABOUT NEWMAN

BIOGRAPHICAL

John Henry Newman. By John Moody. New York: Sheed and Ward, 1945. Pp. ix + 353. Bibliography and index.

BIOGRAPHICAL AND CRITICAL

John Henry Newman. By Charles Frederick Harrold. London, New York, Toronto: Longmans, Green and Co., 1945. Pp. xv + 472. Bibliography and index.

CRITICAL

The Art of Newman's Apologia. By Walter E. Houghton, New Haven: Published for Wellesley College by the Yale University Press, 1945. Pp. ix + 116. Index.

Newman on University Education. Edited by Roger J. McHugh, M.A., H. Dip. in Ed. Dublin: Browne and Nolan, Ltd., 1944. Pp. xlvii + 167. Bibliography.

Oeuvres philosophiques de Newman. Traduction de S. Jankélévitch; préface et notes de M. Nédoncelle. Paris: Aubier, 1945. Pp. 668. Bibliographie. [The material contained in the preface to this work is substantially the same as that presented by M. Nédoncelle in his *La philosophie religieuse de J. H. New-man* (Strasbourg: Sostralib)].

A Preface to Newman's Theology. By Edmond Darvil Benard. St. Louis and London: B. Herder Book Co., 1945. Pp. xv + 234. Bibliography and index.

NEW EDITIONS OF NEWMAN'S WRITINGS

Apologia pro vita sua. By John Henry Cardinal Newman. With an Introduction by Maisie Ward. London: Sheed and Ward, 1946. Pp. xiv + 234.

Favorite Newman Sermons. Selected by Daniel M. O'Connell, S.J. New York: The America Press, 1946 (re-issue.) Pp. xiv + 414.

DOCTRINAL SYNTHESES OF NEWMAN SELECTIONS

Kardinal J. H. Newman. Die Kirche. Erster Band. Uebertragung und Einführung von Otto Karrer. Einsiedeln/Köln: Verlagsanstalt Benziger & Co., 1945. 424 Seiten. Bibliographie.

Kardinal J. H. Newman. Die Kirche. Zweiter Band. Uebertragung und Einführung von Otto Karrer. Einsiedeln/Köln: Verlagsanstalt Benziger & Co., 1946. 428 Seiten.

A Newman Synthesis. Arranged by Erich Przywara, S.J. New York: Sheed and Ward, 1945 (re-issue). Pp. xiii + 379.

COLLECTIONS OF ESSAYS

The Golden Thread of Newman. By William R. Lamm, S.M. Foreword by John Moody. San Antonio, Texas: The Marian Foundation, 1946. Pp. 41. Paper bound. (Referred to below as *Golden Thread.*)

Homage to Newman 1845-1945. Foreword by The Most Reverend Bernard Griffin, Archbishop of Westminster. London: The Westminster Cathedral Chronicle, 1945. Pp. 47. Paper bound. (Referred to below as *Homage.*)

John Henry Cardinal Newman: Centenary 1845-1945. By Henry Tristam, *Cong. Orat.* Edited, with a Foreword, by H. Francis Davis. Birmingham, England, 1945. Pp. 36. Paper bound. (Referred to below as *Davis Centenary.*)

John Henry Newman: Centenary Essays. Introduction by Henry Tristam. Westminster, Md.: The Newman Bookshop, 1945. Pp. 241. (Referred to below as *Centenary Essays.*)

Newman Commemorative Essays. By students in St. Joseph's Seminary, Dunwoodie, N.Y. Foreword by Rev. Florence D. Cohalan. New York: The Paulist Press, 1946. Pp. 57. Paper bound. (Referred to below as *Dunwoodie Essays.*)

Newman and Littlemore. Foreword by The Most Reverend William Godfrey, Apostolic Delegate to Great Britain. Introduction by F. V. Couche, S.C. Littlemore, Oxford: The Salesian Fathers, 1945. Pp. 81. Paper bound. (Referred to below as *Littlemore.*)

A Tribute to Newman. Essays on Aspects of His Life and Thought. Edited by Professor Michael Tierney. Dublin: Browne and Nolan Ltd., 1946. Pp. vi + 360. (Referred to below as *Tierney Tribute.*)

[Note: The promised volume containing the papers read at the National Newman Centenary Conference, held in August, 1945, at Beaumont College, Old Windsor, England, had not yet appeared when this bibliography went to press.]

"NEWMAN ISSUES" OF PERIODICALS

America (New York), LXXIV, 2 (Oct. 13, 1945).

The American Ecclesiastical Review (Washington, D.C.), "Newman Centennial Number," CXIII, 4 (Oct., 1945).

Blackfriars (Oxford), XXVI, 307 (Oct., 1945): "The Life of the Spirit" Supplement (II, 20) is devoted to Newman.

The Clergy Review (London), "Newman Memorial Number," New Series XXV, 10 (Oct., 1945).

The Dublin Review (London), CCXVII, 435 (Oct., Nov., Dec., 1945).

The Epistle (New York), XI, 4 (Autumn, 1945).

The Tablet (London), CLXXXVI, 5500 (Oct. 6, 1945).

PAMPHLETS

The Apostle of the Second Spring (Father Dominic Barberi). By Kenan Carey, C.P. New York: The Paulist Press, 1945. Pp. 48.

John Henry Newman, St. Augustine, St. Thomas Aquinas, St. Thomas More, Matt Talbot. Five "Catholic Hour" addresses (Oct. 28-Nov. 25, 1945) by Rev. Thomas J. McCarthy, Ph.D. Westminster, Md.: The Newman Bookshop; also privately printed, 1946. Pp. 32.

"Newman Booklets" (separate pamphlets): *Christianity and Science.* Pp. 31; *Christianity and the Sceptic.* Pp. 30; *What is Literature?* Pp. 32. Edited by Roger J. McHugh, M.A. Dublin: Browne and Nolan, Ltd., 1944.

ESSAYS AND ARTICLES

BIOGRAPHICAL

GENERAL STUDIES

"John Henry Newman." By Denis Gwynn. *Homage,* pp. 17-24.

"John Henry Newman, 1801-1890." By Denis Gwynn. *Centenary Essays,* pp. 16-35.

"John Henry Newman" (Editorial). *Journal of Religious Instruction,* XVI, 2 (Oct., 1945), 169-72.

"A Newman Pilgrimage in England." By Gordon Wheeler. *Homage,* pp. 7-16.

FORMATIVE YEARS

"The Classics." By Henry Tristam, Cong. Orat. *Tierney Tribute,* pp. 246-78.

ANGLICAN YEARS

"Anglican Background." By P. Rogers. *Tierney Tribute,* pp. 1-26.

"The Church of England in 1845." By Humphrey J. T. Johnson. *The Dublin Review,* CCXVII, 435 (Oct., Nov., Dec., 1945), 147-55.

"Littlemore." By Henry Tristam, Cong. Orat. *Littlemore,* pp. 9-20.

"Newman and Faber at Oxford." By V. Baker, Cong. Orat. Lond. *Littlemore,* pp. 61-65.

"Newman and Oxford." By William Abel Pantin. *Littlemore,* pp. 43-49.

"Newman at Oxford." Anon. *The Epistle,* XI, 4 (Autumn, 1945), 101-106.

"Newman's Church and Other Buildings at Littlemore." By John Rothenstein. *Littlemore*, pp. 74-79.

"The Oxford Background." By Henry Tristam. *The Dublin Review*, CCXVII, 435 (Oct., Nov., Dec., 1945), 136-46.

"Tractarian Oxford." By Jeremiah J. Hogan. *Tierney Tribute*, pp. 27-56.

"The Vicar of St. Mary's." By R. D. Middleton. *Centenary Essays*, pp. 127-38.

THE CONVERSION

"Le centenaire de la conversion de celui qui devait être le Cardinal Newman." By Philippe Lajoie, p.s.s. *Le séminaire* (Montreal, Can.), Dec., 1945, pp. 257-75.

"The Conversion." By Fergal McGrath. *Tierney Tribute*, pp. 57-83.

"The Conversion of John Henry Newman." By Mary Paula Williamson, R.C. *The Epistle*, XI, 4 (Autumn, 1945), 107-10.

"La conversion de Newman." By Jean-Charles Laframboise, o.m.i. *Revue de l'Université d'Ottawa*, XV, 4 (Oct.-Dec., 1945), 408-45.

"The Event of October 9, 1845." By Henry Tristam, Cong. Orat. *Davis Centenary*, pp. 5-14.

"From 'The Tablet' of a Hundred Years Ago." By Douglas Woodruff. *The Tablet*, CLXXXVI, 5500 (Oct. 6, 1945), p. 166.

"Many Mansions: the Conversions of Newman and Faber" (Sermon preached at the London Oratory on June 26, 1945). By Mgr. Ronald Knox. *The Tablet*, CLXXXV, 5486 (June 30, 1945), 310.

"Most Consoling Intelligence from England. . . ." By Edmond Darvil Benard. *The American Ecclesiastical Review*, CXIII, 4 (Oct., 1945), 241-52.

"Psychological Reactions Before Newman's Conversion." By Daniel J. Saunders, S.J. *Theological Studies*, VI, 4 (Dec., 1945), 488-508.

Sermon preached by Mgr. Ronald Knox at the Birmingham Oratory on Oct. 9, 1945. *The Tablet*, CLXXXVI, 5501 (Oct. 13, 1945), 172-73.

CATHOLIC YEARS

"Cardinal Newman in Birmingham." By Henry Tristam, Cong. Orat. *Davis Centenary,* pp. 15-30.

"John Henry Cardinal Newman: I. The Crucible of Trial." By George Carver. *Journal of Religious Instruction,* XVI, 7 (March, 1946), 643-49.

"John Henry Cardinal Newman: II. In Permanent Ascendency." By George Carver. *Journal of Religious Instruction,* XVI, 8 (April, 1946), 731-39.

"John Henry Newman and London." By Vincent Baker. *Homage,* pp. 35-38.

"A Newman Postscript" (1870 correspondence concerning the Revised Version of the New Testament). *Blackfriars,* XXVII, 311 (Feb., 1946), 66-67.

"Some Newman Letters from the Baltimore Cathedral Archives." By John Tracy Ellis. *The Catholic Historical Review,* XXXI, 4 (Jan., 1946), 438-45.

"Was Newman Badly Treated?" By Denis Gwynn. *The Clergy Review,* New Series XXV, 10 (Oct., 1945), pp. 433-44.

NEWMAN IN IRELAND

"Ireland's Debt to Newman." By F. McGrath, S.J. *Littlemore,* pp. 66-73.

"Ireland's Debt to Newman." By W. J. Hegarty. *The Irish Ecclesiastical Record,* Sixth Series LXV, 3 (March, 1945), 150-60.

"John Hungerford Pollen and University Church." By C. P. Curran. *Tierney Tribute,* pp. 207-31.

"Newman in Ireland." By William Noe Field. *The Catholic World,* CLXII, 967 (Oct., 1945), 28-35.

"The Years in Ireland." By Roger McHugh. *Tierney Tribute,* pp. 144-71.

NEWMAN AND DR. CHARLES RUSSELL

"Cardinal Newman and Dr. Charles Russell." By J. M. Flood. *Studies,* XXXIV, 135 (Sept., 1945), 387-96.

"Dr. Russell and Newman's Conversion." By Henry Tristam, Cong. Orat. *The Irish Ecclesiastical Record,* Fifth Series LXVI, 3 (Sept., 1945), 189-200.

NEWMAN AND FATHER DOMINIC

"Apostle of the Second Spring." By Kenan Carey, C.P. *The Sign*, XXV, 3 (Oct., 1945), 8-11. (Also published in pamphlet form; cf. *supra.*)

"Dominic Barberi and Newman's Conversion." By Denis Gwynn. *The Clergy Review*, New Series XXV, 2 (Feb., 1945), 49-58.

"Father Dominic Barberi and the English." By Denis Gwynn. *The Month*, CLXXXI, 948 (Nov., Dec., 1945), 384-92.

"Father Dominic Barberi and Littlemore." By Denis Gwynn. *Littlemore*, pp. 37-42.

"Father Dominic Barberi the Missionary." By Denis Gwynn. *Blackfriars*, XXVI, 308 (Nov., 1945), Supplement II, 21, 145-52.

"Father Dominic and Cardinal Newman." By Henry Tristam. *Homage*, pp. 28-34.

"The Forgotten Priest of the Oxford Movement." By Raymond J. Judge. *The Catholic World*, CLXII, 966 (Sept., 1945), 476-79.

"A Man with a Mission." By M. O'Leary. *The Sword of the Spirit*, 77 (Jan., 1945), 9.

"Newman and Dominic." By Urban Young, C.P. *Littlemore*, pp. 30-31.

"Newman and Father Dominic Barberi." By Denis Gwynn. *Studies*, XXXIV, 135 (Sept., 1945), 347-53.

NEWMAN AND VARIOUS FRIENDS

"Cardinal Newman and Dean Church." By Christopher Hollis. *Centenary Essays*, pp. 68-91.

"Cardinal Newman and Sir William Cope." ("Passages from some Unpublished Letters.") By "A Correspondent." *The Tablet*, CLXXXVI, 5493 (Aug. 18, 1945), 80-81.

"Newman and Pusey." By Robert Sencourt. *The Dublin Review*, CCXVII, 435 (Oct., Nov., Dec., 1945), 156-65.

"Newman's Letters to W. J. Copeland." ("Selections from an Unpublished Correspondence.") With a Commentary by Canon S. L. Ollard. *The Tablet*, CLXXXVI, 5500 (Oct. 6, 1945), 60-64.

PERSONALITY AND WORKS

GENERAL CHARACTER SKETCHES

"The Many-Sided Genius of Newman." By William R. Lamm, S.M. *Golden Thread,* pp. 1-7.

"Newman in His Writings." By Swithin Bowers, o.m.i. *Revue de l'Université d'Ottawa,* XV, 3 (July-Sept., 1945), 265-86.

"The Newman of the Apologia." By K. M. Murphy. *The Capuchin Annual, 1945-6,* pp. 252-62.

"The Sentimental Myth." By Francis Vincent Reade. *Centenary Essays,* pp. 139-54.

NEWMAN THE CONTROVERSIALIST

"The Controversy Between Newman and Gladstone over the Question of Civil Allegiance." By Humphrey J. T. Johnson. *The Dublin Review,* CCXVII, 435 (Oct., Nov., Dec., 1945), pp. 173-82.

"In the Lists with the Abbé Jager." By Henry Tristam. *Centenary Essays,* pp. 201-22.

NEWMAN THE EDUCATOR

"The Background of Newman's 'Idea of a University.'" By Fergal McGrath. *The Month,* CLXXI, 946 (July-Aug., 1945), 247-58.

"Cardinal Newman on Education and Knowledge." By Daniel M. O'Connell, S.J. *The Epistle,* XI, 4 (Autumn, 1945), 120-24.

"Catholic University." By Michael Tierney. *Tierney Tribute,* pp. 172-205.

"The Contribution of the University (With Special Reference to Newman's 'Idea')." By Rev. J. McMackin, M.A. *The Irish Ecclesiastical Record,* Fifth Series, LXVII, 937 (Jan., 1946), 12-22.

"The Legacy of Newman." By Denis Meehan. *The Irish Ecclesiastical Record,* Fifth Series, LXVII, 2 (Feb., 1946), 73-82.

"Newman and the Catholic University of Ireland." By E. V. C. *Dunwoodie Essays,* pp. 22-50.

"Newman and the Liberal Arts." By John E. Wise. *Thought,* XX, 77 (June, 1945), 253-70. Reprinted in *The Catholic Mind,* XLIII, 995 (Nov., 1945), 641-54.

"Newman and Modern Educational Thought." By J. F. Leddy. *The American Ecclesiastical Review*, CXIII, 4 (Oct., 1945), 264-76.

"Newman and Science." By P. J. MacLaughlin. *Tierney Tribute*, pp. 307-36.

"Newman on the College Religion Curriculum." By Charles F. Donovan, S.J. *Journal of Religious Instruction*, XVI, 4 (Dec., 1945), 413-20.

"Newman, l'Universitaire." By Philippe Cornellier, o.m.i. *Revue de l'Université d'Ottawa*, XIV, 3 (July-Sept., 1944), 257-70.

"The Role of the Teacher in Education According to Newman." By Brother Theodore Hoeffken, S.M. *The Catholic Educational Review*, XLIII, 7 (Sept., 1945), 411-16.

"Teaching Possibilities in 'The Dream of Gerontius.'" By Sister Mary William, C.S.J. *Journal of Religious Instruction*, XV, 7 (March, 1945), 633-38.

"University—Actuality or Idea?" By Charles F. Donovan, S.J. *America*, LXXIV, 2 (Oct. 13, 1945), 36-38.

NEWMAN THE HISTORIAN

"Newman and the Catholic Historian." By Aubrey Gwynn, S.J. *Tierney Tribute*, pp. 279-306.

NEWMAN THE PHILOSOPHER

"The Development of Newman's Political Thought." By Alvan S. Ryan. *The Review of Politics* (Notre Dame University), VII, 2 (April, 1945), 210-40.

"Newman as a Philosopher." By Father James, O.F.M. Cap. *Tierney Tribute*, pp. 232-45.

"Newman and Liberalism." By T. S. Gregory. *Tierney Tribute*, pp. 84-116.

"Newman's Warning Words." Anon. *Social Justice Review*, XXXVIII, 9 (Jan., 1946), 306-307.

"A Parallel Between Newman and Thomism." By H. Francis Davis. *Blackfriars*, XXVI, 307 (Oct., 1945), Supplement II, 20, 129-36.

"The Social Philosopher." By Werner Stark. *Centenary Essays*, pp. 155-77.

"The Teaching of Newman on Church and State." By Andrew Beck, A.A. *The Clergy Review,* New Series XXV, 10 (Oct., 1945), 444-53.

"Was Newman a Disciple of Coleridge?" By H. Francis Davis. *The Dublin Review,* CCXVII, 435 (Oct., Nov., Dec., 1945), 165-73.

NEWMAN THE POET

"The Dream of Gerontius: The Poem and its Setting." By Henry Tristam, Cong. Orat. *Davis Centenary,* 31-36.

"Newman as Poet." By John K. Ryan. *Thought,* XX, 79 (Dec., 1945), 645-56.

"Newman's Essay on Poetry." By Geoffrey Tillotson. *Centenary Essays,* pp. 178-200.

"Newman's Verse." By Joseph W. Dunne. *The Clergy Review,* New Series XXV, 10 (Oct., 1945), 453-61.

"On Newman's Verse." By Ronald Moffat. *The Month,* CLXXXI, 948 (Nov.-Dec., 1945), 422-24.

"The Poetry of Cardinal Newman." By D. J. P. *Dunwoodie Essays,* pp. 51-56.

"The Writer and Preacher." By Thomas Wall. *Tierney Tribute,* pp. 337-60.

NEWMAN THE PREACHER

"Do the Laity Read Newman's Sermons?" By Daniel M. O'Connell, S.J. *The Homiletic and Pastoral Review,* XLVI, 3 (Dec., 1945), 182-88.

"Newman, a Light amid Encircling Gloom." By Charles F. Donovan, S.J. *The American Ecclesiastical Review,* CXIII, 5 (Nov., 1945), 366-76.

"The Parochial and Plain Sermons." By M. C. D'Arcy, S.J. *Littlemore,* pp. 50-60.

"The Salvation of the Hearer. . . ." By Eugene M. Burke, C.S.P. *The American Ecclesiastical Review,* CXIII, 4 (Oct., 1945), pp. 288-99.

"Self-Revelation in Newman's Sermons." By Sister Julia of the Trinity, S.N.D. *The Catholic World,* CLXII, 967 (Oct., 1945), 55-60.

NEWMAN'S SPIRITUAL LIFE AND WRITINGS

"Cardinal Newman and the Breviary." By Lancelot Sheppard. *Orate Fratres*, XIX, 7 (May 20, 1945), 292-97.

"La doctrine spirituelle de Newman." Jean-Charles Laframboise, o.m.i. *Revue de l'Université d'Ottawa*, XV, 1 (Jan.-March, 1945), 48-76.

"John Henry Cardinal Newman, Saintly Scholar—Scholarly Saint." By Aloysius McDonough, C.P. *The Homiletic and Pastoral Review*, XLVI, 1 (Oct., 1945), 1-11; and XLVI, 2 (Nov., 1945), 86-94.

"Newman and the Providence of God." By William R. Lamm, S.M. *Golden Thread*, pp. 23-33; and *Journal of Religious Instruction*, XVI, 2 (Oct., 1945), 226-37.

"Newman and the Religious Life." By Walter J. Ong, S.J. *Review for Religious*, IV, 4 (July 15, 1945), 230-42.

"Newman and the Seminarian." By J. E. B. *Dunwoodie Essays*, pp. 15-21.

"Newman's Message in Callista." By William R. Lamm, S.M., with Olive M. Biddison. *Golden Thread*, pp. 34-41.

"Newman's Spiritual Legacy to the Catholic Priest." By William R. Lamm, S.M. *The American Ecclesiastical Review*, CXIII, 4 (Oct., 1945), 277-87; appears as "Newman's Spiritual Legacy to the Catholic Priesthood," with slight additions, in *Golden Thread*, pp. 8-22.

"The Sanctity of Newman." By W. L. D. *Dunwoodie Essays*, pp. 11-14.

"The Spiritual Life of John Henry Newman." By F. Vincent Reade. *The Dublin Review*, CCXVII, 435 (Oct., Nov., Dec., 1945), 99-111.

"The Spirituality of Cardinal Newman." By F. Vincent Reade, Cong. Orat. *Homage*, pp. 46-47.

"With Newman at Prayer." By Henry Tristam. *Centenary Essays*, pp. 101-26.

NEWMAN THE STYLIST

"Newman as a Master of English Prose." By J. Lewis May. *Homage*, pp. 25-27.

"Newman, Master of English Prose." By Margaret R. Grennan. *The Epistle,* XI, 4 (Autumn, 1945), 111-16.

"Newman: a Model for the Literary." By Sebastian Redmond, A.A. *The Clergy Review,* New series XXV, 10 (Oct., 1945), pp. 461-65.

"Quis desiderio—" By J. Lewis May. *Centenary Essays,* pp. 92-100.

NEWMAN THE THEOLOGIAN

"The Ancient Newness of Dogma." By Walter P. Burke, C.S.P. *The American Ecclesiastical Review,* CXV, 3 (Sept., 1946), pp. 169-85.

"L'apologétique de Newman." By Jacques Gervais, o.m.i. *Revue de l'Université d'Ottawa,* XIV, 4 (Oct.-Dec., 1944), 425-39.

"Le Cardinal Dechamps et le Cardinal Newman." By Maurice Becqué, C.SS.R. *Nouvelle revue théologique,* LXVII, 2e partie, 5 (Nov.-Dec., 1945), 532 (1140)-540 (1148).

"The Catholicism of Cardinal Newman." By H. Francis Davis. *Centenary Essays,* pp. 36-54.

"Le centenaire de la conversion de Newman." By Edgar Hocedez, S.J. *Nouvelle revue théologique,* LXVII, 2e partie, 3 (July-Aug., 1945), 296 (904)-310 (918).

"Le document Newman-Perrone et le développment du dogme." By Ferdinand Cavallera. *Bulletin de littérature ecclésiastique,* 2-3 (Apr.-Sept., 1946), 132-42. (This study is to be continued in future issues of the *Bulletin.*)

"The Dream of Gerontius and the Fall of Man." By Rt. Rev. Abbot Horne, F.S.A. *The Dublin Review,* CCXVII, 435 (Oct., Nov., Dec., 1945), 188-93.

"The Essay on Development." By William J. Philbin. *Tierney Tribute,* pp. 116-43.

"John Henry Newman and the Vatican Definition of Papal Infallibility." By Joseph Clifford Fenton. *The American Ecclesiastical Review,* CXIII, 4 (Oct., 1945), 300-20.

"Newman's Essay on Development in its Intellectual Milieu." By Walter J. Ong., S.J. *Theological Studies,* VII, 1 (March, 1946), 3-45.

"Newman: the Marian Doctor." By Liam Brophy. *Ave Maria,* LXI (N.S.), 26 (June 30, 1945), 410-11.

"Newman's 'Moral Governor.'" By James O'Rourke, C.C., M.A. *The Irish Ecclesiastical Record,* Fifth Series, LXIII, 917 (May, 1944), 329-35. Reprinted in *The Catholic Mind,* XLII, 981 (Sept., 1944), 535-41.

"Newman and the Psychology of the Development of Doctrine." By H. Francis Davis. *The Dublin Review,* CCXVI, 433 (April, May, June, 1945), 97-107.

"Aux sources de la pensée chrétienne. Newman théologien." By Jean-Charles Laframboise, o.m.i. *Revue de l'Université d'Ottawa,* XVI, 2 (April-June, 1946), 65-89; and XVI, 3 (July-Sept., 1946), 129-53.

INFLUENCE AND PRESENT-DAY SIGNIFICANCE

"Cardinal Newman and America." By Msgr. Edward Hawks. *America,* LXXIV, 2 (Oct. 13, 1945), 38-41.

"Cardinal Newman and the Apostolate of the Intellect." By Alfred F. Horrigan. *The Catholic School Editor,* XV (Jan., 1946), 4-6.

"Cardinal Newman's Fears and Hopes for the Faith." By Herbert Keldany. *Homage,* pp. 41-42.

"The Critics' Probation." By Ethelbert Cardiff, O.F.M. *Blackfriars,* XXVI, 307 (Oct., 1945), Supplement II, 20, 136-41.

"The Conversion of Mr. Newman" (Editorial). *The Tablet,* CLXXXVI, 5500 (Oct. 6, 1945), 159-60.

"The First Newman Club." By Gerald Kernan. *America,* LXXIV, 11 (Dec. 15, 1945), 291-92.

"For What Do You Remember Newman?" By Fred Smith. *The Catholic World,* CLXI, 3 (June, 1945), 256-58.

"An Idea and an Ideal" (Newman Clubs). By Rev. John S. Dempsey. *The Epistle,* XI, 4 (Autumn, 1945), 124-27.

"Idea for a University" (Newman Clubs). By Courtenay Savage. *Catholic Digest,* X, 1 (Nov., 1945), 68-72. (Condensed from the *St. Joseph Magazine,* Oct., 1945.)

"The Influence of Newman on Modern Catechetics." By Michael Tynan. *The Irish Ecclesiastical Record,* Fifth Series LXVII, 3 (March, 1946), 159-70.

"Newman: Apostle of the Future." By Aodh de Blacam. *The Irish Monthly*, LXXIV (Feb., 1946), 75-83.

"John Henry Newman—His Prophetic Sense." By Robert Wilberforce. *The Catholic World*, CLXII, 970 (Jan., 1946), 336-42.

"Newman and German Catholicism." By Paul Simon. *The Dublin Review*, CCXIX, 438 (July, Aug., Sept., 1946), 75-84.

"Newman and His Age." By Philip Hughes. *The Dublin Review*, CCXVII, 435 (Oct., Nov., Dec., 1945), 111-36.

"Newman and the Modern Age." By Douglas Woodruff. *Centenary Essays*, pp. 55-67.

"Newman's Influence in France." By Louis Bouyer. *The Dublin Review*, CCXVII, 435 (Oct., Nov., Dec., 1945), 182-88.

"Newman's Influence on the Church of England: An Anglican View." By R. D. Middleton. *Homage*, 43-45.

"Newman in Germany: a Note on Theodor Haecker." By Henry Tristam, Cong. Orat. *The Tablet*, CLXXXVI, 5500 (Oct. 6, 1945), 165.

"Newman in Retrospect." By Margaret Devereux Conway. *America*, LXXIV, 1 (Oct. 6, 1945), 6-8.

"Newman and the Sword of the Spirit." By Christopher Dawson. *The Sword of the Spirit*, 84 (Aug., 1945), 1-2.

"Newman's Genius." By Martin D'Arcy, S.J. *America*, LXXIV, 2 (Oct. 13, 1945), 34-36.

"Newman's Place in History." By Christopher Dawson. *Littlemore*, pp. 32-36.

"Newman Today" (Editorial). *America*, LXXVI, 2 (Oct. 13, 1945), 42.

"The Present Significance of Newman" (Editorial). By Joseph J. Reilly. *Thought*, XX, 78 (Sept., 1945), 389-95.

"Recessional for the Tractarians." By Mgr. Ronald Knox. *Littlemore*, pp. 21-28.

"The Significance of Newman." By Joseph Francis Menez. *Ave Maria*, LXII (N.S.), 14 (Oct. 6, 1945), 213-15.

"The Tone of the Centre." By Joseph J. Reilly. *America*, LXXIV, 2 (Oct. 13, 1945), 45-47.

PAPAL LETTER ON NEWMAN

From His Holiness Pope Pius XII to Archbishop (now Cardinal) Bernard Griffin. *Acta Apostolicae Sedis*, XXXVII (1945), 184-86; also *The Clergy Review*, New Series, XXVI, 5 (May, 1946), 269-70. English translation in *The Tablet*, CLXXXVI, 5501 (Oct. 13, 1945), 172.

PERSONAL RECOLLECTIONS OF NEWMAN

"The Oratory School in the 'Sixties." By Viscount Fitzalan, K.G. *The Tablet*, CLXXXVI, 5500 (Oct. 6, 1945), 164.

"A Schoolboy's Reminiscences of Cardinal Newman." By Hugh Pope, O.P. *Blackfriars*, XXVII, 311 (Feb., 1946), 62-66.

"School Days under Cardinal Newman." By J. P. Boland, K.S.G. *Homage*, pp. 39-40.

THE REGIS COLLEGE NEWMAN COLLECTION

"In Quest of Newman." By Hugh F. Blunt. *The American Ecclesiastical Review*, CXIII, 4 (Oct., 1945), 253-63.

ON READING NEWMAN

"Cardinal Newman Is Easy Reading." By Daniel M. O'Connell, S.J. *The American Ecclesiastical Review*, CXIV, 3 (March, 1946), 188-96.

"On Reading Newman." By Henry Tristam. *Centenary Essays*, pp. 223-41.

THE CENTENNIAL CELEBRATION

"The Centenary Conference at Beaumont." By Kenelm Foster, O.P. *Blackfriars*, XXVI, 307 (Oct., 1945), Supplement II, 20, 142-44.

"Newman at Beaumont." By Stephen J. Brown, S.J. *Studies*, XXXIV, 136 (Dec., 1945), 533-38.

"The Newman Centenary." By H. J. Parkinson. *The Sword of the Spirit*, 84 (Aug., 1945), 6.

"Newman Centennial" (Editorial). *The Catholic Mind*, XLIII, 995 (Nov., 1945), 682. Reprinted from *The Catholic Sun*, Syracuse, N.Y., Sept. 13, 1945.

"The Newman Centenary." *The Month*, CLXXXI, 946 (July-Aug., 1945), 230-31.

"The Newman Centenary." *The Month*, CLXXXI, 947 (Sept.-Oct., 1945), 303-304.

MISCELLANEOUS

"Cardinal Newman and The Month." Anon. *The Month*, CLXXXI, 948 (Nov.-Dec., 1945), 312-21.

"Un newmaniste français: Henri Bremond." By Rodrigue Normandin, o.m.i. *Revue de l'Université d'Ottawa*, XV, 2 (Apr.-June, 1945), 157-79.

"Securus Iudicat" (Newman's use of phrase). *The Catholic Mind*, XLIII, 986 (Feb., 1945), 126-27.

"Theodor Haecker: A German Disciple of Newman." By Walter Breitenfield. *The Tablet*, CLXXXVI, 5494 (Aug. 25, 1945, 90.

BIOGRAPHICAL NOTES ON CONTRIBUTORS

Biographical Notes On Contributors

EDMOND DARVIL BENARD

Born in Boston, Massachusetts, on August 9, 1914, the Reverend Edmond Darvil Benard was educated at Holy Cross College (A.B., 1936), at the Grand Seminary, Montreal, (S.T.B., 1940; S.T.L., 1941), receiving the doctorate in sacred theology from the University of Montreal in 1942, and at the Catholic University of America (M.A., 1943). He was ordained in Springfield, Mass., in 1941. Dr. Benard began his teaching career at the Séminaire de Philosophie in Montreal and since 1943 has been on the faculty of the School of Sacred Theology at the Catholic University of America, where he conducts courses in fundamental dogmatic theology and homiletics. In 1945 he published *A Preface to Newman's Theology,* and he is also the author of *The Appeal to the Emotions in Preaching* (1944). He is an associate editor of *The American Ecclesiastical Review* and is the author of numerous articles upon theological and related subjects.

EUGENE M. BURKE

The Reverend Eugene M. Burke, C.S.P., was born in Los Angeles, California, on June 10, 1911, and received his early education in that city at Immaculate Heart of Mary school and the Cathedral high school. His college courses were taken at St. Joseph's College, Mountain View, California, and at the Paulist House of Studies in Washington, D.C. A member of the Congregation of St. Paul, he was ordained to the priesthood on April 2, 1938, and was assigned to pursue courses in graduate theology at the Catholic University of America. Upon the completion of these courses in 1941, Dr. Burke became a member of the faculty of the university's School of Sacred Theology. In 1944 he was also appointed to the faculty of Trinity College, Washington, D.C. Articles and reviews by him have appeared in *The American Ecclesiastical Review, The Catholic World, The Catholic Educational Review,* and *National Liturgical Week.*

WALTER P. BURKE

The Reverend Walter P. Burke, C.S.P., was born in Los Angeles, California, on September 19, 1916. His elementary training was received at the Immaculate Heart of Mary school in Hollywood. He completed his high school and junior college courses at Los Angeles College in 1937. After spending a year at the Paulist novitiate at Oak Ridge, N.J., he entered St. Paul's College in Washington, D.C., September, 1938. While there as a member of the Paulist community he received his B.A. degree, completed his major seminary training, and was ordained to the priesthood on December 26, 1943. After a year spent in parish work in Los Angeles and also trailer mission work in Texas, he returned to Catholic University of America for further studies in theology. Having been awarded the S.T.L. degree, he is now engaged in writing his doctoral thesis in theology. As a writer, Father Burke has been a contributor to *The Catholic World* and *The American Ecclesiastical Review.*

CHARLES F. DONOVAN

The Reverend Charles F. Donovan, S.J., was born in Boston in 1912 and was educated at the Boston Latin School, Boston College (A.B., 1933; M.Ed., 1945), Fordham University (A.M., 1943), and Weston College. He entered the Society of Jesus in 1933 and was ordained at Weston in 1943. Father Donovan has taught English at Boston College and is the author of articles that have been published in *America, The Commonweal, The American Ecclesiastical Review, The Journal of Religious Instruction,* and *The Journal for Religious.*

JOHN TRACY ELLIS

The Reverend John Tracy Ellis was born in 1905 at Seneca, Illinois, and was educated at St. Viator College (A.B., 1927), the Catholic University of America (A.M., 1928; Ph.D., 1930), and at Harvard University and the University of Chicago. Dr. Ellis was ordained a priest in 1938. He has taught history at St. Viator College, the College of St. Teresa, and, since 1935, at the Catholic University of America, where he is now associate professor of American church history. He served as director of the university's southern branch summer school at

San Antonio, Texas, from 1935 to 1937. Since 1941 he has been managing editor of *The Catholic Historical Review* and secretary of the American Catholic Historical Association. Dr. Ellis is the author of *Anti-Papal Legislation in Medieval England, 1066-1377* (1930); *Cardinal Consalvi and Anglo-Papal Relations, 1814-1824* (1942); *The Formative Years of the Catholic University of America* (1946); and of numerous articles in scholarly journals. He is also co-author of *The Catholic Church and Peace Efforts* (1942).

Joseph Clifford Fenton

The Very Reverend Joseph Clifford Fenton was born in 1906 in Springfield, Massachusetts, and was educated at Holy Cross College (A.B., 1926) and the Grand Seminary in Montreal (J.C.B. and S.T.L., 1930). He was ordained in Springfield in 1930. After graduate studies at the Gregorian University in Rome (S.T.D., 1931), he taught at St. Ambrose College, Davenport, Iowa, and St. Bernard's Seminary, Rochester, New York, before going to the Catholic University of America, where he is associate professor of dogmatic theology in the School of Sacred Theology. Dr. Fenton is the author of *The Theology of Prayer* (1939); *The Concept of Sacred Theology* (1941); *We Stand With Christ* (1942) and *The Calling of a Diocesan Priest* (1944). He is the editor of *The American Ecclesiastical Review* and is the author of numerous articles upon theological subjects.

Edward Hawks

The Right Reverend Edward Hawks was born in Crickhowel, Wales, in 1878, and was educated in private schools and at the University of London, Bishops' College, Quebec, Nashotah House, and St. Charles Seminary, Overbrook, Pa. A member of the Companions of the Holy Saviour and an Anglican minister, he was one of the group of clergymen who became Catholics at the time of the Open Pulpit controversy in 1908. Ordained a priest in 1911, Monsignor Hawks has held various positions in the archdiocese of Philadelphia, where he has been rector of St. Joan of Arc church since 1919. He served as chaplain in the Canadian Expeditionary Force in France and Belgium in 1917-19. In 1936 he was given the rank of domestic prelate and he is an officer of the French Academy. Among Monsignor Hawks's writings are *Conversions of 1908* (1930); *William McGarvey and the Open Pulpit* (1935); *Difficulties of Myron Digby* (1936); *The Pedigree of Protestantism* (1936); *History of St. Joan of Arc Parish* (1937); *Difficulties of Father Callaghan* (1939); and *How It Looks Now* (1940).

J. F. Leddy

Professor of classics, head of the department of classics, and director of the summer school at the University of Saskatchewan, Dr. J. F. Leddy was born in Ottawa, Ontario, in 1911. His higher education was received in the universities of Saskatchewan, Chicago, and Oxford. From Saskatchewan he received the M.A. degree and from Oxford the B. Litt. and D. Phil. degrees. Among his publications is "Newman and His Critics," which appeared in the report of the Canadian Catholic Historical Association for 1942-1943.

Daniel M. O'Connell

Born in Louisville, Kentucky, in 1885, the Reverend Daniel M. O'Connell, S.J., was educated at St. Mary's College, Kansas, St. Louis University, and Fordham University (Ph.D., 1930). He joined the Society of Jesus in 1903, was ordained in 1918, and has served in various positions as teacher and official within his community. Father O'Connell is at present librarian at the University of Detroit. He has long specialized in Newman studies and has published two prayer books drawn from Newman's writings, *Heart to Heart* (1938) and *Kindly Light* (1941), *Favorite Newman Sermons* (1932), and editions of *The Present Position of Catholics in England* (1925) and the *Apologia Pro Vita Sua* (1930).

Joseph J. Reilly

Born in Springfield, Massachusetts, in 1881, Joseph J. Reilly was educated at Holy Cross (A.B., 1904; M.A., 1906), Columbia (M.A., 1909), and Yale (Ph.D., 1912). He has taught at Fordham, the College of the City of New York, Yale University, and Hunter College, where he is professor of English and librarian. Among Dr. Reilly's books are *Lowell as Critic* (1915); *Newman as a Man of Letters* (1925); *Masters of 19th Century Prose*

1930); *The Fine Gold of Newman* (1931); and *Dear Prue's Husband and Other People* (1932).

JOHN K. RYAN

A member of the faculty of the School of Philosophy at the Catholic University of America and of the staff of Trinity College in Washington, the Reverend John K. Ryan was educated at St. Thomas Academy, St. Paul, Minn., Holy Cross College (B.A., 1920), the St. Paul Seminary, the American College, Rome (S.T.B., 1921), and the Catholic University of America (M.A., 1931; Ph.D., 1933). He was ordained priest in 1924. He is the author of *Modern War and Basic Ethics* (1933; 2nd edition, 1940); *Basic Principles and Problems of Philosophy* (3rd edition, 1944); *Valor Is Not Suicide* (1943); and *The Ideal of the Catholic School* (1947). He is co-author of *God and My Heart* (1938) and *My Communion* (1935); and has written chapters for *Essays in Thomism* (1942) and *Essays on Catholic Education in the United States* (1942). Associate editor of *The New Scholasticism*, Dr. Ryan has contributed many articles on philosophical subjects to *The Modern Schoolman, The Forum, America, Thought, The Commonweal, Columbia, The Catholic World,* and other magazines.

DANIEL J. SAUNDERS

Born in Somerville, Massachusetts, in 1910, the Reverend Daniel J. Saunders, S.J., was educated at Boston College (A.B., 1934), St. Louis University (M.A., 1936), and Weston College (S.T.D., 1944), where he was ordained in 1940. Father Saunders has taught theology at Weston and is now studying in Rome. He has contributed to *Theological Studies*.

JOHN E. WISE

Dean of the evening school at Loyola College, Baltimore, since 1945, the Reverend John E. Wise, S.J., was educated at Georgetown University (A.B., 1926), Woodstock College (A.M., 1931), the Gregorian University, Rome, (Ph.D., 1939), St. Louis University and Fordham University (Ph.D., 1945), where his doctoral dissertation was entitled *The Nature of the Liberal*

Arts. He taught English and Latin at Fordham Preparatory School from 1931 to 1934 and was dean of freshmen at Georgetown from 1939 to 1943. Father Wise has published articles in *America, Thought, The American Ecclesiastical Review, The Educational Forum,* and *School and Society.*

INDEX

Index